T0215076

Harley Hahn's Emacs Field Guide

Harley Hahn

Apress®

Harley Hahn's Emacs Field Guide

Harley Hahn
www.harley.com

ISBN-13 (pbk): 978-1-4842-1702-3   ISBN-13 (electronic): 978-1-4842-1703-0
DOI 10.1007/978-1-4842-1703-0

Library of Congress Control Number: 2016938804

Managing Director: Welmoed Spahr
Lead Editor: Jeffrey Pepper
Technical Reviewer: Dmitry Shkatov
Copyeditor: Lydia Hearn
Editorial Board: Steve Anglin, Pramila Balan, Louise Corrigan, Jonathan Gennick, Robert Hutchinson, Celestin Suresh John, Michelle Lowman, James Markham, Susan McDermott, Matthew Moodie, Jeffrey Pepper, Douglas Pundick, Ben Renow-Clarke, Gwenan Spearing
Coordinating Editor: Mark Powers
Compositor: SPi Global
Indexer: SPi Global
Artist: SPi Global

Distributed to the book trade worldwide by Springer Science+Business Media New York, 233 Spring Street, 6th Floor, New York, NY 10013. Phone 1-800-SPRINGER, fax (201) 348-4505, e-mail orders-ny@springer-sbm.com, or visit www.springeronline.com. Apress Media, LLC is a California LLC and the sole member (owner) is Springer Science + Business Media Finance Inc (SSBM Finance Inc). SSBM Finance Inc is a **Delaware** corporation.

For information on translations, please e-mail rights@apress.com, or visit www.apress.com.

Apress and friends of ED books may be purchased in bulk for academic, corporate, or promotional use. eBook versions and licenses are also available for most titles. For more information, reference our Special Bulk Sales–eBook Licensing web page at www.apress.com/bulk-sales.

Any source code or other supplementary materials referenced by the author in this text are available to readers at www.apress.com/9781484217023. For detailed information about how to locate your book's source code, go to www.apress.com/source-code/. Readers can also access source code at SpringerLink in the Supplementary Material section for each chapter.

Printed on acid-free paper

To Maria, for love and support.

And to Sadie (my dog) and Max (Maria's dog),
for being such good company.

Contents at a Glance

Contents

About the Author

Harley Hahn is a writer, philosopher, humorist, abstract artist, musician and computer expert. Hahn has written 33 books, including three university-level Unix/Linux textbooks. In all, Hahn's books have sold more than 2 million copies, including *Harley Hahn's Internet Yellow Pages*, the first Internet book in history to sell more than 1 million copies.

Hahn is the best-selling Internet author of all time, and has had three of his books nominated for a Pulitzer Prize. His work—including a complete set of his books—is archived by the Special Collections Department of the library at the University of California at Santa Barbara.

In addition to books, Hahn has written numerous articles, essays, and stories on a wide variety of topics, including romance, philosophy, money and economics, culture, medicine, and biology. Much of his writing is available on his Web site www.harley.com.

Hahn has a degree in Mathematics and Computer Science from the University of Waterloo (Canada), and a graduate degree in Computer Science from the University of California at San Diego. He has also studied medicine at the University of Toronto Medical School, and has been the recipient of a number of honors and awards, including a prestigious National Research Council (Canada) post-graduate scholarship, and the 1974 George Forsythe Award from the ACM (Association of Computer Machinery).

Of all his endeavors, Hahn most enjoys writing books, because "I get to sleep in, and I like telling people what to do."

Web Site for This Book

For online support for *Harley Hahn's Emacs Field Guide*, please visit:

`http://www.harley.com/emacs`

At this Web site, you will find a variety of useful information. You can also send a message to Harley Hahn.

About the Technical Reviewer

Dmitry Shkatov has an MA in Philosophy from Moscow State University, Russia, and a PhD in Computer Science from the University of Nottingham, England. Shkatov lives in South Africa, where he is a Senior Lecturer in Computer Science at the University of the Witwatersrand, Johannesburg.

Acknowledgments

Writing a book requires me to spend many, many hours at home for months at a time, researching, composing and rewriting, alone at my desk, with only my dog Sadie to keep me company. (Sadie is a three-year-old border collie, who doesn't understand why we don't spend every day running around outside.) Publishing a book, however, is a team effort, so if you have a moment, I'd like to introduce you to my team.

Let's start with Lydia Hearn. Lydia and I have worked on books together for a long time, and I have found her to be a truly remarkable person. She is a tenured professor at De Anza College in Cupertino, California, where she teaches English. For this book, Lydia was my copy editor, which means that it was her job to find and correct any writing mistakes I might have made. This is harder than you might imagine, because writers think so fast that their fingers can't keep up with their thoughts, which means it is easy to make mistakes, many of which are subtle and hard to find. That is why I need Lydia, a tireless perfectionist (actually, a tired perfectionist) with boundless enthusiasm and enormous skill. Moreover, Lydia is the only person in the world that I will, voluntarily, let make changes to what I write.

Next comes Jeff Pepper, the lead editor for this book. Jeff and I started publishing books together a long, long time ago, and it is through his efforts that I have been able to create many of my most successful, high-quality books. Whenever I start a new project with Jeff, I know that he will be there with lots of advice, experience, and a good-natured approach that comes from dealing with authors and publishing people all day long, for many years. In addition, for this particular book, Jeff put in many hours—often late at night and under pressure — processing the files I would send him to ensure that everything was done just right.

The other editor on our team is Mark Powers, who served as managing editor for this book. This means that Mark handled a lot of details, including a schedule that seemed to have a life of its own. Mark has a background, not only in book publishing, but in writing graphic novels and comic books, which makes him uniquely qualified to work with the more esoteric parts of this book.

Then there is Dmitry Shkatov, a very special person whose job it was to help me look for technical mistakes. Dmitry teaches computer science at the University of the Witwatersrand in Johannesburg, South Africa. In fact, if it weren't for Dmitry, this book would never have been written. Here is how it happened.

On July 20, 2015, Dmitry wrote me the following letter:

Dear Harley,

I was wondering whether it would be possible to somehow get access to the chapter on Emacs from the 2nd edition of your "Student Guide to Unix", which was sadly left out of the 3rd edition.

It's the best introduction to Emacs I have ever seen (and that's how I came to love Emacs), and now that I'm teaching computer science to South African undergraduates, I'd like to be able to share it with my students.

Your assistance would be highly appreciated not only by me, but I am sure, by my students as well.

Not long afterwards, Jeff Pepper contacted me about writing a new book. I showed him Dmitry's letter, and we agreed that it would be a good idea for me to write a book focusing only on Emacs. We asked Dmitry if he would be the technical editor for the book, and he said yes. This was a stroke of luck for me, because you would have to search long and hard to find someone as smart as Dmitry, who has as much experience with Emacs. Dmitry not only read everything I wrote, making important suggestions, he also took the time to discuss all manner of Emacs-related ideas, which helped me enormously.

Speaking of help, I thank Ron Lockwood-Childs and Stephanie Lockwood-Childs, highly accomplished engineers and programmers, who helped me with advice on how to set up a Linux system to run on a virtual machine, specifically for testing Emacs. In addition, I thank Jebi Koilpillai, for helping me understand and test the technical issues involved in installing Emacs under Mac OS X.

As a writer, I always hope for production people who share my desire to create the best possible book. As such, I wish to thank several hard-working, skillful employees of SPi Global, an international business service provider. These three people are Mercy Thomas (account manager), Dulcy Nirmala Chellappa (project manager), Parameswari Balasubramaniyan (page layout artist), and Samuel Devanand (production editor). Without the time-consuming, detailed work of people like Mercy, Dulcy, Parameswari, and Samuel, it would not be possible to produce high-quality books like this one. I am lucky to have had their help.

For the final acknowledgments, I call upon the wisdom of the ancient Roman poet Juvenal who once observed, if you are going to spend hours a day for months at a time writing an Emacs book, you had better make sure that you get a lot of high-quality exercise, or you are going to have a lot of trouble. (Actually, the way he put it was *Mens sana in corpore sano*, which means "A healthy mind in a healthy body".)

With this in mind, I thank Sandrine Rocher-Krul, my cardioboxing teacher, for helping me to stay fit, alert, and healthy. I have taken a lot of classes in my life — as a child, as an undergraduate, in grad school, and in medical school — and without a doubt, Sandrine is the best teacher I have ever had. She has a rare confluence of motivation, skill, and creativity, which she demonstrates daily. For the same reason, I am grateful to the other students with whom I have been taking cardioboxing for so long. In particular, I thank Miguel Trujillo and Abe Solis for their continued encouragement and their help.

A Personal Note from Harley Hahn

You are floating down a narrow, winding river. Much of the time you move slowly, drifting with the current. You have been drifting a long time. Although the current is steady, the water is warm and comfortable, and you don't even notice it anymore. It just is. Warm, comfortable, predictable.

You are floating peacefully. Still, every now and then, you find yourself wondering: Is something missing? Am I bored? Is that all there is?

One day, you notice that the river is about to bifurcate into two different streams, and you need to make a choice. Which way do you want to go? You look carefully, squinting your eyes against the bright sun, trying to notice the details you are used to taking for granted.

Straight ahead, the water is calm. Do nothing, and you will keep drifting, safely and predictably. And why not? After all, your journey is far from over, and everything seems to be working out just fine. Part of you wants nothing more than to lay back and relax.

To the left, however, the water looks unusual. The current is faster and, in the distance, you see some rapids, although nothing you can't handle. A memory comes back: Years ago, you used to love the rapids, bouncing up and down for a short time, then resting to catch your breath. You were living in the moment, over and over and over, just being. How long has it been since you had that feeling of really being alive? You can't remember.

You close your eyes and imagine the map of the river, the map you thought you had memorized. However, you can't recall a place where one river turns into two. You open your eyes, feeling puzzled, and you see that, soon, you must make a decision.

Here is a promise. If you decide to turn and travel down the unknown branch of the river away from the current, you will find me there, waiting for you, and we will explore together. In fact, I have a map that we will share. There is a lot ahead of us, and I can tell you now that what is just around the bend will take effort. However, I can also tell you it will change your life.

What to do? Should you push against the current and explore the unknown, unexpected branch of the river? Or should you keep drifting in a slow, safe, predictable direction? Even doing nothing is a decision.

My advice? Go to Chapter 1 of this book and read the first three sections.

Then make your choice.

HARLEY HAHN

CHAPTER 1

■ ■ ■

All About Emacs

Section 1.1: Getting Started Together

Emacs is a powerful, computer-based tool, created a long time ago by smart people *for* other smart people. At its core, Emacs is a "text editor", a program you use to work with files that contain plain text. (We'll talk more about this in Section 1.2.) However, the Emacs text editor is part of a larger, more complex working environment and, in fact, there are many people — especially programmers — who happily spend most of their day working within Emacs.

In this book, I will teach you the basics of using Emacs. Although I will not be able to explain everything there is to know about Emacs — that would take several books — I will show you most of what you need to know for straightforward day-to-day work. In addition, before we get into a lot of technical details, you and I will discuss the environment in which Emacs was created and how it affects you even today. My goal is to ensure that, as you learn and use Emacs, you have a deep understanding of what you are doing and why.

Before we start working together, I'd like to get acquainted by talking about what I assume about you, my reader, and what I assume about the software you will be using. I will then tell you what you need to know about me.

Generally speaking, here is what we can say about the type of people who like to use Emacs (and because you are reading this book, I am assuming that these three statements apply to you):

1. Emacs users are smart.
2. Emacs users like to use computers.
3. Emacs users enjoy teaching themselves how to use complicated, powerful tools.

In addition, there is one more assumption I would like to make:

4. You are able to learn on your own by reading and practicing.

© Harley Hahn 2016
H. Hahn, *Harley Hahn's Emacs Field Guide*, DOI 10.1007/978-1-4842-1703-0_1

This is important because, out of the 7.28 billion other people in the world, there is nobody who is ever going to teach you Emacs in person. You will have to teach it to yourself by reading and practicing.[1]

■ **Note** It wasn't always this way. In the 1970s, programmers and researchers worked in rooms with shared terminals, and programming was a much more social activity. Today, no one is going to teach you how to use Emacs in person, so you will have to teach yourself. Of course, you do have this book, so you aren't completely alone.

As you read the book you will, of course, need access to some type of Emacs, so you can practice and use what I will be teaching you. It will help a lot if you already have some experience using a computer with a keyboard.[2] Don't worry if Emacs is not already bundled (included) with your system: it is easy to find and it is always free.

There are a number of different versions of Emacs but, by far, the most widely used is GNU Emacs (which we will discuss in Section 1.4), so that is the version of Emacs we will be discussing in this book. GNU Emacs will work with just about every version of the Unix operating system — including Linux (all types), FreeBSD, NetBSD, OpenBSD, Mac OS X, Solaris — as well as with Microsoft Windows.

Once you have Emacs up and running, it works the same on any computer, under any operating system. For example, suppose you learn how to use Emacs with Windows. You then decide to change to Linux. The operating system and the working environment will be a lot different — but Emacs will look and function exactly the same.

Nevertheless, there are two important topics that do differ from one operating system to another: user interfaces and installation procedures. So when we cover these topics, I will be sure to show you how the details differ depending on your operating system. (Remember, though, Emacs itself will work the same.) In particular, since so many people use Emacs with some type of Unix (especially Linux), we will spend some time talking about operating systems in general (Section 2.1), and Unix and Linux in particular (Section 2.2).

To conclude this section, let's talk for a moment about what I can promise you. First, you can assume that I understand what I am teaching you, and that I have personally tested all the examples in the book.

Second, you can assume that I am experienced enough to explain highly technical details in a way that will be easy for you to understand and fun to read. My intention is that you should find learning Emacs to be an interesting and useful experience.

---

[1] See Personal Note #1, "Teaching Yourself Emacs" (Appendix A). From time to time, as you read as you read this book, you will see notes like the one above. In addition, there are also *personal* notes, which I hope you will find interesting and useful. For your convenience — and so I don't distract you — all the personal notes are collected in Appendix A.

[2] See Personal Note #2, "Computer With a Keyboard" (Appendix A).

Third, you can assume that I wrote this book very carefully, to be both a teacher and a reference. Specifically, there are 102 short sections, and everything you read in every section is something I want you to know. The very best way to use this book is to let it be your teacher. Start with the very first page and read straight through, in order, until you have finished all 102 sections. As you read, do not hurry. It will take a while to get to the part of the book where we actually start using Emacs. However, once we get there, please take the time to practice by trying all the examples, especially the many different key combinations, on your own computer. Although this may not seem necessary, it is the fastest and best way to learn Emacs. Taking time to practice the examples makes it easy for your brain to make the changes necessary for you to think like an Emacs person. (This is not a metaphor: you will need to give your brain time to change on the cellular level in order to use Emacs well.)

However, if this plan does not suit your needs, remember that this book is also a reference. If you so choose, you can skip around the book reading whatever sections you want in whatever order you want. As you read, you will find many forward- and backward-references to other sections, so if you encounter something you don't understand, it will be easy for you to find the information you need quickly.

As you read through the book, you will, from time to time, see two types of notes. First, you will see short notes (like the one below), useful and interesting comments placed within the text. Second, in the footnotes, you will see references to Appendix A, which contains longer (and more distracting) "personal notes". You will also see a few short discussions called "What's in a Name?", in which I explain the meaning of a specific name. For example, in Section 2.2, you will learn where the name "Linux" came from, and how to pronounce "Linus", the name of the person who started the Linux Project.

Finally, whenever I define the meaning of a new term, I will write it in capital letters, for example: EMACS is a sophisticated text editor within a complex and powerful work environment.

Note   Emacs is difficult to learn, but easy to use.

Section 1.2: Emacs Is a Text Editor

What is Emacs?

Before I answer that question, let me take a moment to review some basic terminology.

Broadly speaking, there are two types of data that you can work with using your keyboard, mouse, and screen: text and graphics.

TEXT refers to data that consists only of characters that you can type on a keyboard: letters, numbers, punctuation, spaces and tabs. The old term for TEXT, which you will often encounter, is ASCII TEXT. (The name refers to one of the original systems used to represent characters stored as computer data, ASCII: the "American Standard Code for Information Interchange".)

GRAPHICS refers to any type of data that can be displayed on a screen, often using colors: not only characters, but images (photos or drawings); shapes (rectangles, circles); lines, dots, and so on.

A FILE is a collection of data that has a name and is stored on a disk or other storage device. Thus, a TEXT FILE or an ASCII FILE is a file that contains only text. A TEXT EDITOR (or more simply, an EDITOR) is a program used to create and modify text files.

EMACS is a text editor.

Text files have many different uses, so Emacs can be used for many different purposes. For example, you can use Emacs to write a story or an article, to make a grocery list or take notes during a lecture, or to edit system configuration files on a Linux system. In fact, any time you need to manipulate textual data directly, you need a text editor and Emacs is a good choice. In addition, Emacs is also capable of displaying images in a limited way.

■ **Note**   When you start Emacs within a graphics environment (see Section 2.5), it will display a logo, which is an image. When you start Emacs within a text-only environment, you see only characters.

From the beginning, however, the most important use of Emacs has been to write programs, including shell scripts, and that is still the case today. Indeed, many people consider Emacs to be the best programmer's editor ever created. (I'll explain why in Section 1.3.)

■ **Note**   A shell, also called a command processor, is the program that interprets the commands you type. A shell script is a list of such commands stored in a file. Shell scripts are commonly used to automate procedures or to write relatively simple programs. With Linux, the most commonly used shell is called Bash (see Section 2.2).

What else is Emacs used for? That depends on the state of technology and what people need at the time. For example, from the mid 1970s through the 1990s, many people used Emacs to compose email messages and to participate in Usenet (the global system of thousands of discussion groups). Today, using Emacs in these ways is obsolete.

Why? Today, almost everyone sends and receives email using a Web based-service or a modern email client (I use Eudora), all of which have built-in text editors, making Emacs unnecessary for email. Similarly, for over 25 years, Usenet was used by a very large number of people around the world to post messages discussing every topic you can imagine, as well as to develop and share software. Many people used Emacs to create their messages, and a related program (**gnus**) to participate in Usenet discussion groups. Eventually, however, both discussions and software distribution migrated to the Web, which has no need of an external text editor.[3]

So how is Emacs used today?

Aside from programming, general note-taking, and so on as we discussed, you will find that many people use Emacs to create and modify files containing MARKED-UP TEXT: character-based information embedded with instructions as to how that information should be presented. The two most common examples are LaTeX files for typesetting documents, especially technical documents and research papers; and HTML and CSS files for creating Web pages.

The basic idea I want you to understand is that Emacs has always worked so well that, for over four decades, it has been used by smart people everywhere to work on whatever tasks arise in their lives that require a well-designed, powerful text editor. This is why learning how to use Emacs is such a good use of your time.

Note   No matter what happens to come along in the future, you will always have a use for Emacs (as will your grandchildren).

Section 1.3: Emacs Is a Working Environment

There is a story in the Bible that relates what happened when the Queen of Sheba met King Solomon.[4] People had told the Queen that Solomon and his household were pretty hot stuff, but she was skeptical. Her attitude was that words are cheap, so she had better go to Jerusalem with some expensive gifts (just in case) and check things out for herself. When she got there, however, she was astonished: Solomon and his accomplishments were even more impressive than she had been told. When she finally met the king, she told him in person about all the stories she had heard and then remarked: "I believed not the words until I came, and mine eyes had seen it: and, behold, the half was not told me."

Well, that is what it is going to be like for you as you get more and more experienced with Emacs. In Section 1.1, I introduced Emacs to you as a text editor. But, as the Queen of Sheba might put it, the half was not told unto you: Emacs is more, a lot more. Here is why.

The text editor part of Emacs runs inside a framework that is highly customizable and very powerful. In fact, I would venture to say that Emacs is unlike anything you have ever seen or used before in your life. If you want to take the time, you can customize Emacs to work just the way you want and you can integrate Emacs with the other programs you use. In this way, you can build yourself an all-encompassing world in which you can spend all of your working time (and many people do).

---

[3] See Personal Note #3, "Usenet, Emacs, and the Internet" (Appendix A).
[4] Old Testament, 1 Kings 10:7.

■ **Note** For many people, Emacs is a way of life, like religion or football.

When you use Emacs on a Unix system, such as Linux, you can use any Unix command you want without leaving the program. For example, you can manipulate files and directories, test and run programs, download files from the Internet, install new software, and much, much more. You can also start a new shell (that is, open a new command line) whenever you want.

■ **Note** You can do pretty much the same thing using Emacs under Windows. However, the Windows command line is not nearly as powerful as the Unix command line.

In addition, Emacs is designed to make it very easy for you to change its behavior to suit your needs. For example, you can tell Emacs to work in a way that is suitable for the specific programming language you are using: indentation, syntax highlighting, and so on. You do this by setting what is called a "major mode" (see Section 11.2). For example, you can set major modes for programming in Assembly Language (x86), C, C++, Fortran, Go, Lisp, Java, JavaScript, MATLAB, Perl, Python, Ruby, and many other languages. Moreover, Emacs stays up to date. Whenever a new programming language starts to become popular, the Emacs community will create a major mode for it.

You can also set major modes for other types of editing, such as working with LaTeX, HTML and CSS files; multimedia files; picture files (including ASCII art!); and various types of data (such as CSV, comma separated value, files). In addition, there are many other modes (including the "minor modes", which we will discuss in Section 11.4) that enable you to fine-tune exactly how Emacs works for you.

If you are a programmer, you may be familiar with an IDE, or integrated development environment. An IDE provides a number of important programming tools with a common interface, in a way that makes them easy to use together:

- Text editor: to create and modify source code
- Debugger: to help track down and fix problems
- Build automation tool: to create a large program out of many components
- Help facility: to display documentation and reference material

For large projects, you will also use:

- Version control: to keep track of different versions of a program

---

■ **Note** SOURCE CODE, or more simply, CODE, refers to a collection of computer instructions written in a human-readable programming language, usually as text.

There are many different IDEs and, in a lot of cases, using one of them will be the best way to go. This is because they are complete packages, ready to go as soon as you install them. All you have to do is find the one that works best with the type of project on which you are working. However, with Emacs, it is possible to create your own, custom IDE. In fact, once you have enough experience with Emacs and Unix, you can set up your personal environment so that it is easy to access tools like the ones I mentioned above without ever having to leave Emacs.

For example, for some programming languages — such as C, C++, Python, and Java — Emacs is tightly integrated with build tools (**make**), a debugger (**gdb**), version control tools (Git), documentation tools, and so on. Emacs is also tightly integrated with all the programming languages that are part of the GCC. As a result, many programmers are able to work all day within the Emacs environment, leaving only to go to the bathroom or walk the dog.

Note   As we will discuss in Section 1.5, GNU Emacs is part of the GNU Project from the Free Software Foundation (FSF). The FSF also maintains a compiler system, called GNU COMPILER COLLECTION or GCC. GCC is a complex, powerful tool that can compile a variety of programming languages (C, C++, Objective-C, Fortran, Java, Ada, Go) and generate code for many different processor architectures.

The more experience you have, the better you can set up Emacs to work exactly as you want it to, and you can change it instantly as your needs dictate. For example, Emacs lets you create as many "buffers" (work areas) as you want, each of which can be set up for a different task. This makes it easy to switch back and forth seamlessly between completely different types of work, according to what you want to do from one moment to the next. (We will talk about buffers in Section 6.2 and Section 7.7.)

If you are so inclined, you can extend Emacs by using a programming language, called Emacs Lisp, which is integrated into Emacs. Using Emacs Lisp, you can create what are called MACROS to enhance Emacs to suit your needs. A MACRO is a tool that you can create and use to perform a specific function according to your personal needs. Macros can be used for just about anything you can imagine, from simple abbreviations to use when you are typing, to complex tools that are actual programs in their own right. One of the most common uses of macros is to automate tasks that would otherwise be time consuming or error prone.

Finally, because Emacs is free, open source software, anyone can look at and modify the source code (the actual programs that make up Emacs) and contribute their own changes and improvements. This means that if you are willing to learn Emacs Lisp, you not only can customize your work environment up the wazoo, you can change Emacs itself by creating new tools and features, which you can then share with other users.

When I first introduced you to Emacs, I told you it is a text editor, which is true. However, we can now expand upon this definition: EMACS is a sophisticated text editor within a complex and powerful work environment.

There is a lot more I could say but we need to keep moving, so I'll end this section by quoting a short poem, called "Happy Thought", written by the Scottish poet Robert Louis Stevenson for the Queen of Sheba to explain to her the pleasure that comes from using Emacs:

> *The world is so full of a number of things,*
> *I'm sure we should all be as happy as kings.*[5]

■ **Note**　If you want to master Emacs, it helps to believe in reincarnation, because there is no way you are going to learn it all in a single lifetime.

Section: 1.4: Where Did Emacs Come From?

Many people believe that Emacs is of divine origin, but that is only partially correct.

The original Emacs was developed by Richard Stallman at MIT in 1975. At the time, Stallman was working in the MIT Artificial Intelligence Lab on an operating system called ITS, the Incompatible Time-sharing System, using a PDP-10 computer. (The name was coined to make fun of CTSS, the Compatible Time-sharing System, a more mainstream system that had been developed at the MIT Computation Center.)

One of the programs used by many ITS users was a text editor named TECO. Although TECO was useful, it was complex and difficult to use, driving even experienced programmers to the point of dementia. To make their lives simpler, some of the programmers developed collections of macros whose purpose was to make TECO easier to use. (As we discussed in Section 1.3, a macro is a tool that you can use to perform a specific function according to your personal needs.) In 1976, Stallman organized and extended the various sets of TECO macros into a coherent collection, which collectively, were referred to as the Emacs text editor. (The name is explained below.)

Since then, Emacs has been rewritten as a separate program many times, and greatly improved. It is available in a number of versions, the most popular being GNU Emacs, a product of the Free Software Foundation (FSF), which we discuss in Section 1.5. This is the version of Emacs you are most likely to encounter on a Unix system. Most of GNU Emacs is written in Emacs Lisp; the rest is written in C.

---

[5] Robert Louis Stevenson. *A Child's Garden of Verses*, 1885.

▧ **What's in a Name?**

TECO, Emacs

The original version of Emacs was a set of editing macros written to run under the TECO editor. Originally, the name TECO stood for "Tape Editor and Corrector". Later, the official name was changed to "Text Editor and Corrector".

Emacs is a simple abbreviation for "Editing Macros".

Section 1.5: The Free Software Foundation

In 1985, ten years after he released the first version of Emacs, Richard Stallman founded the FREE SOFTWARE FOUNDATION or FSF, based on the belief that high-quality software should be readily available without the usual commercial restrictions. Toward this end, Stallman wrote a manifesto (see Section 1.6) in which he set forth his philosophy regarding "free software". Stallman's influential and enduring contributions to programming culture were based on an observation:

• Programmers, by their nature, like to share their work.

From which he formed two core beliefs:

• When programmers have such freedom, the world benefits.
• Software licensing restrictions should reflect this reality.

It is important to understand that Stallman did not mean that all software should be available for no cost, with no restrictions. Rather, in calling for "free" software, Stallman was referring to freedom, not price. (At the time, it was popular to say that Stallman used the word "free" as in "free speech", not "free beer".) By definition, FREE SOFTWARE refers to programs that are distributed with a license specifying that anyone in the world is allowed to read the source code, modify the code, and share the results of their work freely. Moreover, any program based on free software must itself be licensed as free software. Another name commonly used for free software is OPEN SOURCE SOFTWARE.[6] (Programs that are not free of such restrictions are called PROPRIETARY SOFTWARE.)

To describe this philosophy, the FSF created the GNU GENERAL PUBLIC LICENSE or GPL, which mandates that any program derived from free software is itself free software. This is why any version of Emacs you will ever find is free software: all versions of Emacs are derived, at least indirectly, from GNU Emacs, which is distributed using the GPL.

However, in starting the Free Software Foundation, Stallman had more in mind than being able to distribute Emacs as free software. His goal was much more ambitious: to create a complete, free version of a Unix-like operating system, which he called GNU, to be licensed under the GNU General Public License.

---

[6] See Personal Note #4, "Free/Open Source Software" (Appendix A).

■ **What's in a Name?**

GNU

GNU is the name Richard Stallman chose to describe the Free Software Foundation's project to develop Unix-like tools and programs. The name GNU is an acronym for GNU's Not Unix.[7]

GNU is pronounced "ga-new", to rhyme with the sound that you make when you sneeze.

Section 1.6: Excerpts From *The Gnu Manifesto*

As I mentioned, Richard Stallman (Figure 1-1) wrote a manifesto whose philosophy forms the foundation of the Free Software Foundation. His basic idea — that *all* software should be shared freely — is, at best, naive. However, with the rise of the Internet, the development and distribution of free software and open source software has become an important economic and social force in our world. There are literally tens of thousands of programs available for free, and their contribution to the world at large (and to the happiness of their programmers) is beyond measure.

The FSF has been one of the leaders in this area, not only with Emacs, but with a C compiler (`gcc`), a C++ compiler (`g++`), a powerful debugger (`gdb`), a Unix shell (`bash`), and many, many other tools. All of this software — which is part of the GNU project — is used around the world and is considered to be of the highest quality.

Stallman's public declaration was not as sophisticated as other well-known manifestos, such as *95 Theses* (Martin Luther, 1517), or *The Playboy Philosophy* (Hugh Hefner, 1962-1966). Still, the

FIGURE 1-1. Richard Stallman, 2014.

Since 1975, Richard Stallman (1953-), the creator of Emacs and founder of the Free Software Foundation, has been a tireless and influential advocate for the importance of free software.

work of the Free Software Foundation continues to make an important contribution to our culture and, for this reason, you may be interested in reading a few excerpts from Stallman's 1985 essay.

If you want to read the entire *GNU Manifesto* (it's not long), it is easy to find online: just search for "gnu manifesto". You can also read it within Emacs by displaying the "Manifesto" section of the online Emacs manual. Here is how to do it. (These instructions will make sense once you learn some basic Emacs commands.)

---

[7] See Personal Note #5, "GNU's Not Unix?" (Appendix A).

1. Start Emacs
2. Start the Info facility: type <Ctrl-H> i
3. Jump to the menu item named "Emacs": type **m** then `emacs`
4. Jump to the menu item named "Manifesto": type **m** then `manifesto`
5. To move around as you read: press <PageUp> and <PageDown>
6. To quit: press <Ctrl-X> <Ctrl-C>

In addition to *The GNU Manifesto*, there is another important essay, called *The GNU Project*, also written by Richard Stallman,that will give you the flavor of the thinking behind Emacs and the Free Software Foundation. If you are interested in the philosophy behind free software, you can find this essay online by searching for "about the gnu project". You can also read it from within Emacs, as follows:

1. Start Emacs
2. Start the "About Emacs" part of the Help facility: type <Ctrl-H> then `g`
3. To move around as you read: press <PageUp> and <PageDown>
4. To quit: press <Ctrl-X> <Ctrl-C>

To finish this section, I have included, below, a few passages from the original GNU Manifesto. Note that when Stallman says software should be free he does *not* mean that anyone — including for-profit corporations — should be able to use any program for no money. He means that no one should have to pay for *permission* to use a program, although there may be a charge for distribution or support.

The following are excerpts from *The GNU Manifesto*:

"I consider that the golden rule requires that if I like a program I must share it with other people who like it. Software sellers want to divide the users and conquer them, making each user agree not to share with others. I refuse to break solidarity with other users in this way. I cannot in good conscience sign a nondisclosure agreement or a software license agreement. For years I worked within the Artificial Intelligence Lab to resist such tendencies and other inhospitalities, but eventually they had gone too far: I could not remain in an institution where such things are done for me against my will. So that I can continue to use computers without dishonor, I have decided to put together a sufficient body of free software so that I will be able to get along without any software that is not free. I have resigned from the AI lab to deny MIT any legal excuse to prevent me from giving GNU away..."

"Many programmers are unhappy about the commercialization of system software. It may enable them to make more money, but it requires them to feel in conflict with other programmers in general rather than feel as comrades. The fundamental act of friendship among programmers is the sharing of programs; marketing arrangements now typically used essentially forbid programmers to treat others as friends. The purchaser of software must choose between friendship and obeying the law. Naturally, many decide that friendship is more important. But those who believe in law often do not feel at ease with either choice. They become cynical and think that programming is just a way of making money..."

"Copying all or parts of a program is as natural to a programmer as breathing, and as productive. It ought to be as free..."

"In the long run, making programs free is a step toward the post-scarcity world, where nobody will have to work very hard just to make a living. People will be free to devote themselves to activities that are fun, such as programming, after spending the necessary ten hours a week on required tasks such as legislation, family counseling, robot repair and asteroid prospecting. There will be no need to be able to make a living from programming..."

CHAPTER 2

Unix for Emacs Users

Section 2.1: Operating Systems

I have already mentioned Unix several times. Unix is the name of a family of operating systems, and it is important to us for three reasons. First, most people who use Emacs do so with a Unix system such as Linux (which is a type of Unix). Second, Emacs was developed — and still lives — within the Unix culture. Finally, operating systems are important, and Unix and Linux are interesting in their own right. So before we get into the details of using Emacs, I'd like to take some time to talk about operating systems generally, and Unix and Linux in particular. I'm going to start with a few basic ideas, so if you are already an experienced programmer, please be patient. Although you might already be familiar with this material, I would ask you to at least skim it, just to make sure.

Whenever a human being uses a "computer system", there are three fundamental parts of the system that interact with one another: the computer itself, the programs that run on the computer, and the person who uses the programs. These three parts are inter-dependent:

- Computers (machines) run programs in order to perform tasks for people and provide services to other programs.
- Programs bring life to what would otherwise be inert machines.
- People use computers for a large variety of purposes, including writing more programs to run on computers.

When we talk about these ideas, we generally use more technical, impersonal terms. Specifically, we call the machines HARDWARE; we call the programs SOFTWARE; and we call the people USERS. The important idea I want you to appreciate is that computer systems are complex entities, created by a melding of hardware, software, and users. Since you are the user, you are affected by the hardware and the software that you choose to use. And, whether you realize it or not, one of the most important choices you make in your life is which operating system you will be using.[1] So let's talk about that for a moment.

---

[1] See Personal Note #6, "Our Tools Shape Our Minds" (Appendix A).

© Harley Hahn 2016
H. Hahn, *Harley Hahn's Emacs Field Guide*, DOI 10.1007/978-1-4842-1703-0_2

An OPERATING SYSTEM is a complex master control program that makes a computer work. Every computer, from the smallest phone to the largest supercomputer uses an operating system. Traditionally, the most important jobs for an operating system are:

1. To make efficient use of the hardware.
2. To furnish an environment for software, offering resources to the various programs as they run.
3. To provide an interface for users to interact with the software.

Since most operating systems are bundled (packaged) with a large number of tools, we can add one more item to our list:

4. To offer a variety of basic tools (useful programs) for users.

There are a large number of different operating systems. However, the ones that you and I are likely to encounter are almost always from one of two very different families: Unix and Windows.

WINDOWS, more formally, MICROSOFT WINDOWS, is the name of a family of commercial operating systems, first released in 1985. Since then, Microsoft has created many versions of Windows to run on a large variety of different types of hardware. Windows is a commercial product, created and controlled by Microsoft. If you want to use Windows, you (or someone) has to pay for it. UNIX is a general term, referring to a large number of operating systems that are based on a large set of specific principles and specifications developed over many years. Unix is not owned by a single company. Moreover, there are many versions of Unix that are available for free.

The important thing to appreciate is that, as long as you are using a computer that has a keyboard (not a tablet, phone, or touchpad), Emacs is available — for free — to run on whatever system you are likely to be using. And (you will have to believe me here) it will be good for your brain to learn how to use Emacs.

However, before we get into the details of installing and using Emacs, I want to take some time for us to talk about Unix.

Section 2.2: Unix and Linux

Unix is the name of the world's largest family of operating systems.

The first primitive version of Unix was created in 1969 by Ken Thompson, a programmer at the Bell Labs research facility in New Jersey, owned by AT&T.[2] Within a short time, Unix became popular among the Bell Labs' and other East Coast researchers. The two main Unix pioneers at Bell Labs were Ken Thompson and Dennis Ritchie. (Their names are worth remembering.) Throughout the 1970s and into the early 1980s, Thompson, Ritchie, and other programmers expended a great deal of effort expanding and improving Unix.

---

[2] See Personal Note #7, "AT&T" (Appendix A).

In 1974, the use of Unix began to spread to the West Coast, when a computer science professor from the University of California at Berkeley visited Bell Labs and brought back a copy of Unix. In 1975, Ken Thompson went to Berkeley from Bell Labs for a year-long sabbatical. As a result of Thompson's visit, a graduate student named Bill Joy became interested in Unix and began to work on his own version. The result was a new Unix, called BSD (an acronym for Berkeley System Distribution), which became popular among computer scientists and programmers around the world.[3] In fact, today, there are still a variety of Unix systems based on BSD, the most important being FreeBSD, NetBSD, OpenBSD, and DragonFly BSD. In addition, Apple's Mac OS X operating system (often referred to as OS X) is, to a great extent, also based on BSD. (See the footnote in Section 2.3.)

By the early 1980s, AT&T — the company that owned Bell Labs — became increasingly impatient to start making money from Unix. To do so, in 1983, AT&T turned Unix into a commercial product called System V (pronounced "system five"). Throughout the rest of the 1980s, a large number of different Unix systems were developed, based on either System V (what we might call East Coast Unix) or BSD (West Coast Unix). The System V-based versions of Unix were commercial products, developed and sold by computer companies, including AT&T. Most of the BSD-based versions of Unix, on the other hand, were non-commercial and were distributed for free.[4] In this way, BSD gathered a large following of computer scientists, researchers, and programmers around the world.

By 1991, personal computers had been around for 10 years, and many programmers now had their very own computers. (The IBM Personal Computer was introduced in August 1981.) However, there was still no operating system that ran on a PC that was attractive to the type of programmer whose idea of fun was to take things apart and modify them.[5] Nevertheless, the world was ready. What follows is a long, interesting story, very much related to Emacs. However, in the interest of brevity I will shorten it.

In 1985, Richard Stallman started the Free Software Foundation (FSF). As we discussed in Section 1.4, one of Stallman's goals was to create a free version of Unix — which he named GNU — that would be available to anyone who wanted to modify, use, or distribute it in any way. Nevertheless, by 1991, GNU was not nearly ready. To explain what happened next, I have to make a quick technical digression. However, it's an important digression, so stay with me.

As we have discussed, operating systems such as Unix are very complex. To simplify a bit, the *basic* functionality of a Unix system is provided by two different parts: the kernel and the utilities. The KERNEL, which is always running, is the central part of the operating system. As such, it provides essential services as they are needed. The UTILITIES consist of a wide variety of separate programs, distributed

---

[3] See Personal Note #8, "Early Unix on the West Coast" (Appendix A).
[4] See Personal Note #9, "BSD Unix in the 1980s" (Appendix A).
[5] See Personal Note #10, "Hackers and Geeks" (Appendix A).

along with the kernel as part of the entire system. Where the kernel is the heart of an operating system, the utilities provide functionality to the users and to other programs. To summarize:

Kernel + Utilities → basic operating system

Unix Kernel + Unix Utilities → basic Unix system

Modern Unix systems come with, literally, hundreds of different utilities, each of which provides a different function. The most important utility is the SHELL — also known as the COMMAND PROCESSOR — the program that provides the primary user interface into Unix. The job of the shell is to process Unix commands as they are entered by a user. The shell can also process a list of commands stored in a file, called a SHELL SCRIPT. Over the years, there have been a variety of different Unix shells. Today, the most popular shell — the one you will probably use — is called BASH.[6] (In Section 2.7, we'll talk about how to enter commands for the shell.)

To return to our discussion: By 1991, the world was ready for a completely free operating system that programmers could run on their own PCs for fun, for experimenting, and to modify and share — without cost — with other programmers around the world. (The Microsoft and Apple operating systems, Windows and Mac OS respectively, didn't fill this need because they were — and still are — purely commercial products that are kept under tight control by the companies that own them.) To be sure, the FSF had done a lot of work towards creating an open version of Unix for personal computers. By 1991, they had created a great deal of high-quality, free software, including many of the traditional Unix utilities (and Emacs). However, the FSF did not, as yet, have a kernel. And until such a kernel was created, there would be no free Unix system for PCs.

However, on August 25, 1991, Linus Torvalds (Figure 2-1), a second-year computer science student at the University of Helsinki (Finland) announced via Usenet,[7] that he was developing his own freely shared Unix-like kernel for PCs. Torvalds started this project just for fun, and asked for volunteers. He realized that all he really needed was a kernel, because the FSF had already created a free version of the most important Unix utilities, which he could adapt easily to his own system.

In September 1991, Torvalds and his collaborators released the first-ever free Unix kernel to run on a PC. It was then a relatively easy job to adapt the FSF utilities to work with the new kernel, giving birth to a brand new version of Unix, which came to be known as LINUX. Linux is free,[8] open source software, licensed primarily under Version 2 of the GNU General Public License (GPLv2). (We discussed the GPL in Section 1.5.)

---

[6] See Personal Note #11, "Bash" (Appendix A).
[7] The worldwide system of discussions groups. See Personal Note #3, "Usenet, Emacs, and the Internet" (Appendix A).

FIGURE 2-1. Linus Torvalds, 2004.

Linus Torvalds (1969), the original creator of the Linux kernel. In 1991, Torvalds founded the project that resulted in the first-ever, free Unix kernel. Torvalds combined his kernel with the Free Software Foundation's utilities to create Linux, the first free Unix system for personal computers. Today, there are a very large number of different Linux systems, running on virtually every type of computer.

Today, there are many, many different versions of Linux — often referred to as Linux DISTRIBUTIONS — running on virtually every type of computer: from tiny computers that are smaller than your hand, to the largest supercomputers.

Note   If you would like to try Linux and you are not sure which distribution to choose, my advice is to start with Ubuntu Linux.

---

[8] See Personal Note #12, "Linux is Free" (Appendix A).

17

▓ **What's in a Name?**

Linux

When Linus Torvalds was working on his first kernel, he sometimes referred to it informally as Linux, the name being a contraction of "Linus' Minix". (Minix was a small, Unix-like operating system created by the Dutch computer scientist Andrew Tannenbaum.) However, when it came time to release the new kernel, Torvalds had decided to name it Freax, for "free Unix". Here is where fate steps in.

In September 1991, it happened that another programmer, Ari Lemmke, convinced Linus to distribute the kernel files using an FTP (file sharing) server maintained by Funet, a Finnish academic/research network. However, Lemmke didn't like the name Freax and when he received the files from Torvalds, he uploaded them to a directory he called `linux,` and the name stuck.

Today, the name Linux refers to any operating system that uses the Linux kernel. Many Linux systems still use the FSF utilities and, for this reason, you will sometimes see Linux referred to as GNU/Linux.

The name Linux is pronounced to rhyme with "bin'-ex".

The name Linus is pronounced "Lee'-nus".

Section 2.3: Unix Terminals and Userids

In Section 1.4, I told you that the most popular type of Emacs is GNU Emacs, and that it runs under a variety of different operating systems, including Microsoft Windows. However, almost everyone who uses Emacs does so under some type of Unix. Specifically, GNU Emacs is available in specific versions for Linux, FreeBSD, NetBSD, OpenBSD, Mac OS X,[9] and Solaris. For this reason, I am going to assume that there is a good chance that you, too, will be using Emacs on a Unix system. To prepare you properly, there are important Unix concepts I want to make sure you understand.

What we are about to cover in the rest of this chapter is particularly relevant to learning how to use Emacs skillfully. However, it is, necessarily, a brief, abbreviated overview of Unix. There is a *lot* more to learn and, unfortunately, I am not able to cover it all in this book. The best way to learn how to use Unix/Linux well is to read my book *Harley Hahn's Guide to Unix and Linux.*[10] As you read this chapter, you might wonder, is all this really necessary? The answer is, yes. I can assure you that people who are skilled at using Emacs know everything I will be covering. Please take the time to read through all the material.

---

[9] See Personal Note #13, "Mac OS X Is Unix" (Appendix A).

[10] *Harley Hahn's Guide to Unix and Linux*, McGraw-Hill Higher Education, 2008. The ISBN is 0073133612.

To start, I'll remind you that Unix was developed in the 1970s (see Section 2.2), before programmers were able to have their own personal computers. To work with Unix, a person would use a terminal to connect to a host. The TERMINAL was an electronic box with a keyboard and a screen, or a keyboard and a printer.[11] The HOST was the computer to which the terminal connected. The connection could be either via a cable (which was relatively fast), or via a modem and telephone line (which was very slow). Such terminal/host systems were called TIME-SHARING SYSTEMS or MULTIUSER SYSTEMS, because they could support multiple users who were "sharing" the computer's time, so to speak.

Thus, from the very beginning, the architecture of Unix was based on a terminal/host time-sharing system and — believe it or not — that is still the case today. I want to spend a moment talking about this paradigm because it will help you understand what happens when you use Unix in general and Emacs in particular.

Let's pretend for a moment that we are going to take a time-travel trip back to the late 1970s. Close your eyes and pretend that it is 1976, and you and I are visiting the computer science department at U.C. San Diego.[12] We want to use one of the Unix systems so we visit the SYSTEM ADMINISTRATOR, the person who runs the system we want to use. The system administrator sets up a Unix account that will enable us to use the system. The ACCOUNT includes a variety of information including a userid and a password.

A USERID (pronounced "user-eye-dee") is a one-word name, usually all lowercase, that is used to identify a user to the system. A PASSWORD is a (hopefully) difficult-to-guess series of characters that provides security for a particular userid. Passwords are secret; userids are not.

As an example, let us say that the system administrator gives us the userid **harley** and a password **kajsaanka**.[13] Whenever we want to use Unix, we must find a terminal and identify ourselves to the system. To do so, we LOG IN by typing our userid (so the system knows which account we will be using), followed by our password (to prove that we are allowed to use that account).

After logging in, we can now make use of the Unix system by entering commands. As we discussed in Section 2.2, the program that interprets our commands is called the shell. Each time we log in, a shell is started for us automatically. It then sits there quietly, waiting to serve us. We enter commands, one after another, and when we are finished using the system, we LOG OUT by terminating the shell. We do this by entering the **logout** command, or by pressing a special key combination (<Ctrl-D>) to tell the shell there are no more commands.[14] Once we have logged out, someone else can use the terminal.

---

[11] See Personal Note #14, "Terminals That Print" (Appendix A).

[12] See Personal Note #15, "Why U.C. San Diego in 1976?" (Appendix A).

[13] Kajsa Anka is a real name. Look it up.

[14] Pressing <Ctrl-D> sends an **eof** signal, which indicates that there is no more data (see Section 2-6).

Aside from keeping track of our userid and password, our account also specifies what level of privileges we are allowed to use. Generally speaking, there are two types of userids: the system administrator's and everyone else's. The system administrator has a special userid with its own password that allows him to do *anything he wants*. When a person logs in using this userid, we say that he or she becomes SUPERUSER. To protect the integrity of the system, all the other accounts have restricted privileges: they are able to use the system for regular work, but they do not have enough power to cause harm to the system or to other people's files. Being superuser is so powerful that it must be used sparingly to protect the integrity of the system and to keep everyone's files safe.

▪ **Note**   Traditionally, the name of the system administrator userid is `root`. The name was chosen because the main directory in the Unix filesystem is called the root directory (see Section 2.16).

Typically, a system administrator will use a regular account for his own personal work. He or she will only use the superuser account when absolutely necessary. In our example, when we asked the system administrator for a Unix account, he would have paused what he was doing, logged in as superuser, created a new account for us, and then logged out as superuser.

So that is how it worked in 1976. To use a Unix system, we had to ask the system administrator to create an account for us, with a userid and password. We then had to find a terminal attached to that system, and log in. We would use the system by typing commands, one after the other, which would be processed by the shell. When we were finished, we would log out. If something important had to be done that required special privileges, the system administrator was required to log in as superuser, at least long enough to carry out that particular task.

The reason I am telling you all this is because — believe it or not — decades later, Unix still works the same way. And since Emacs developed within a Unix environment, the Unix way of thinking is deeply connected to the Emacs way of thinking.

Consider the following metaphor. Let's say you want to learn how to speak a new language. Ideally, you want more than to simply speak the language; you want to speak it without an accent. It's the same with Emacs. No matter what operating system you use to run Emacs; no matter how much time you spend with it; no matter what you use it for — if you don't learn basic Unix, you will never be able to speak Emacs without an accent.

Eventually, this will all make sense. For now, just trust my judgment and keep reading as we move towards our next goal: to discuss the various environments ("user interfaces") that you can use to run Emacs. However, for that discussion to make sense, we first need to take a few minutes to talk some more about terminals.

Section 2.4: Types of Terminals

The very first computer terminals, dating from the 1960s, were PRINTING TERMINALS that printed their output on paper: either a continuous roll or a stack of folded, perforated pages (called COMPUTER PAPER). You can see two such terminals in the photo in Figure 2-2. This photo, taken around 1970, shows Dennis Ritchie and Ken Thompson working on a PDP-11 computer at Bell Labs. It is likely that this is the very computer used by Ritchie and Thompson to create the first version of Unix.

FIGURE 2-2. Dennis Ritchie (standing) and Ken Thompson (sitting), circa 1970.

This photo, taken at Bell Labs sometime around 1970, shows Dennis Ritchie (1941-2011) and Ken Thompson (1943-). Ritchie and Thompson, the original developers of Unix, are working on a DEC PDP-11 computer. The terminals that Thompson is using are Teletype Model 33 ASRs.

By the early 1970s, printing terminals were being replaced by VIDEO DISPLAY TERMINALS. Instead of using paper, video display terminals displayed their output on a built-in monitor. The terminal worked with a set number of rows, and each new line of text was written to the bottom row of the monitor. As this happened, all the other lines were moved up one row, while the (old) top line disappeared.

The DEC VT52 terminal (introduced in July 1974) had 24 rows, each of which could display 80 characters. A few years later, the VT52 was replaced by a more powerful terminal, the DEC VT100 (August 1978), which displayed either 24 rows of 80 characters or 14 rows of 132 characters.[15] Since this type of terminal can display only characters, we refer to them as TEXT TERMINALS. You can see a photo of a VT100 in Figure 2-3.

As I mentioned, the original video display terminals displayed new data only on the bottom row, causing all the lines to move up (similar to a printing terminal). However, as text terminals were improved, it became possible for the software to display or erase characters in any position on any row. This meant that programmers now had more choices. Instead of simply displaying output on the bottom line — causing all the other lines to move up — terminals such as the DEC VT100 made it possible for programs to use the entire screen at once, typically 1,920 separate characters (24 lines x 80 characters/line). This enabled programmers to create a new type of interface. We'll talk about the details in Section 2.5. For now, I'll just say that this is the type of interface that was used to create Emacs.

Over the years, better and better video display terminals were developed: not only text terminals but, eventually, GRAPHICS TERMINALS that could display both text and images. A few of the more widely used graphics terminals were the IBM 2250 (introduced in 1964), the DEC GT40 (1972), the IBM 3270 (1977), the Textronix 4010 family (1972-1974), and the latecomer DEC VT240 (1984).

FIGURE 2-3. VT100 terminal.

The DEC VT100 terminal was introduced in 1978 by the Digital Equipment Company. In the late 1970s and early 1980s, these VT100 family of terminals were very popular. To this day, their basic characteristics are preserved in most terminal emulators.

Graphics terminals were important because they made it possible for programs to display images, lines, curves and other shapes, as well as plain text. Graphics terminals also made it possible to share graphical programs over a network, a capability that was especially important to universities and research organizations. However, compared to text terminals, graphics terminals were very expensive and required much more complicated software to connect to a host computer. One

---

[15] See Personal Note #16, "80- and 132-character Lines" (Appendix A).

reason was that every type of graphics terminal had its own distinctive requirements, and it was a lot of work to make even a simple program work with different types of graphics terminals. This is because displaying graphical output requires special-purpose hardware and extra computing power.

In the late 1980s, however, these limitations began to change because of an ambitious and, ultimately, very successful project called X Window, started at MIT in 1984 by Bob Scheifler and Jim Gettys. At the time, there were many MIT programmers, using a large variety of different types of hardware. What X WINDOW offered was a standard way for people to use the keyboard, monitor and mouse on their own computer to interact with programs that were running on any computer in their network. Moreover, X Window offered portability. Once a program was written to work with X Window, it could be used by anyone whose computer had X Window software.

Because personal computers with graphics capabilities were now readily available, it wasn't long before computers running X Window obviated the need for expensive, complex graphics terminals. Within a short time, X Window became an industry standard that, over the next few years, led to a revolution that would change forever the way most people used their computers.

What fueled this revolution was the growing realization that it was not the case that people interact with hardware. Rather, people *use* hardware to interact with programs. Although this might seem obvious to you now, this idea was an important insight that took years for people to appreciate. Why this was so important and, specifically, how it influenced the development of Emacs, is the topic of Section 2.5.

Section 2.5: User Interfaces

On August 12, 1981, at the Waldorf Astoria ballroom in New York City, an event occurred that would, in retrospect, be recognized as changing the world. At an IBM press conference, an executive named Phil Estridge announced the brand new IBM 5150 computer, nicknamed the IBM Personal Computer or IBM PC. Since the late 1970s, other companies had been making relatively inexpensive computers to be used exclusively by one person at a time. The most popular machines were the Commodore PT, Apple II, TRS-80 and Atari 400. However, IBM was, by far, the largest computer company in the world, and it wasn't until they finally announced their own personal computer, along with a new set of industry standards, that the age of personal computing finally began.

■ **Note**   The cost of the original IBM PC was $1,565 (a bit more than $4,000 in 2016 dollars). The original IBM PC came with 16 kilobytes of memory (0.000016 gigabytes) and no hard disk. Instead it had a disk drive that used floppy disks which could store up to 160 kilobytes of data.

By the end of the 1980s, personal computers became more affordable and more powerful, and Unix programmers had shifted from using terminals to using their own computers. Specifically, many people were using Unix on inexpensive IBM PC COMPATIBLE personal computers, machines that adhered to standards based on the IBM PC family. Other people, who needed more power and larger monitors, used expensive, high-end Unix machines called WORKSTATIONS.[16]

Remember, however, Unix had always been a multiuser, terminal/host time-sharing system (and it still is). As we discussed in Section 2.3, in the early 1980s, to use Unix you needed a terminal to access a Unix host. But with a personal computer, all the hardware is part of a single machine. So the question arises: When you use Unix on your own computer, where is the terminal and where is the host?

The answer to this question involves two important inventions: "terminal emulators" to use with text-based programs and "graphical user interfaces" to use with graphics-based programs. We'll start with the text-based programs.

When you run a text-based program on your own Unix computer, even today, you need a terminal to connect to a host. That's the way Unix was designed in the early 1970s, and it has never been changed. As you might guess, your computer is the host. But where is the terminal?

Obviously, you don't use a real terminal. Instead, you use a special program that utilizes your computer's keyboard and monitor to simulate the functionality of a terminal. In this way, you can log in, enter as many commands as you want, run as many programs as you want, and log out, just as if you were using an actual physical terminal.

When a program simulates the functionally of a physical device, we say that it EMULATES that device. So a program that acts as a terminal is called a TERMINAL EMULATOR. There are many different terminal emulators in use today and, believe it or not, they are all based on the old DEC VT100 family of terminals we discussed in Section 2.4. This means that, even today, when you type a Unix command or run a text-based Unix program, you are using a technology that was first introduced in 1978.[17] Moreover, as far as Unix is concerned, the terminal/host system is working just fine, the way it has always worked, because your programs don't know whether you are using a terminal emulator or a real terminal. This concept is important because the underlying technology has a strong influence on how you interact with your programs. Let me be more specific.

To communicate with a program that is running, we use what is called a USER INTERFACE. There are two basic text-based interfaces, which means that there are two different ways in which you might find yourself working with text-based programs. (Graphics-based programs work differently, as you will see in a moment.)

---

[16] See Personal Note #17, "Unix Workstations" (Appendix A).
[17] See Personal Note #18, "Time Travel" (Appendix A).

The simplest text-based interface is the COMMAND-LINE INTERFACE or CLI. When you use a CLI, you type one line at a time and then press the <Enter> (or <Return>) key. As you type, the characters are displayed on the bottom line of the screen. When you press <Enter>, whatever you have typed is sent to the program, and all the lines on the screen scroll up one row. In the same way, when a CLI-based program writes output for you to read, it does so one line at a time on the bottom line of your screen. As each line is displayed, all the other lines scroll up one row.

When you use a CLI, you use only a keyboard for input, not a pointing device. The most common example would be typing Unix commands, one at a time, for the shell to interpret. (This is where the name "command-line interface" comes from. The bottom line of the screen where your input is displayed is called the COMMAND LINE.)

The second text-based interface is more sophisticated. It is called a TEXT-BASED USER INTERFACE or TUI. With a TUI, a program can read and write characters anywhere on the screen, not just on the command line. As a result, TUI-based programs have a different look and feel: they take over the entire screen, so you have the feeling that you are working "within" the program. The more sophisticated TUI programs may display colors, and will use the various parts of the screen in different ways. For example, a TUI-based program may arrange data into columns, or even create rudimentary windows.

Some TUI programs will let you use a mouse, most commonly to access simple menus to make selections. Still, with a TUI-based program, pull-down menus are generally not very important. Most of the time, you will be using your keyboard to control the program, which means that you will need to memorize a lot of different commands. The reason I am telling you all this is because Emacs is a TUI-based program. In fact, it is one of the most powerful TUI-based programs ever written.[18]

When you work with graphics-based programs, you use a GRAPHICAL USER INTERFACE or GUI, which is a lot different than a CLI or TUI. A GUI manages the entire screen, or multiple screens if you have more than one monitor. With a GUI, you typically run multiple programs at the same time, each program in its own window. Whenever you change to another program — usually by clicking on its window — we say that you move the FOCUS to that program. (At any moment, the program that has the focus is the one that reads the input from your keyboard.)

When you use a GUI, you will see all the typical graphical elements: windows, icons, menus, scroll bars, buttons, and so on. The background on which these elements appear is called the DESKTOP. (For example, you might say, "I have three windows open on my desktop.") For this reason, a GUI-based working environment is often referred to as a DESKTOP ENVIRONMENT. More specifically, a desktop environment refers to the design of all the graphical elements, how they work, and

---

[18] See Personal Note #19, "Midnight Commander" (Appendix A).

how they interact; as well as all the tools that are included as part of the GUI package, such as a file manager, a terminal emulator, tools to help you change your system's settings, and much more.

When you install Linux, you create a master account by specifying a userid and password. Each time you start Linux, you will be asked to enter your userid and password, at which point the GUI will start automatically. In the world of Unix, there are many GUIs, but they are all based on the X Window system we discussed in Section 2.4. With Linux, the most popular GUIs are Unity, Gnome and KDE.[19] Each of these GUIs has its own desktop environment. However, because they more or less follow the same general principles, if you can use one, it's not hard to learn how to use another.

When you use a CLI or a TUI, you control a program by typing at it. With a GUI, you do use your keyboard, but mostly to enter data. Generally, you control your programs by using a pointing device, such as a mouse, trackball, touchpad, or pointing stick. For example, you would use a pointing device to pull down menus and make a selection; to manipulate objects by dragging and dropping; and so on.

Now back to Emacs. Every time Emacs starts it checks what type of interface you are using and acts appropriately. If you start Emacs while you are working within a GUI, Emacs runs as a graphics-based program inside a window. If you start Emacs from a text-based terminal, Emacs takes over the terminal's screen and runs as a TUI program. Nevertheless, no matter what system you are using (Unix, Windows, or Macintosh) and regardless of how you run the program, Emacs always works the same. Here is why.

Like so many other enduring programs, Emacs is a product of the times during which it was created. To be sure, over the decades, Emacs has been rewritten more than once and enhanced many, many times. Still, the program remains surprisingly close to its roots, and if you really want to understand it you need to have a sense of the historical conditions under which it arose.

Emacs was designed to work well with the hardware and software limitations of its time and, in the environment in which Emacs was developed, people interacted with programs by typing one command after another.

Realize then, that when you use Emacs today you are, literally, copying the keystrokes of programmers who, decades ago, decided which key combinations worked best for what they wanted to do. This is important to remember so when you set out to learn how to use Emacs, you don't think that what you are learning is unnecessarily complicated and arbitrary. Emacs is well-designed and, I promise you, you will see that, but it will take a while. Along the way, if you ever get discouraged

---

[19] See Personal Note #20, "KDE and Gnome" (Appendix A).
[20] Compared to your phone or tablet, which is easy to learn but hard to use.

or confused remember what I told you in Section 1.1: Emacs is difficult to learn, but easy to use.[20]

For this reason, no matter where and how you run Emacs, you will always control the program by typing at it — and the key combinations will always be the same. This means that the Emacs skills you learn from this book will last you forever.[21] That's the way it was designed back in the late 1970s (see Section 1.4), and the design still works well. Emacs is, arguably, the best TUI-based program ever written, and there is no need to change it. Indeed, changing Emacs from a text-based, command-driven program that requires you to learn a huge number of key combinations into an "easy-to-use", GUI-based program with icons and menus would be like sending Donald Duck to charm school.[22]

Section 2.6: Using a Unix Terminal

So far, we have discussed why the terminal/host system is a basic part of Unix (Section 2.3) and why you need a terminal to work with text-based programs (Section 2.5). The most important such program is the shell, the command processor that reads and interprets your commands (Section 2.2). Because the shell is a text-based program, you need to have access to a terminal in order to use Unix commands. You also need access to a terminal to use Emacs.

The specific details I am about to show you below are based on Ubuntu Linux, a very popular Linux distribution. However, most of what you read here will work with all Linux systems, and the general ideas apply to any type of Unix.

As we have discussed, no one uses real terminals anymore. Instead, we use terminal emulators. So whenever you hear people talk about a "terminal", you can assume that they are referring to a terminal emulator, not a real terminal. For example, if I say, "I am going to show you how to use a Linux terminal", what I mean is, I am going to show you how to use a Linux terminal emulator.

There are two different types of terminal emulators: virtual terminals and terminal windows. When you use a VIRTUAL TERMINAL, the terminal emulator uses your entire screen to provide you with a totally text-based experience. When you use a TERMINAL WINDOW, the terminal emulator runs in a window within a GUI (graphical user interface).[23]

Note   For historical reasons, you will sometimes see a virtual terminal referred to as a VIRTUAL CONSOLE.

---

[21] Or until you die, whichever comes first.
[22] It's not going to work, and all you are going to do is annoy the duck.
[23] See Personal Note #21, "Aren't All Terminals Virtual?" (Appendix A).

27

Linux systems come with six built-in virtual terminals (and you can create more if you need them). To access the six built-in terminals, you use the key combinations shown in Figures 2-4 and 2-5.

Terminal	Key Combination
1	<Ctrl-Alt-F1>
2	<Ctrl-Alt-F2>
3	<Ctrl-Alt-F3>
4	<Ctrl-Alt-F4>
5	<Ctrl-Alt-F5>
6	<Ctrl-Alt-F6>

FIGURE 2-4. Accessing a Virtual Terminal From the GUI.

To switch from the GUI to a specific virtual terminal, use <Ctrl-Alt-F1> through <Ctrl-Alt-F6>. To return to the GUI, use <Alt-F7> or <Ctrl-Alt-F7>.

Terminal	Key Combination
Next	<Alt-Right>
Previous	<Alt-Left>
1	<Alt-F1> or <Ctrl-Alt-F1>
2	<Alt-F2> or <Ctrl-Alt-F2>
3	<Alt-F3> or <Ctrl-Alt-F3>
4	<Alt-F4> or <Ctrl-Alt-F4>
5	<Alt-F5> or <Ctrl-Alt-F5>
6	<Alt-F6> or <Ctrl-Alt-F6>
Return to GUI	<Alt-F7> or <Ctrl-Alt-F7>

FIGURE 2-5. Changing From One Virtual Terminal to Another.

To switch from one virtual terminal to another, you have several choices. <Alt-Right> changes to the terminal with the next highest number. <Alt-Left> changes to the terminal with the previous number. <Alt-F1> through <Alt-F6> changes to a specific terminal. Finally, <Alt-F7> will return you to the GUI (the Desktop Environment). Please note that, for convenience, the function key combinations can use either <Alt> or <Ctrl-Alt>.

To use a virtual terminal, you must log in by typing your userid and your password. To log out, you can either use the **logout** command, or press <Ctrl-D> to send an **eof** signal. (We will discuss signals and **eof** in Section 2.11.)

The advantage of using a virtual terminal is that it looks and works pretty much the same as if you were using a real terminal. Specifically, the display is all text and uses the entire screen, which makes the characters easy to read. Moreover, there are no windows or icons or other elements to distract you, so it is easy to focus on one thing at a time.

You can switch from one virtual terminal to another by pressing the appropriate key combination.[24] For example, let's say you are working with the GUI and you want to use virtual terminal #1. You would use:

<Ctrl-Alt-F1>

After a while, you want to pause what you are doing to use a different virtual terminal. To switch to virtual terminal #2:

<Alt-F2>

Later, you decide to switch back to virtual terminal #1. Either of the following will work:

<Alt-Left>
<Alt-F1>

Finally, you decide to switch back to the GUI (which will be exactly how you left it):

<Alt-F7>

The second way to access a terminal is by using a terminal window. Unlike virtual terminals, terminal windows run within the GUI in their own window, like regular programs. The advantage of using a terminal window is that, as you work, you are within the GUI, so you can use all the other GUI-based tools that are part of your desktop environment. You can also have multiple windows open, each with its own program. If you want to work with more than one terminal at a time you can open more than one terminal window and, because everything is running within the GUI, you can copy and paste between a terminal window and any other window. (This is not the case with virtual terminals. Because each virtual terminal runs in its own environment, you can't copy and paste from one virtual terminal to another; and you can't copy and paste from a virtual terminal to the GUI, or from the GUI to a virtual terminal.)

Starting a terminal window is easy. However, before I give you the instructions, I want to take a moment to give you a brief introduction to the Ubuntu GUI and the default desktop environment, named Unity (see Section 2.5).

The Unity desktop environment (see Figure 2-6) is particularly easy to use. The column of icons on the far left (under the words "Ubuntu Desktop") is called the LAUNCHER. You use the Launcher to start programs. The top icon in the Launcher is the Ubuntu logo. You click it to open the DASH, a tool that lets you search for anything you want.

---

[24] If your function keys don't respond properly, check your keyboard. You may have to hold down a special key (such as <Fn>) to make your function keys work.

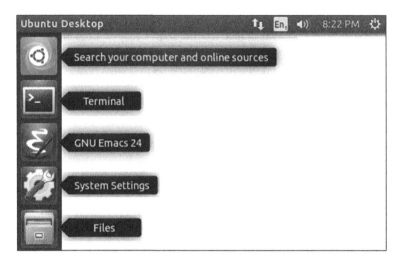

FIGURE 2-6. The Ubuntu Desktop.

The default Ubuntu desktop environment, Unity, is particularly easy to use. The column of icons on the left, under the words "Ubuntu Desktop", is called the Launcher. It is used to start programs. For example, to start a terminal window, just click on the Terminal icon. To start Emacs (once it is installed), click on the Emacs icon. The top icon in the Launcher is the Ubuntu logo. You can click it to open the Dash, which enables you to search for anything you want.

The easiest way to start a terminal window is to click on the Terminal icon in the Launcher (see Figure 2-6). Clicking on this icon will open a program (a terminal emulator) called TERMINAL inside a window of its own. If you want to start another, separate terminal window, just right-click on Terminal Icon and select "New Terminal". In this way, you can start as many terminal windows as you want.

If for some reason you don't see the Terminal icon in the Launcher, it is easy to find. Click the top icon on the Launcher to open the Dash and then type "terminal". You will see the Terminal icon, which you can click to start the program.[25]

■ **Note**

If the Launcher doesn't already have a Terminal icon, it is easy to put one there. Use the Dash to find and start the Terminal program. Once it starts running, its icon will appear in the Launcher. However, it will disappear when the program ends.

To make an icon stay in the Launcher permanently, right-click on the icon and select "Lock to Launcher".

To delete an icon from the Launcher, right-click on the icon and select "Unlock from Launcher".

Once an icon is in the Launcher, you may want to change its position. To do so, use your mouse and — in one smooth motion — drag the icon away from the Launcher, then up or down to the place you want to move it, and then back into the Launcher. (After you do it once, it's easy.)

---

[25] See Personal Note #22, "Ubuntu Terminal Emulators" (Appendix A).

Section 2.7: The Unix Command Line

The COMMAND LINE is a facility provided by an operating system that enables you to enter commands, one at a time. These commands are then processed by the shell (see Section 2.2). The command line is important because it enables you to use many of the tools that come with your operating system. (These tools are the "utilities" we talked about in Section 2.2.) When you use Unix, these tools are referred to as UNIX COMMANDS. With Windows, they are called WINDOWS COMMANDS.

As a smart person who wants to use his or her computer well, it behooves you to master the intricacies of the command line. In addition, it will help you to understand how to use the more important Unix commands (tools). As an Emacs user, it is especially important, because you can access the command line from within the Emacs environment, which makes it possible to use any of the commands you want — and there are hundreds of them — without having to leave Emacs. Before that can happen, however, you need to understand how to use the command-line on its own.

To use the command line well requires a lot of knowledge and takes a lot of experience, so I can't teach you everything right now. What I can do is make sure you know the basics, at least enough to get you started. If you are an experienced programmer, you may already know what I am about to explain. If so, it's probably better to not skip this part of the book. (Just read it quickly. Who knows, you may find something that is new to you.)

In the next few sections, I am going to show you how to use the Unix command line. What you are about to read will work for any type of Unix, including Linux and Mac OS X. If you use Windows, the basic ideas will be the same, but the details and the commands will be different.[26]

To access the command line, you must be using a terminal. If you are using Linux, just follow the directions in Section 2.6 and open either a terminal window or a virtual terminal. With a terminal window, you will be logged in automatically. With a virtual terminal, you will have to enter your userid and password to log in manually.

▨ **What's in a Name?**

Command Line

In Unix, the term "command line" is used in two different, but related, ways.

First, "command line" refers to the facility that lets you enter Unix commands to be processed by the shell. Example: "To learn how to use Unix well, you need to master the command line."

Second, when you use a terminal, the bottom line of the display is called the "command line". This is because, as you type a command, this is where you see the characters you are typing.

---

[26] See Personal Note #23, "How to Access the Command Line with Mac OS X and Windows" (Appendix A).

31

Section 2.8: The Shell Prompt

As you use a terminal, the shell will indicate when it is ready for you to enter a command. It does this by displaying a special series of characters called the SHELL PROMPT. Every shell has a default prompt, which you can change if you want. Here is an example using Bash on one of my Linux systems:

```
harley@kajsa:~$
```

Although you can't see it, there is a space after the **$** (dollar sign) character. The space is there to create a bit of room between the prompt and the command you will be typing. For example, if you were to type the **date** command (to display the time and date), it would look like this:

```
harley@kajsa:~$ date
```

By convention, the second-last letter of the prompt (before the space) identifies the type of shell. Broadly speaking, there are two main families of shells in common use: the Bourne Shell family and the C-Shell family. If your shell is a member of the Bourne Shell family, you will see a **$** character, as in the examples above. If your shell is a member of the C-Shell family, you will see a **%** (percent-sign) character:

```
harley@kajsa:~%
```

If you are logged in as superuser (see Section 2.3), no matter what shell you are using you will see a **#** (number sign) character:

```
harley@kajsa:~#
```

A prompt that ends with # is telling you to be very careful: you are superuser and, if you make a mistake, you could cause a lot of damage.

■ **Note**

The most popular shells in the Bourne Shell family are Bash (**bash**) and the Korn Shell (**ksh**) in that order. The most popular shell in the C-Shell family is **tcsh** (pronounced "tee-see-shell").

The default shell for Linux systems and for Mac OS X is Bash. The default shell for BSD-based system is either **tcsh** or the Korn Shell. If you don't like your default shell, you can change it by using the **chsh** (change shell) command.

The first shell prompt I showed you is the default Ubuntu Linux prompt. Let's take a moment to dissect it:

```
harley@kajsa:~$
```

First, you see the name of my userid (**harley**). Then you see the **@** (at sign) character, followed by the name of my computer (**kajsa**), and a : (colon). Following the colon is a ~ (tilde) character. (It has a special meaning that I will get to in a moment.) Next, you see a **$** (dollar sign) character. This indicates that your shell is a member of the Bourne Shell family (in this case, Bash). Finally, at the very end of the prompt is a space, which you can't see.

■ **Note**   In the default Bash shell prompt, the @ (at sign) and : (colon) characters are delimiters. A DELIMITER is an otherwise meaningless character that divides a string of characters into sections. For example, in the phone number 202-456-1414, the hyphens are delimiters.

So what is the meaning of the ~ (tilde) character? It is actually the pathname of your "current directory". (We will discuss this in Section 2.17.)

At any time, you can think of yourself as working within a directory. For now, I'll just tell you that the tilde stands for your personal "home directory". As you move from one directory to another, this part of the prompt will change to show where you are. For example, let's say that I changed from my home directory to the **Documents** subdirectory. The shell prompt would become:

`harley@kajsa:~/Documents$`

And let's say that this directory had a subdirectory of its own called **archive**. If I change to that subdirectory, the shell prompt would become:

`harley@kajsa:~/Documents/archive$`

Finally, if I changed to the **/usr/include/protocols** directory, the prompt would change to:

`harley@kajsa:/usr/include/protocols$`

To review, the general format of the default Bash shell prompt with Ubuntu Linux is:

userid@ *computer* : *current-directory*$

Section 2.9: What Unix Commands Look Like

Whenever you see the shell prompt, you can enter commands one at a time. When you are finished typing a command, you tell the shell to process it by pressing the Enter key (or the Return key on a Macintosh keyboard). As an example, here's the command that you would use to start Emacs (once it is installed) to edit a file named **important**:

`emacs important`

As a general rule, most Unix commands have the following format:

command-name short-options long-options parameters

In the example above, the command name is **emacs**; there are no short options or long options, and there is one parameter, **important**.

Short options start with a single – (hyphen) character. Long options start with two hyphen characters in a row. Let us analyze the following example using the **ls** command lists (used to display information about files).

```
ls -l --classify Documents Music
```

The command name is **ls**. There is one short option (**-l**) , one long option (**--classify**), and two parameters (**Documents** and **Music**).

If a command has more than one short option, you can put them together with a single hyphen. For example, let's say you want to use the **ls** command with three short options (**-a -l -d**). The following commands are equivalent:

```
ls -ald
ls -a -l -d
```

When we talk about such commands out loud, there are two conventions we follow. First, for short, two-letter commands, we pronounce the separate letters. For example, when we talk about the **ls** command, we call it the "L S" ("ell-ess") command; and the name of the **vi** text editor is pronounced "V I" ("vee-eye").

Second, when we talk about options, we pronounce the – (hyphen) character as either "minus" or "dash". For example, let's say you wanted to tell someone to use the following command:

```
ls -l
```

You would say "Use the L S minus L command" or "Use the L S dash L command".

■ **Note**   Unix considers upper- and lowercase letters to be completely different characters. If you are used to Windows or Mac OS X, remember this when you type commands. For example, the **-a** option is completely different from the **-A** option (see Section 2.18).

Section 2.10: Making Corrections as You Type Commands

As you type a Unix command, there are keys you can use to modify the command or to make corrections. The most important is the Backspace key. As you type, whenever you make a mistake, just press <Backspace> as many times as necessary and fix the mistake.

You can also make changes by using the two arrow keys, <Left> and <Right>, to move the cursor within the command. You can then use <Backspace> to delete the character to the left of the cursor, or <Delete> to delete the character at the cursor.

If you are used to a PC keyboard you probably already know how to use these keys. However, Unix also uses two other keys you may not know about. To delete the previous word, press <Ctrl-W>. To delete the entire line, press <Ctrl-U> (on some systems, <Ctrl-X>). For a summary of these keys, see Figure 2-7.

Key	Function
<Left>	Move cursor left one position
<Right>	Move cursor right one position
<Backspace>	Delete character to the left of the cursor
<Delete>	Delete character at the cursor
<Ctrl-W>	Delete the previous word
<Ctrl-U>	Delete the entire line (on some systems <Ctrl-X>)

FIGURE 2-7. Keys to Make Corrections When Typing a Command.

As you enter a command, here are the most important keys you can use to make corrections. These keys work with all Unix systems, including Mac OS X. The first four keys also work when you type commands with Microsoft Windows. However, <Ctrl-W> and <Ctrl-U> do not work with Windows, as they are Unix keys.

Note

On a Macintosh keyboard, there is no Backspace key. To delete to the left, you use the primary Delete key at the top-right corner of the main part of the keyboard. To delete at the cursor, you use the secondary Delete key, the one to the left of the End key.

The secondary Delete key is available only with a full-sized keyboard. If you have a compact keyboard, you won't have this key. Instead, use <fn-Delete> or <Control-D>.

Section 2.11: Two Important Keys: <Ctrl-C> and <Ctrl-D>

To enter a command, you type it and then press the Enter key. When you press <Enter>, you are telling the shell to process the command.

A small number of commands are built in to the shell. When you enter such a command, the shell handles it on its own. Most commands, however, require the shell to run another program on your behalf. For example, if you enter the **date** command (to display the time and date), the shell will start a program named **date**. The shell then places itself on hold, waiting for the program to finish. The moment the program finishes, the shell regains control. It then displays the shell prompt and waits for you to enter another command.

The same thing happens when you enter the **emacs** command. The shell starts Emacs and then puts itself on hold. When you quit Emacs, the shell regains control and displays the shell prompt.

From time to time you may want to quit (stop) a program that is running. How you do so depends on which user interface the program uses.

Programs that use a TUI (text-based user interface) take over the screen and create their own environment. Such programs will have a quit command that you use to end the program. For example, when you run Emacs, it will keep control until you stop it deliberately. (The most common way to do this is by pressing <Ctrl-X> <Ctrl-C>.) Here is another example. In Section 2.11, I will show you how to access the Unix manual. If you are displaying information from the Unix manual and you want to stop, you use the q (quit) command.

Programs that use a CLI (command-line interface) are different. They don't take control of the screen. Instead, they write each line of output to the bottom of the screen, causing all the other lines to scroll up.

With many commands, the output is short and the command finishes quickly. This is the case, for example, when you enter the **date** command. Within an instant, the shell runs the date program, the time and date are displayed, the program ends, and you see the next shell prompt.

Some CLI programs, however, may not stop on their own, either by design or if they run into a problem. When this happens, you will have to interrupt the program to get it to stop. You do so by sending it a SIGNAL, a special notification that is sent to a program that is running. Specifically, to stop a program, you press <Ctrl-C> to send the program an **intr** signal (INTERRUPT SIGNAL). Most CLI programs will stop instantly when they detect an **intr** signal.

If you want to try this, enter the following command:

ping www.harley.com

The **ping** command sends a PING SIGNAL to another computer to see if it responds, and then displays technical information about the response (or lack of response). If you use **ping** without any options, it will keep sending the signal and displaying output indefinitely. To stop **ping**, simply send an **intr** signal by pressing <Ctrl-C>.

■ **Note**

When you are working with Emacs, <Ctrl-G> acts a lot like <Ctrl-C> does with CLI-based programs. Pressing <Ctrl-G> won't stop Emacs (because it is a TUI-based program), but it will cancel any action you may have started within Emacs.

We will discuss this later, so don't worry about it right now. Just file it away as a useful piece of information that will come in handy one day: <Ctrl-G> with Emacs is similar to <Ctrl-C> with the Unix command line.

Some CLI programs invite you to enter data for the program to process, and as long as you keep entering data the program will keep running. An interesting example is the **factor** program. Once you start **factor**, it waits for you to enter a whole number. It then breaks the number down into prime factors, which it displays.

For example, if you enter the number 68, **factor** will calculate that 68 = 2 x 2 x 17, and respond with:

68: 2 2 17

At this point, the program waits for you to enter another number. On its own, **factor** will never stop. To stop such programs, you must indicate that there is no more data. To do so, you press <Ctrl-D> to send an **eof** signal (END OF FILE SIGNAL).

If you want to try this, enter the command:

factor

Then enter any whole number you want followed by <Enter>, over and over, as long as you want. When you want to stop, press <Ctrl-D>.

As we have discussed, when you use the shell, you enter one command after another. The shell processes each command appropriately and then waits for you to enter another one. Because the shell is a CLI program, you can press <Ctrl D> to indicate that there is no more data. When you do this, the shell, like all CLI programs, will stop. The moment the shell stops, your userid is logged out automatically.

Thus, when you are using a terminal, whenever you see a shell prompt, you can log out by pressing <Ctrl-D>. (You can also enter the **logout** command.)

■ **Note** If a CLI program is waiting for data and pressing <Ctrl-D> doesn't stop the program, you can press <Ctrl-C> and send it an **intr** (interrupt) signal. Most well-behaved programs will then quit. (Of course, programs are like people. Not all of them are well behaved.)

Section 2.12: The History List; Command Line Editing

As you use the command line, the shell maintains a list of the commands you enter. This list is called the HISTORY LIST. At any time, you can recall commands from the history list, which you can then modify and reuse.

For example, let's say you want to use the **ls -l** command to display information about the files in the directory named **/usr/include/protocols**. The command you want is:

ls -l /usr/include/protocols

However, by accident, you enter:

ls -l /usr/include/protcols

This won't work because you forgot to type the second "o" in **protocols**.

Instead of typing the entire command again (and probably making another mistake), you can recall what you just typed from the history list. It will then be the work of a moment to fix the mistake and re-enter the corrected command. (I'll show you how in a moment.)

You can do a lot with the history list and the details are complex. However, because it is worth learning, I will describe a few of the basic techniques. Afterwards, I will explain how this is all connected with Emacs.

Think of the history list as an invisible file containing your most recent Unix commands. Each time you enter a new command, it is inserted into the bottom of the history list. So the last line of the invisible file is always the last command you entered.

The simplest way to move up and down through the invisible file is to use the <Up> and <Down> (arrow) keys. As you do, the shell displays the command to which you are pointing within the invisible file. When you press <Up>, the current command vanishes and is replaced by the previous command, as if you were going back in time. If you go too far, you can press <Down> to move back down the list.

Once you display a command from the history list, you can modify it however you want. You then press <Enter> to tell the shell to process the newly modified command. Let's consider our example.

To start, let's say you enter the following, incorrect `ls` command:

```
ls -l /usr/include/protcols
```

Because you made a spelling mistake, you see the following error message:

```
ls: cannot access /usr/include/protcols: No such file or
directory
```

To recall the incorrect command from the history list, press the <Up> arrow once. You now see, once again, the incorrect command:

```
ls -l /usr/include/protcols
```

To fix it, press <Left> four times to move the cursor between the `t` and the `c` in `protcols`. Then press `o` to insert the letter "o". You now see:

```
ls -l /usr/include/protocols
```

To enter the corrected command, press <Enter>.

As I said, there is a lot you can do with the history list and it is all worth learning. However, it will take you some time to learn. At the very least, however, here are the basic ideas I want you to remember:

1. The history list is an invisible file containing your recently entered Unix commands.

2. To move up and down through the list, use the Up key and the Down key. As you move through the history list, the shell will show you the appropriate command.

3. To move the cursor within a command, use <Left> and <Right>.

4. As you make corrections and changes, you delete characters by using <Backspace>, <Delete>, <Ctrl-W>, and <Ctrl-U> (or <Ctrl-X>). For a summary of these keys, see Figure 2-8.

Unix Keys	Function
<Up>	Display previous line in history list
<Down>	Display next line in history list
<Left>	Move cursor left one position
<Right>	Move cursor right one position
<Backspace>	Delete character to the left of the cursor
<Delete>	Delete character at the cursor
<Ctrl-W>	Delete the previous word
<Ctrl-U>	Delete the entire line (on some systems <Ctrl-X>)

Emacs Keys	Function
<Ctrl-P>	Display previous line in history list
<Ctrl-N>	Display next line in history list
<Ctrl-A>	Move cursor to beginning of the line
<Ctrl-E>	Move cursor to end of the line
<Ctrl-B>	Move cursor left (backward) one position
<Ctrl-F>	Move cursor right (forward) one position
<Alt-F>	Move cursor right (forward) one word
<Alt-B>	Move cursor left (backward) one word
<Ctrl-K>	Delete from cursor to end of the line
<Ctrl-A> <Ctrl-K>	Delete the entire line

FIGURE 2-8. Key Combinations to Use When Typing a Command.

The top list shows the keys we discussed in Section 2.10 that you can use to make corrections when you are typing a command. The bottom list shows some of the key combinations copied from Emacs as part of the GNU Readline facility. You can use the keys in both these lists to move within the current line and the history list, and to help you make changes.

The shell has a powerful, built-in facility called COMMAND LINE EDITING. In fact, it is command line editing that enables you to modify commands as you type, to access the history list, and to use autocompletion (which we won't go into here).

You will recall that, in the last few sections, I showed you how to enter commands and make corrections as you were typing. I then explained how to move within the history list, recall a previous command, modify it, and enter it again. What I was showing you was actually basic command line editing. What you didn't realize is that I was also showing you basic Emacs editing commands. (So if you were following along on your own computer, you were actually using a few Emacs keys.)

This is not as strange as you might think. The Emacs editing commands are so powerful and (once you master them) so easy to use, that many other programs also use them. In particular, the most popular shells (Bash, **tcsh**, Korn Shell) all recognize Emacs key combinations that you can use for command line editing, that is, for moving through the history list and modifying commands, and for autocompletion. These capabilities are provided by a software library called GNU Readline. For reference, some of these Emacs key combinations are shown in Figure 2-8.

This means that, as you learn the Emacs key combinations, you can immediately use them with the shell for command line editing: just another reason why, the more you learn Emacs, the closer you are to becoming a totally fulfilled and actualized human being.

However, none of this is a substitute for the real thing, so let's move on. We still have more to cover before we can actually start using Emacs.

Section 2.13: The Unix Manual

All Unix commands and programs are documented in the UNIX MANUAL, a part of every Unix system. When a Unix person talks about THE MANUAL, they always mean the Unix manual. For example, if you ask your grandmother how to use the **ls** command, she might tell you, "Look it up in the manual, and let me know if you have any questions."

The Unix manual is considered to be authoritative, the definitive reference when it comes to basic information about a particular command or program. As such, when a programmer changes a program — say, to add a new option — he or she is expected to update the entry for that program in the manual.

Each entry in the Unix manual is called a MAN PAGE. Don't take this term literally, though: most man pages are much longer than the size of a printed page. (Here is an extreme example: if you printed the Bash man page, a particularly long one, it would take 155 printed pages.)

To display a man page, you use the **man** command. Type **man** followed by the name of the command or program you want to learn about. For example, to read the man page for the **ls** command, enter:

```
man ls
```

To learn about the **man** command itself, use:

```
man man
```

To look up something on the Bash shell man page, use:

```
man bash
```

▪ **Note:**

The Unix manual is a *reference* manual, not a teaching guide. At a minimum, each page shows you:

- Name of the command
- Description (usually only a few words)
- Syntax summary
- Options (description of all the options)

The SYNTAX of a command is the formal description of all the different ways you can enter the command and its options.

Section 2.14: Using the less Pager Program

When you use a terminal to display man pages, you are working in a text-based environment using a CLI (command line interface). As such, the **man** command writes its output to the bottom line of the terminal screen, causing previous output to scroll up. This works fine if the man page is short enough to fit on your screen. However, most man pages are much too long. Without a tool to display the output in a controlled fashion, most of the text would scroll off the top of the screen so quickly, you wouldn't be able to read it.

To make the output readable, the **man** command does not write it directly to the screen. Instead, it sends it to a special tool called a PAGER PROGRAM or, more simply, a PAGER. The job of a pager is to take all the output and display it one screenful at a time. This lets you read the output in a controlled fashion. In fact, you can use the pager to move backwards and forwards, to search for a particular string of characters, to jump to the beginning or the end of the page, and much more.

The default Unix pager is called **less**.

▤ **What's in a Name?**

less

The original Unix pager was a simple program named **more**, written in 1978 by Dan Halbert, then a grad student at U.C. Berkeley. Halbert wrote **more** to display text one screenful at a time. If there was more to come, it would display a message at the bottom of the screen:

-- More --

Using **more** was easy. After you read what was on the screen, you would press <Space> to display more. Thus, you could read an entire file, one screenful at a time, simply by pressing the <Space> bar.

The biggest problem with **more** is that it could only move forward. In 1983, a programmer named Mark Nudelman was working with large log files, and he needed a pager that could move forward and backward. He and his colleagues used to joke that what they needed was a "backwards **more**", so when he wrote a replacement for **more** that could move backwards, he called it **less**.

When **less** is running, it controls the entire screen. It starts by displaying the first screenful of output, with an informative message on the bottom line of the screen (the command line). It then waits for you to enter a command, of which there are many.

▤ **Note**

It is interesting to note that, the moment **less** takes control of the screen, it changes your experience from using a command-line (CLI) interface to using a text-based interface (TUI). That is what enables it to use the entire screen in order to control the flow of the output. Emacs does exactly the same thing, as do many other programs.

For a discussion of the three basic user interfaces (CLI, TUI, GUI), see Section 2.5.

As I said, **less** has many commands that you can use while you are reading text. If you want to see them all, look at the **less** man page:

man less

(As you do, you will be using **less** to read about **less**.)

For reference, Figure 2-9 shows the basic **less** commands. The three most important ones are:

- Press the <Space> bar to display the next screenful of text
- Press the **q** key to quit the program
- Press the **h** key to display help information

Notice that you can navigate by using either single-letter commands, or by using the special keys <Home>, <End>, <PageDown>, and <PageUp>.

When you have a moment, enter the **man** command above and spend some time practicing with **less**. This is a program that you need to learn how to use, because it is the key that unlocks the Unix manual.

Letters	Function
h	Display help information
q	Quit the program
g	Go to first line of text
G	Go to last line of text
<Space>	Move forward (down) one screenful
b	Move backward (up) one screenful
/pattern	Search forward for specified pattern
?pattern	Search backward for specified pattern
n	Repeat search in the same direction (next)
N	Repeat search in the opposite direction
! *command*	Run the specified shell command

Special Keys	Function
<Home>	Go to first line of text
<End>	Go to last line of text
<PageDown>	Move forward (down) one screenful
<PageUp>	Move backward (up) one screenful

FIGURE 2-9. Commands to use with less.

*The default Unix pager program is named **less**. The purpose of **less** is to display text, one screenful at a time. While you are reading, there are many commands you can use. Here are the most important ones.*

Section 2.15: The Three Types of Unix Files

As we discussed in Section 1.2, the primary use of Emacs is to create and modify text files: programs and scripts, data files, HMTL files, LaTeX documents, logs, and so on. For this reason, it is important to understand how files are organized. Specifically, I want to make sure you are familiar with the idea of a hierarchical filesystem, as well as the basic concepts that support it: files, directories, and subdirectories. I also want you to know the names of the Unix commands we use to work with files and directories.

Being able to manage your files is a basic skill you need if you are to use Emacs well. To do so, there are two sets of tools, and I want you to be skillful with both of them. First, you can use the standard Unix file and directory commands that everyone learns. Second, you can use a TUI-based file management program called Dired (Directory Editor) that is part of Emacs. (We will talk about Dired in Section 12.6.) In either case, you will need to know the basic concepts, so let's start with files.

There are three types of Unix files: ordinary files, directories, and pseudo files. An ORDINARY FILE is what most people think of when they use the word "file": a collection of data that has a name and is stored on a disk or other storage device. With Emacs, we generally work with text files, ordinary files that contain the characters you can type on a keyboard: letters, numbers, punctuation, spaces and tabs.

A DIRECTORY is used to organize groups of files. For instance, you might create a directory named `circus` to hold a collection of photos from a trip to Centerboro, New York, where you saw Boomschmidt's Stupendous and Unexcelled Circus.[27] When we talk about a directory, we say that it CONTAINS or HOLDS other files. Literally, this is not the case. Directories contain information about files, not the actual files themselves.

The reason directories are so important is that they can contain other directories, as well as ordinary files. This allows you to create a hierarchy of directories to organize your data. When a directory contains another directory, with respect to one another we call the first one the PARENT DIRECTORY and the second one a SUBDIRECTORY.

For example, if you have a lot of photos in your `circus` directory, you might organize them by using three subdirectories: `animals`, `friends` and `martians`. In this case, `circus` is the parent directory of `animals`, and `animals` is a subdirectory of `circus`.

Traditionally, the term "directory" is used by people who are comfortable working with a command-line interface. People who use a GUI (graphical user interface) tend to refer to directories as FOLDERS and subdirectories as SUBFOLDERS.

---

[27] See Personal Note #24, "Freddy and the Men From Mars" (Appendix A).

■ **Note**

If you ever decide to use an online dating service, I suggest you specify, "I prefer someone who organizes their directories well."

By using the word *directories* instead of *folders*, you will eliminate all the Windows and Mac users whose desktops are filled with icons.

A moment ago, I told you that when most people think about a file, they consider it to be "a collection of data that has a name and is stored on a disk or other storage device". This description is certainly accurate for both ordinary files and directories. As a definition, it is intuitive and for some systems, such as Microsoft Windows, it works just fine. With Unix, however, the concept of a file is much more generalized. Specifically, a Unix FILE is any source from which data can be read, or any target to which data can be written.

There are different types of Unix files, but they all fall into one of three categories: ordinary files, directories, or pseudo files. Unlike ordinary files and directories, PSEUDO FILES do not store data. Instead, they provide services to programs using the same methods that are normally used to read and write data from ordinary files. As such, pseudo files are part of the Unix filesystem and, like ordinary files, they are organized into directories. The three most important types of pseudo files are special files, named pipes, and proc files.

SPECIAL FILES (also called DEVICE FILES) represent physical or emulated devices. NAMED PIPES connect the output of one program to the input of another. PROC FILES provide technical information about the system itself.

Although we don't need to get into a lot of details, it is important that you understand the general concept: pseudo files do not store data in the regular manner, but they can be used for input and output in the same way as you would use an ordinary file.[28]

■ **What's in a Name?**

File

Strictly speaking, a Unix file is any input source or any output target. As we have discussed, there are three types of files: ordinary files, directories, and pseudo files (which include device files). However, when people talk about ordinary files, they rarely bother to use the word "ordinary". However, the meaning should be clear from the context.

For example, if I were to tell you, "Files and directories require storage space, I am referring to ordinary files. However, if I say, "You can use the `ls` command to display a list of the files in a directory," I am referring to any type of file, including ordinary files, subdirectories, and pseudo files.

One last example. The title of Section 2.18 is "File and Directory Names". I hope it is clear from the context that, when I wrote the title, I was referring to ordinary files and directories.

If this idea is new to you, I suggest that whenever you see the word "file" used, you take a moment to ask yourself: In this context, does the word "file" refer to any type of file, or just to ordinary files? After a while, it will become second nature, and you will just know.

[28] See Personal Note #25, "Special Files and Proc Files" (Appendix A).

Section 2.16: The Tree-Structured Filesystem

Most people run Emacs on some type of Unix system, such as Linux, FreeBSD, NetBSD, or OpenBSD. However, you can also use Emacs with Mac OS X (which is actually Unix) and Microsoft Windows (which is most definitely *not* Unix). There are some differences between how filesystems work with Linux and BSD compared to OS X and Windows, and we will talk about them in Section 2.17. What's most important, however, is that all of these operating systems organize files into a hierarchy, a basic paradigm I want to make sure you understand.

A typical Unix system contains well over 300,000 files. (I am not exaggerating.[29]) These files are organized into a TREE-STRUCTURED FILESYSTEM in which one main directory, called the ROOT DIRECTORY, serves as the parent directory for the entire filesystem. The root directory is — directly or indirectly — the parent of all the other directories in the system. (Think of a tree where the trunk is the root directory, and all the branches are subdirectories.)

When we write the name of the root directory, we don't use the name "root". Instead, we simply write a single / (slash) character. Here is an example using the `ls` (list) command, which is used to display information about a directory. The following command displays the names of the files in the root directory:

```
ls /
```

The basic way to write the name of a directory is to simply trace the path from the root directory, through every subdirectory that leads to the target directory. Within the sequence of directories, we use / characters as delimiters, to separate one directory name from another. Here is an example.

Let's say the root directory contains a subdirectory named **home**, which contains a subdirectory named **harley**, which contains a subdirectory named **circus**, which contains a subdirectory named **animals**. We would write the full name of the **animals** directory as follows:

```
/home/harley/circus/animals
```

To display the contents of this directory, we can use the following `ls` command:

```
ls /home/harley/circus/animals
```

■ **Note** When you say directory names out loud, you pronounce the "slash". Thus, the directory name above is pronounced: "slash home slash harley slash circus slash animals".

If we want to reference the name of an ordinary file, we simply put another / at the end of the last directory and add the file name onto the end of the list.

---

[29] See Personal Note #26, "How Many Files Are on Your Unix System?" (Appendix A).

For example, let's say there is a file called `leo.jpg` in the `animals` directory. We can reference it as follows:

`/home/harley/circus/animals/leo.jpg`

When we use this pattern to specify a sequence of directories (possibly with a file at the end) separated by / characters, we call it a PATHNAME or, more simply, a PATH. If a pathname ends with a file, we call that part of the path a FILENAME. For instance, the example above is a pathname. The last part, `leo.jpg`, is a filename.

You will have noticed that our example used the directory **home**, which is a subdirectory of the root directory. Each time a userid is created, the system creates a HOME DIRECTORY for the person using that userid to store his or her personal files. Each userid's home directory is a subdirectory of **/home**, and its name is the same as the userid. For example, let's say that a system is used by four different people whose userids are **harley**, **lydia**, **jeff** and **dmitry**. Their home directories will be:

```
/home/harley
/home/lydia
/home/jeff
/home/dmitry
```

Each of these people can create their own subdirectories within their home directory. In this way, every Unix user is able to design a personal directory tree to organize his files in a way that make sense to him or her. As an example, let's say that, within the **/home/harley** directory, there is a **circus** subdirectory, and within that, three subdirectories named **animals**, **friends** and **martians**. We have the following personalized directory tree:

```
/home/harley
/home/harley/circus
/home/harley/circus/animals
/home/harley/circus/friends
/home/harley/circus/martians
```

The **/home** directory is only one of many built-in subdirectories of the root directory. There are also **/bin**, **/dev**, **/etc** and more. It is these "first-level" subdirectories that define the shape and function of the Unix filesystem. Many (but not all) of these subdirectories are the same from one Unix system to another. Once you get used to the basic plan, it will be generally the same no matter what system you use to run Emacs as long as it is Unix: including Linux, any BSD system, or Mac OS X. (Microsoft Windows, however, is different in that it uses a completely separate file system for each storage device.)

Note

If you want to see the directory organization used with your system, you look at the **hier** (hierarchy) man page:

man hier

Whenever you use a new system, take a few moments to look at the **hier** man page to see how the filesystem is organized.

Although there is no universal master plan that all Unix systems are required to follow, there is a widely recognized plan called the FILESYSTEM HIERARCHY STANDARD, or FHS, that is used with most Linux systems. (In fact, the FHS is maintained by the Linux Foundation.) For reference, Figure 2-10 shows the most important directories within the Filesystem Hierarchy Standard, Version 3.0.

Directory	Description
/	Root directory
/bin	Essential user commands (binaries)
/boot	Boot loader files
/dev	Device files (special files)
/etc	System configuration files
/home	User home directories
/lib	Essential shared libraries and kernel modules
/media	Mount point: removable media
/mnt	Mount point: temporarily mounted filesystems
/opt	Application programs ("optional" software)
/proc	Proc files
/root	Home directory for the root userid (superuser)
/run	Temporary data used by programs that are running
/sbin	System programs (binaries)
/srv	Data for system services
/tmp	Temporary files, not preserved between reboots
/usr	Sharable, read-only data
/var	Variable (changeable) system data

FIGURE 2-10. The Most Important Directories Within the Filesystem Hierarchy Standard.

All Unix systems organize files and directories into a tree-structured filesystem using a single root directory. The Filesystem Hierarchy Standard is the basic plan followed by Linux systems. To see the details for your particular system, look at the **hier** *man page.*

▩ **What's in a Name?**

root, **root**

In Unix, the word "root" has two meanings. First, the root directory is the name of the top-level directory for the entire filesystem.

To help you with the metaphor, think of a Unix filesystem as a very, very large tree growing from a single root. The many levels of directories and subdirectories are the branches of the tree. The ordinary files are leaves, and the pseudo files are imaginary leaves. (If you want to see a visual representation of a Unix filesystem, look for a photo of a large *Tipuana tipu* tree.)

The second meaning: **root** is also the name of the userid for the superuser (see Section 2.3). The superuser userid was named after the most important directory in the filesystem.

Section 2.17: The Current Directory and Pathnames

At all times, one specific directory is designated as your CURRENT DIRECTORY, also called your WORKING DIRECTORY. Informally, this is the directory in which you are working at that moment. When you log in, your current directory is set to your home directory. For example, my userid is **harley**, so when I log in, my current directory is set to **/home/harley**.

In Section 2.16, we discussed how to specify pathnames. Starting from the root directory (/), you specify each subdirectory (or filename) using / characters as delimiters. For example:

`/home/harley/circus/animals/leo.jpg`

A pathname that begins with a / character starts from the root directory. This is called an ABSOLUTE PATHNAME. If the pathname doesn't begin with a /, the pathname starts from your current directory. This is called a RELATIVE PATHNAME. Here is an example.

Let's say that, at this moment, your current directory is **/home/harley**. The following two paths are equivalent:

```
/home/harley/circus/animals/leo.jpg
circus/animals/leo.jpg
```

Because the second pathname does not begin with a /, it starts from your current directory, which is **/home/harley**.

The concept of a current directory is important because it means that you rarely have to type long, absolute pathnames. Once you set your current directory to wherever you want to work, you can use shorter pathnames relative to that directory (as I did in the last example).

For convenience, there are three standard abbreviations you can use when you type pathnames. First, the tilde (~) character is a synonym for your home directory. For example, if your home directory is **/home/harley**, typing ~ at the beginning of a pathname is the same as typing `/home/harley`. Thus, the following two `ls` commands would be equivalent. (The command `ls -l` displays information about a file.)

```
ls -l /home/harley/circus/animals/leo.jpg
ls -l ~/circus/animals/leo.jpg
```

The other two abbreviations are `.` (a single period) and `..` (two periods in a row), pronounced "dot" and "dot-dot" respectively. The `.` abbreviation stands for your current directory. For example, let's say that your current directory is:

```
/home/harley/circus/animals
```

The following two commands both refer to the file `leo.jpg` in this directory:

```
ls -l leo.jpg
ls -l ./leo.jpg
```

You might ask, why would you want to type a `.` character at the beginning of a pathname? Normally, you wouldn't because it's not necessary. However, there are times you do need to use it. For example, if you want to run a program from your current directory, and that directory is not in your search path, you must use `./` to specify the path explicitly. (If you don't understand what I just said, you can ignore it.)

The final abbreviation `..` stands for the parent directory. You use it when you want to go "up" one level within a pathname. For example, let's say that the `circus` directory has three subdirectories: `animals`, `friends` and `martians`. The `martian` directory contains a file named `chirp-squeak.jpg`. You want to display information about the file `chirp-squeak.jpg` in the `martians` directory, and your current directory is:

```
/home/harley/circus/animals
```

The following two commands are equivalent:

```
ls -l /home/harley/circus/martians/chirp-squeak.jpg
ls -l ../martians/chirp-squeak.jpg
```

The first command uses an absolute pathname that starts from the root directory. The second command uses a relative pathname that starts from the current directory (`animals`), goes up one level (to `circus`), and then goes down one level (into `martians`).

At this point, you may be wondering, at any moment, how do you know what directory is your current directory? There are two ways.

First, you can use the `pwd` command. The name stands for "print working directory":

```
pwd
```

Remember this command: if you ever get lost, `pwd` will tell you where you are.

■ **What's in a name?**

Print

As we discussed in Section 2.3, the oldest Unix terminals produced output by printing on a continuous roll of paper. Eventually, printing terminals were replaced by video terminals, and the idea of "printing data" changed into "displaying data". Nevertheless, it is still traditional among Unix people to use the term "print" to refer to displaying output.

For example, if you look at **pwd** man page, the description of this command is given as: "Print the full filename of the current working directory."

The second way to find out the name of your current directory is to look at your shell prompt. As we discussed in Section 2.8, it is likely that, by default, your shell prompt will display the name of your current directory. For example, the default Ubuntu Linux shell prompt is:

userid@ *computer*: current-*directory*$

This means that, unless you have changed your shell prompt, it will always show you where you are in the directory tree.

Here are some examples using the **cd** command, which is used to change your current directory. (All you do is specify the directory to which you want to change.)

■ **Note**   When you use the **cd** command without specifying a directory, it will, by default, change to your home directory. Thus, the following two commands are equivalent:

cd
cd ~

In the following examples, I will include the shell prompt so you can see how the current directory is changing. Before we start, I will tell you that my userid is **harley** and my computer is named **kajsa**.[30]

The examples start just after I log in, at which time my current directory is set to **/home/harley**. I then use **cd** to move from one directory to another. Take your time to read the examples slowly, and make sure you understand exactly what is happening. As you read, remember that ~ stands for the home directory, and .. refers to the parent directory.

```
harley@kajsa:~$ cd circus
harley@kajsa:~/circus$ cd animals
harley@kajsa:~/circus/animals$ cd ../martians
harley@kajsa:~/circus/martians$ cd ~
harley@kajsa:~$ cd /usr/share/man/man1
harley@kajsa:/usr/share/man/man1$ cd ..
harley@kajsa:/usr/share/man$ cd ..
```

---

[30] After my dog Kajsa Anka, also known as Sadie.

```
harley@kajsa:/usr/share$ cd ..
harley@kajsa:/usr$ cd ..
harley@kajsa:/$ cd ..
harley@kajsa:/$ cd
harley@kajsa:~$ cd circus/martians
harley@kajsa:~/circus/martians$ cd ../..
harley@kajsa:~$
```

Notice that you can use more than one .. in a row to go up more than one level at a time (second line from the bottom). Notice also that when you try to go up from the root directory nothing happens (fifth line from the bottom).

To finish this section, I have created two reference lists to show you the most important file and directory commands. Figure 2-11 shows the most important commands to use with ordinary files. Figure 2-12 shows the most important directory commands.

Command	Description
cat	Display a very short file
cat	Combine (catenate) multiple files
chmod	Modify (change) file permissions
cmp	Compare two files to see if they are the same
cp	Copy files
du	Display disk usage for files
file	Analyze file type
find	Search for files in directory tree, then process results
head	Display the beginning of a file
less	Display contents of file, one screenful at a time
ls	Display (list) information about files
ls -l	Display full information (long listing) about files
mv	Move files
mv	Rename files
od	Display contents of a binary file (octal dump)
pwd	Display name of current directory
rm	Delete (remove) files
tail	Display the end of a file
touch	When file does not exist: create brand new empty file
touch	When file exists: update access and modification times
whereis	Find files associated with a command

FIGURE 2-11. **The most important file commands.**

When you use Emacs there will be many times when you need to manipulate your files. Sometimes you can do it from within Emacs, but a lot of the time, it will be easier and faster to use the standard Unix file commands. These are the most important ones, and I recommend you learn how to use them all. (Notice that **cat**, **mv**, *and* **touch** *each perform two different functions.)*

Command	Description
cd	Change your current (working) directory
chmod	Modify (change) directory permissions
du	Display disk usage for directories
ls	Display (list) information about directories
ls -l	Display full information (long listing) about directories
mkdir	Create (make) a directory
mv	Move directories
mv	Rename directories
pwd	Display name of current directory
rmdir	Delete (remove) an empty directory
tree -d	Display a diagram of a directory tree

FIGURE 2-12. The most important directory commands.

*Unix uses a very large, tree-structured file system. Within that file system, starting from your home directory, you can build a tree structure of your own in a way that suits you. This will become more and more important, as you develop a facility with Emacs. Here are the commands you can use to build, maintain, and use your own personal directory tree. (Notice that **mv** performs two different functions.)*

Why do I list all these commands? Emacs is linked tightly to Unix and to the Unix command line, and understanding how to use files and directories is a basic skill you need to know. If you talk to anyone who is a skilled Emacs user, it is likely that he or she will know how to use all the commands I have listed in these two tables.

Section 2.18: File and Directory Names

To complete our discussion about Unix and its file system, I want to spend a few minutes talking about how to name files, specifically, ordinary files and directories. There are small differences with Mac OS X, and larger differences with Microsoft Windows, which we will talk about in Section 2.19.

Before we start, I want to take a moment to remind you that the topics we have covered in this chapter give you the basic knowledge about Unix you need to use Emacs. However, there is a lot more to learn about Unix, and it will take time and experience for you to do so. If you want a more comprehensive Unix reference, please get a copy of my book *Harley Hahn's Guide to Unix and Linux.*[31] This is a book you will want to keep as a permanent reference, so I recommend you look for an actual printed book, not an electronic copy.

Now, to continue. There are four important ideas you need to remember about naming files and directories.

---

[31] *Harley Hahn's Guide to Unix and Linux*, McGraw-Hill Higher Education, 2008. The ISBN is 0073133612.

1. LENGTH

File and directory names can be up to 255 characters long. However, unless you have a good reason to use a long name, stick with names that are short, so they will be easy to type.

2. CHARACTERS

When you name a file, choose from the following characters:

- Lowercase letters: **a b c**... **z**
- Uppercase letters: **A B C**... **Z**
- Numbers: **0 1 2 3 4 5 6 7 8 9**
- Hyphen: **-**
- Underscore: **_**
- Period: **.**

Unix is very flexible, and you can use almost any character you want in a file name, even spaces and tabs. However, don't do it. Your life will be a lot easier if you stick with the characters I listed above.

Note Remember, when you pronounce file names, the hyphen is called "minus" or "dash", and the period is called "dot".

If you end up with file names that have spaces, tabs, or most other special characters, you will have to put quotes around the names to make your commands work properly. For example, let's say you have created a directory named:

photos from the circus

Every time you use it in a command, you will need quotes around it:

ls -l 'photos from the circus'

If you don't use quotes, the shell will think you are referring to four separate files: **photos, from, the** and **circus**.

Note When you type a command and you want to indicate that certain characters are to be taken literally, you use either single quotes (like I did above) or double quotes ("like this"). For technical reasons, single quotes work better, so unless you are doing something that you know requires double quotes, get in the habit of using single quotes.

---

3. UPPER AND LOWER CASE

With respect to the letters of the alphabet, capital letters are called UPPERCASE, and small letters are called LOWERCASE. If a filesystem distinguishes between upper- and lowercase letters, we say that it is CASE SENSITIVE. If a filesystem does not distinguish between upper- and lowercase letters, we say that it is CASE INSENSITIVE.

The Unix filesystem is case sensitive. For instance, the letter **a** is completely different from the letter **A**. In the following example, all the file names are considered to be completely different:

harley Harley HARLEY haRLey

___

▓ **Note** Unless you have a good reason, use only lowercase letters for file names. Some people like to use a single uppercase letter at the beginning of a directory name, but anything more than that is too much.

___

4. DOTFILES

There are many files that, for one reason or another, you will want to ignore most of the time. For example, some programs will put a configuration file in one of your directories. The program will use this file silently, which is fine, but *you* don't want to look at it every time you display the contents of the directory.

By default, the **ls** command will not display the names of files whose names begin with a **.** (dot) character. Such files are called DOTFILES or HIDDEN FILES. If you want to see dotfiles, you use **ls** with the **-a** (all) option. This means that, if you have a lot of configuration files (which are normally dotfiles), you don't have to look at them unless you really want to.

As an experiment, try this. Use **cd** to make sure you are in your home directory. Then use ls to display all the files and directories that are not dotfiles. Then use **ls -a** to display *all* your files, including dotfiles, and notice how many there are.

```
cd
ls
ls -a
```

If you use Bash for your shell, you will see several dotfiles that are the Bash configuration files. For reference, I have listed them in Figure 2-13. I'm showing these to you for two reasons. First, they are a good example of how dotfiles are used. Second, you may want to use Emacs to edit one or more of these files to customize your command line environment. If so, start by looking in the files to see what is already there, figure out what you want, and make your changes carefully.

File	Description
.bash_profile	Login file
.bash_login	Login file
.profile	Login file (POSIX mode)
.bashrc	Environment file
.bash_logout	Logout file

FIGURE 2-13. Bash Configuration Files.

Many programs use dotfiles to hold configuration information. These are the files used by Bash, the default shell on many Unix systems (including most types of Linux as well as Mac OS X). Once you learn how to use Emacs, I suggest that you take some time to learn about these files and customize them.

Note

When you are using the command line, you see dotfiles by using the **ls -a** command.

With a GUI-based file manager, if you want to see dotfiles, you will have to turn on a specific option. For example, with Nautilus (the file manager used with Ubuntu Linux),[32] if you want to see dotfiles, you need to pull down the View menu and select "Show hidden Files". (The shortcut key is <Ctrl-H>.)

Section 2.19: File and Directory Names: OS X and Windows

What we have discussed in Section 2.18 applies to virtually all types of Unix. To finish our discussion, I'd like to take a moment to tell you the differences you will find with Mac OS X and with Windows.

MAC OS X:

Unlike other types of Unix, the OS X filesystem is case insensitive. In other words, it does not distinguish between upper- and lowercase letters. If you are used to Unix, this will be strange to you. For example, with other types of Unix, if you want to use, say, the **ls** command, you must spell it exactly. With OS X, you can use **ls** or **LS** or **lS** or **Ls**.

Similarly, with other types of Unix, you must spell file names exactly. For example, the file **harley** is different than the file **Harley**. With OS X, they are considered to be the same. Thus, with OS X, the following commands are all equivalent:

```
ls harley
LS HARLEY
Ls Harley
lS harLEY
```

---

[32] In September, 2012, Nautilus was renamed "Gnome Files". However, this is such a boring name, most people still call the program "Nautilus".

However, and this is important, when you type options with OS X, they *are* case sensitive. So, with OS X, the following commands are different:

```
ls -a harley
ls -A harley
```

Another difference between OS X and other types of Unix is that the Mac culture encourages the use of names that include spaces. This means that when you use the command line, you are likely to encounter file and directory (folder) names that have spaces. If so, when you need to reference them in a command, remember to put the entire name in single quotes. For example:

```
cd 'New Programs'
```

MICROSOFT WINDOWS:

Windows, like OS X, is also case insensitive. When you type commands and filenames, you can use either upper- or lower case. The same goes for options (which have a different format than Unix options.)

When you are using commands and you encounter a file with a name that contains spaces, you must put quotes around the file name. However, unlike Unix, you must use double quotes, not single quotes. For example:

```
dir "Saved Games"
```

This Windows command lists the contents of a directory named **Saved Games**.

The last important consideration has to do with the filesystem itself. As we discussed in Section 2.16, Unix has one large filesystem, starting from a single root directory. Windows uses a different filesystem for each device. For example, if you have two hard disks, a CD drive, and a memory stick, each device will have its own filesystem with its own root directory.

CHAPTER 3

■ ■ ■

Installing Emacs

Section 3.1: Installing Software: Packages vs. Manual Installation

In this chapter, I will show you how to install Emacs with Linux, OS X, and Microsoft Windows. Before we get to the details, however, I want to discuss the various ways in which Emacs, and software in general, can be installed. Even if you already have Emacs on your computer, I would like you to take a few minutes and read this entire chapter (which is short). There are two reasons.

First, I am going to explain important concepts that I want you to understand. This is because what we will be talking about is generally applicable to installing all types of software, not just Emacs. Second, regardless of which operating system you are using, I think you will find it interesting to see how software installation differs with Unix and Linux, OS X, and Windows.

Emacs is widely available for free: all you have to do is find it and install it. There are a number of different versions of Emacs but, by far, the most widely used is GNU Emacs (see Section 1.4), and that is the version of Emacs we will be discussing in this book. However, because basic Emacs doesn't vary much, if you are using another type of Emacs, what you learn in this book will work just fine on your system.

Emacs has been adapted to run on a very large number of operating systems. My conservative estimate is that, over the years, various versions of GNU Emacs have run on well over 100 different types of operating systems. (And when I quote you that number I am counting *all* the different Linux distributions as one.) As I write this (2016), the most important operating systems on which GNU Emacs is supported officially are:

- Linux (all distributions)
- FreeBSD
- NetBSD
- OpenBSD
- OS X on the Mac
- Solaris
- Microsoft Windows

© Harley Hahn 2016
H. Hahn, *Harley Hahn's Emacs Field Guide*, DOI 10.1007/978-1-4842-1703-0_3

In most cases, you will find that installing GNU Emacs is fast and easy. However, the installation details depend on what operating system you are using. There are two basic ways to install Emacs: using a package management system, or doing a manual installation. I'd like to take a minute to discuss each of these methods briefly, so you understand how they work. Before we start, I'd like to define a few technical terms.

An ARCHIVE is a file that acts as a container for multiple files. The data within an archive is usually compressed to save storage space. When you process an archive in order to access the contents, we say that you EXTRACT the files.

Using an archive is an easy way to store and share any type of file. For instance, you might use an archive to store the full collection of all the photos you have ever taken of your cat. You could then send a copy of the archive — one single file — to your friends. Once they receive the archive, it is easy for them to extract all 739 separate cat photos to enjoy on their own computer.

The most common use of archives is software distribution. In such cases, an archive contains all the programs, data, and metadata (see below) that someone will need to install a specific program on their computer. For example, the Free Software Foundation (FSF) distributes Emacs by using archives. All you need to do is download the appropriate archive for your particular system. You can then extract the files and install them on your system (as long as you know what you are doing).

METADATA refers to information about the contents of the archive. In a software archive, metadata generally consists of helpful comments to be read by humans, as well as directory information, time stamps, file permissions, and file ownership data. You may also see information related to error detection/correction and encryption.

Generally speaking, the programs within a software archive will be either source files or binary files. SOURCE FILES contain programs that need to be COMPILED (processed) before they can be installed and used. BINARY FILES are compiled programs that are ready to run. With Unix (and Linux) systems, programs are generally distributed as source files, so they can be compiled to run on a specific system at the time of installation. Windows programs, on the other hand, can run on other Windows systems, so they are distributed as binary files, which makes the installation quicker and simpler.

With Unix, archives are most commonly created as TARBALLS. The name indicates that the archive is created by the Unix **tar** program. Although you will see variations, a typical tarball will have a file name that ends in **.tar.gz**. For example, the tarball that contains the archive for GNU Emacs version 24.5 is called **emacs-24.5.tar.gz**.

In this example, the **tar** program was used to put all the files needed to install GNU Emacs version 24.5 into a container file named **emacs-24.5.tar**. This is called a TARFILE. The tarfile was then compressed by the **gzip** data compression program to create the tarball named **emacs-24.5.tar.gz**.

With Windows, software archives are most commonly shared as ZIP FILES. Conceptually, a zip file is similar to a tarball, in that it is a compressed file containing a collection of other files. However, the underlying technology is different. Moreover, as I mentioned, when archives are used to distribute software, you will find that Windows zip files contain binaries, where Unix tarfiles generally contain source files.

A moment ago, I told you that an archive contains everything you need to install specific software *as long as you know what you are doing.* That is a big "if", because installing software manually on a Unix system requires knowledge and experience.

To make software installation faster and easier, virtually all Unix systems come with a PACKAGE MANAGEMENT SYSTEM or PACKAGE MANAGER to do the work. A package manager automates the various processes required to install, upgrade, configure, and uninstall software. All you have to do is tell the package manager what you want, and everything is done automatically.[1] As a general rule, each Linux distribution uses a specific package manager. By far, the most popular ones are APT and RPM. However, you will also see Pacman, Pgktool and Portage. The various BSD versions of Unix use either **pkg** or **pkg_add**.

A package manager installs software by using a PACKAGE: a file containing an archive, as well as extra information needed to guide the installation process. There are tens of thousands of different packages, which means it is easy to download and install tens of thousands of different programs. Most packages are shared online in public REPOSITORIES, which are free for anyone to use. (Please take a moment to reflect on this. In fact, the invention of public repositories was one of the main reasons Linux became so important and so popular.)

Each package manager uses its own type of packages. For example, if you want to install Emacs on a Linux system that uses APT, you need an APT Emacs package; if you have a system that uses RPM, you need an RPM Emacs package. However, this isn't something you need to worry about. All you need to do is tell your package manager what you want, and it will search the appropriate online repositories, find the package you want, download it, and install the software for you. Everything is automatic — and free.

If, for some reason, the program you want is not available as a package but you can find it in the form of an archive — a tarball for Unix or a zip file for Windows — you can download it yourself and do a manual installation. I'll show you how to do this for Emacs in Section 3.3 (Linux) and Section 3.5 (Windows).

Finally, installing Emacs with OS X uses a completely different procedure, which I will show you in Section 3.4.

---

[1] See Personal Note #27, "Comparing Unix Packages to Commercial Apps" (Appendix A).

Section 3.2: Installing Emacs Using a Linux Package Manager

Each type of Linux uses a specific package management system (package manager). There are a variety of Linux package managers, the most widely used being APT and RPM. For reference, Figure 3-1 shows you the Linux package managers you are most likely to encounter. As you can see, APT is used by all Debian-based Linux distributions,[2] and RPM is used by Fedora-based and SUSE-based distributions. Figure 3-2 shows you the package managers used by the three most popular BSD operating systems.

Package Manager	Linux Family	Linux Distributions
APT	Debian-based	Debian, Mint, Ubuntu
RPM	Fedora-based	Fedora, Mageia, Manjaro, RHEL, CentOS
RPM	SUSE-based	OpenSUSE
Pacman	Arch-based	Arch
Portage	Gentoo-based	Gentoo
pgktool	Slackware-based	Slackware

FIGURE 3-1. Linux Package Management Systems.

To make software easy to share and download, most Unix systems use a package management system. The most widely used Linux package managers are shown in this table.

Package Manager	BSD System
pkg	FreeBSD
pkg_add	NetBSD
pkg_add	OpenBSD

FIGURE 3-2. BSD Package Management Systems.

This table shows the package managers you are most likely to encounter when you use a BSD-based version of Unix.

The package managers I have mentioned are all CLI-based programs. That is, you use them by typing commands. For completeness, I will mention that some types of Linux also have GUI-based programs. (For example, Ubuntu has a GUI-based package manager named Synaptic.) However, I won't be discussing them here because the CLI-package managers are more widely used and, in my opinion, are more fun to use.

---

[2] Debian Linux was created in 1993 and is still actively developed. Over the years, Debian has spawned a large number of derivative Linux distributions, including the popular Ubuntu and Mint families.

In this section, I will show you how to install Emacs using APT and RPM. If your operating system uses a different package manager, you can look it up online to see how it works, or you can use the information in Section 3.3 to install Emacs manually.

Installing Emacs using a package manager is easy. All you have to do is enter the appropriate command and everything will be done for you automatically.

Installing Emacs with APT

To install software with the APT package manager, you use the `apt-get` program. To install Emacs, the command to use is:

```
sudo apt-get -y install emacs
```

Let's discuss this command, one piece at a time:

- `sudo` runs the command as superuser, so you will have permission to install software on the system. You will need the superuser/administrator password to run this command. (We discussed the superuser in Section 2.3.)

- `apt-get` is the program you want to run.

- The `-y` option: During the installation process, `apt-get` will pause and ask your permission to proceed with various tasks. The `-y` option automatically answers "yes" to such prompts, so `apt-get` will not pause. If you so desire, you can leave out this option and respond to the prompts manually.

- `install` tells `apt-get` that you want to install software.

- `emacs` is the name of the package you want to install.

Once you have installed Emacs, you can test it by starting the program:

```
emacs
```

To quit Emacs, press <Ctrl-C> <Ctrl-X>.

To uninstall Emacs, use the following command:

```
sudo apt-get -y remove emacs
```

Using `remove` deletes the package but leaves its configuration files, which were used to help install the software.

By default, these files are left alone in case you have modified them. However, if you do not plan to reinstall the program or install a new version of the program, you may want to delete both the package and its configuration files. To do so, use:

```
sudo apt-get -y remove --purge emacs
```

Installing Emacs with RPM

To install software with the RPM package manager, there are two programs you might use. The best choice is DNF. To install Emacs, the command to use is:

```
sudo dnf -y install emacs
```

To uninstall Emacs, use the following command:

```
sudo dnf -y erase³ emacs
```

DNF is a replacement for an older program called YUM. DNF is better than YUM, so it should be your first choice.[4] However, if your system uses RPM but it doesn't have DNF, you can use YUM. The syntax is the same as DNF:

```
sudo yum -y install emacs
udo yum -y erase emacs
```

Once you have installed Emacs, you can test it by starting the program:

```
emacs
```

To quit Emacs, press <Ctrl-C> <Ctrl-X>.

Section 3.3: Installing Emacs Manually With Linux

The following instructions show you how to install GNU Emacs manually on a Debian-based Linux system (this includes the Ubuntu and Mint families). A manual installation involves downloading a tarball from the GNU Emacs archive, and then unpacking, compiling, and installing the program. Normally, you would use a package manager, which is a lot easier. However, in some cases, you will want to do a manual installation. Here is an example.

When I was working on this book, the most up-to-date version of Emacs was 24.5. At the time, the latest version of Emacs for which there was a package in the Debian repository was 24.4. (It can take a while for a package to be created when a new version is released.) I could use **apt-get** to install Emacs 24.4 but, for technical reasons, I wanted to test 24.5, so I had to install it manually.

Below I will show you the procedure I followed. Although the details (such as version numbers) will change as time passes, the general principles won't, so you can modify the following commands to suit your needs.

---

[3] You can use either **erase** or **delete**, but **delete** is deprecated.

[4] For example, DNF is much better at handling dependencies.

When you read my annotated procedure for installing Emacs by hand, do take a moment to make sure you understand each step. At the end of the section, I will give you all the commands in a quick list, to make it easy for you to enter them one after another. So don't do anything right now. Just read through my comments until you get to the list of commands at the end of the section.

1. Before you start, be sure to uninstall any existing Emacs programs that may already be on your system. For example, if you have previously installed Emacs using **apt-get** you can use the command:

sudo apt-get -y remove emacs

2. On Debian systems, the tools you need to build a program from source code are not installed by default. So before you can compile and install anything, you need to install these tools (compilers, libraries, and so on). They are in a package called **build-essential**. The command to use is:

sudo apt-get install build-essential

IMPORTANT: Be sure to type **essential**, not **essentials**.

3. Make sure your system satisfies the build dependencies for Emacs version 24:

sudo apt-get build-dep emacs24

IMPORTANT: Be sure to specify only the major version number. Do not include the minor number. In our example, I used **emacs24**, not **emacs24.5**. If you include the minor number (**24.5**) it won't work, and it will take a long time to figure out why.

Note

When you run the **apt-get build-dep** command for the first time, you may reach a point where the program pauses to ask you to specify the "Postfix Configuration". (Postfix is a mail server, a program that delivers email over a network. Configuring Postfix is important if you plan to send email from Emacs.)

You will see a text menu with several choices. Use the Tab key to move to the configuration type that best describes your system. Then press <Enter> to make your selection. If you are not sure what to do, select "No configuration".

---

3. Change to your home directory and create a subdirectory to hold the installation files:

cd && mkdir emacs-24.5-install

4. Change to the installation directory:

cd emacs-24.5-install

63

5. Download the tarball you need to install Emacs. First, use your Web browser to visit the GNU Emacs FTP server:

`http://ftp.gnu.org/gnu/emacs/`

Look for the appropriate tarball, and download it using **wget** (a program to retrieve content from Web servers):

`wget http://ftp.gnu.org/gnu/emacs/emacs-24.5.tar.gz`

The file will be downloaded into the current directory (in this case, `emacs-24.5-install`).

6. Extract the installation files from the tarball.

`tar -xvzf emacs-24.5.tar.gz`

At this point, the Emacs source programs will be in a subdirectory with the name taken from the tarball: in our case, `emacs-24.5`.

7. Change to the subdirectory that holds the installation files:

`cd emacs-24.5`

8. Configure the Emacs software:

`./configure`

9. Build the Emacs software:

`make`

10. Install Emacs:

`sudo make install`

11. Test to see if Emacs is installed properly, by starting the program:

`emacs`

To quit Emacs, press <Ctrl-C> <Ctrl-X>.

For reference, here are all the commands in an easy-to-read list. Remember, before you start, make sure that you have uninstalled any existing version of Emacs:

`sudo apt-get -y remove emacs`

Also, visit the GNU Emacs FTP server and find the tarball you want:

`http://ftp.gnu.org/gnu/emacs/`

In our example, it is `emacs-24.5.tar.gz`. In the commands below, change the version numbers appropriately.

Here are the commands you need to install Emacs manually on a Debian-based Linux system:

```
sudo apt-get install build-essential
sudo apt-get build-dep emacs24
cd && mkdir emacs-24.5-install
cd emacs-24.5-install
wget http://ftp.gnu.org/gnu/emacs/emacs-24.5.tar.gz
tar -xvzf emacs-24.5.tar.gz
cd emacs-24.5
./configure
make
sudo make install
```

To see if Emacs is installed properly, enter:

```
emacs
```

To quit Emacs, press <Ctrl-C> <Ctrl-X>.

Section 3.4: Installing Emacs With OS X

Installing Emacs with OS X is a multi-step process. First you modify your system settings to allow you to run a program downloaded from the Internet. Then you download and mount a disc image of the Emacs installation software. You then install Emacs, and create an icon for it in the Dock. Finally, you start Emacs to make sure it works.

1. ENABLE THE RUNNING OF PROGRAMS DOWNLOADED FROM THE INTERNET

Before you can install Emacs with OS X, you need to make sure your settings allow you to run programs downloaded from the Internet.

a. Open Finder, click "Applications", then double-click "System Preferences". The "System Preferences" will open.

b. Within "System Preferences", click "Security & Privacy". The "Security & Privacy" window will open.

At the bottom of the General Tab where it says "Allow apps downloaded from:" If "Anywhere" is selected, that is fine. Close the window.
If not, you need to change the setting to "Anywhere".

c. Click the icon of a lock next to "Click the lock to make changes". You will be asked to type your password. Type the password you use to log in to your account, then click "Unlock".

d. At the bottom of the General Tab where it says "Allow apps downloaded from:", select "Anywhere".

e. If you see a warning message, read it and then click "Allow From Anywhere".
    If you see a window with a warning that this setting will change back after 30 days,
    click "Allow From Anywhere" to approve the change.

f. To finish, lock the setting by clicking the icon of the lock next to "Click the lock to
    prevent further changes".

g. Close the "Security & Privacy" window.

2. DOWNLOAD A DISK IMAGE OF THE INSTALLATION SOFTWARE

To install Emacs, you must download a DMG ("disk image") file. A DMG file
holds the image of an optical disc, so you can think of it as a virtual disc. (A DMG file
is the Mac version of an ISO file.)

The Web page to download a DMG file containing Emacs for OS X is:

`http://www.emacsformacosx.com/`[5]

Start your browser, visit this page, and download the DMG file. The file should end
up in your Downloads folder. If you can't find it there, check your desktop. Once you
are sure the file is downloaded, you can close your browser.

3. MOUNT THE DMG FILE

When you MOUNT a disc image file, it emulates your putting a real disc into
your CD or DVD device. If you have any experience using ISO files with Unix or
Windows, you will see that mounting a DMG file on a Macintosh is like mounting an
ISO file, only easier.

All you need to do is use Finder to open the Downloads folder. Then double-
click on the DMG file and wait. Your disc image will be mounted automatically. As
this happens, you will see a notice that the DMG file is being opened. Once the DMG
file is mounted, you will see an icon for the program (in this case, an Emacs icon).

4. INSTALL EMACS

Drag the Emacs icon to your Applications folder. It is that easy.

5. CREATE A DOCK ICON

Use Finder to open the Applications folder. Find the Emacs icon, and drag it to
the Dock for easy access. You can now close the Applications folder. (The Dock is like
the Ubuntu Launcher or the Windows Taskbar.)

---

[5] If this Web site doesn't work, search online for: `installing emacs "os x"`.

6. START EMACS TO MAKE SURE IT WORKS

Click the Emacs icon in the Dock to start the program. If your permissions have not been set up properly, you will see:

"Emacs" can't be opened because it was not downloaded from the Mac APP store

If so, simply follow the instructions in Step 1 above. Otherwise, the first time you run Emacs, you will see:

"Emacs" is an application downloaded from the Internet. Are you sure you want to open it?

Click "Open" to start the program. If necessary, bring the focus to the Emacs window by clicking on it.

7. QUIT EMACS

To quit Emacs, press: <Control-X> <Control-C>. (Be sure to use <Control>, not <Command>.)

8. "EJECT" THE DISC IMAGE

Now that you are finished with the virtual disc, you can "eject" it. Look on your Desktop for a white and gray icon with the name Emacs. This represents the mounted DMG file.

Click on the icon. Then press <Command-E>, which will instantly "eject" the virtual disc, at which time the icon for the mounted DMG file will disappear.

9. DELETE THE DMG FILE

Use Finder to open the Downloads folder. Drag the DMG file to the Trash folder. If you want, empty the Trash. Close Finder.

UNINSTALLING EMACS

If you ever want to uninstall Emacs, the process is easy: just drag the Emacs icon from the Applications folder to the Trash.

To remove the Emacs icon from the Dock, right-click on the Emacs icon and select Options, and then "Remove from Dock".

67

■ **Note**

When you use a mouse, there are two basic ways to click: a regular "click" and a "right-click". On a Macintosh, these two types of clicks are referred to formally as a PRIMARY CLICK (click) and a SECONDARY CLICK (right-click). When I instructed you (above) to right-click on the Emacs icon, I was referring to a secondary click.

With a Macintosh two-button mouse, one button sends the primary click; the other sends a secondary click. If you have a one-button mouse, to create a secondary click (a right-click), hold down the Control key as you click.

With a Macintosh touchpad, one of the following should work:

- Touch the touchpad with two fingers.
- Touch the bottom right corner of the touchpad.
- Touch the bottom left corner of the touchpad.

It is a good idea to set the primary and secondary clicks on your system to suit your preferences. To do so, use Finder to open the Applications folder. Then open "System Preferences", and choose either Mouse or Trackpad.

Section 3.5: Installing Emacs With Microsoft Windows

To install Emacs with Microsoft Windows you don't run a setup program, as is usually the case with Windows software. Instead, you download the appropriate archive and then extract its contents. You can then pin the Emacs program to your Taskbar or create an icon for it.

Before you start, you need to choose a directory into which you will install Emacs. If you don't have a master plan for your directory structure, I suggest you use `C:\Emacs`, which is what I will use in the examples below.

■ **Note** During this procedure, you will need to use the Windows file manager. In Windows 7, the file manager is Windows Explorer. In Windows 8 and Windows 10, it is File Explorer.

1. CREATE AN EMACS DIRECTORY

Use the Windows file manager to create the directory `C:\Emacs`.

2. DOWNLOAD THE EMACS ARCHIVE

Use your Web browser to visit the GNU Emacs FTP server where the Windows archives are stored:

```
http://ftp.gnu.org/gnu/emacs/windows/
```

Look for the version of Emacs you want to install. (I suggest the latest version.) In our example, I will use:

`emacs-24.5-bin-i686-mingw32.zip`

Click on this link to download the file to your computer. Be sure to save the file to the `C:\Emacs` directory (not to your Downloads directory).

Note

When you download an archive (or a setup program) for Microsoft Windows, it will contain binary files, all ready to run. This is convenient, but it also makes it easier to infect your computer with malware, such as viruses or trojans. With binary files, there is no way of knowing what's inside the installation package. With source files, anyone can look inside the programs, so the programs are open to the world.

For this reason, before you install any Windows program, it behooves you to use an up-to-date antivirus program to check the installation file for malware.

---

3. EXTRACT THE CONTENTS OF THE ARCHIVE

Use the Windows file manager to navigate to `C:\Emacs`. Look for the archive (zip file) you just downloaded. To extract its contents, right-click on the file name and choose "Extract All".

You will see a dialogue asking you to select the directory to hold the contents of the archive. Before you proceed, make sure that there is a checkmark next to "Show extracted files when complete".

You will see a suggestion to create a directory with the same name as the first part of the zip file. In our example, it is:

`C:\Emacs\emacs-24.5-bin-i686-mingw32`

Unless you have a good reason to use another directory, accept the default choice. To process the archive, click Extract.

Once the extraction process is finished, you will see a file manager window showing you the contents of the destination directory. Specifically, you should see four directories: `bin`, `libexec`, `share` and `var`. Within these directories are some subdirectories and a large number of files.

At this point, your Emacs installation is complete.

In a moment, you will be running Emacs. The first time you run the program, you may see a warning:

The publisher could not be verified.
Are you sure you want to run this software?

As long as you downloaded the Emacs archive from the official GNU Emacs FTP site, it is safe to uncheck the box next to "Always ask before opening this file". That way, you won't be bothered every time you want to run the program.

3. START EMACS TO MAKE SURE IT WORKS

Within the file manager, change to the **bin** directory. In our example:

```
C:\Emacs\emacs-24.5-bin-i686-mingw32\bin
```

You will see a number of executable programs (**.exe** files). To start Emacs, run the program **runemacs.exe**. Once Emacs is running, you can quit it by pressing <Ctrl-X> <Ctrl-C>.

4. MAKE EMACS EASY TO RUN

To make Emacs easy to run whenever you want, you can pin it to the Taskbar. To do so, use the file manager to navigate to the Emacs bin directory. Right-click on **runemacs.exe** and select "Pin to Taskbar".

To create an Emacs icon, run the program **addpm**.exe. (It's in the same directory.)

5. CLEAN UP

You can now delete the Emacs archive file. In our example, it is:

```
emacs-24.5-bin-i686-mingw32.zip
```

CHAPTER 4

■ ■ ■

The Emacs Keyboard

Section 4.1: A Strategy for Learning Emacs

In the first three chapters of this book, we discussed:

- What is Emacs, and where did it come from?
- Basic Unix skills and how they relate to Emacs.
- Installing Emacs on your own computer.

At this point, you are now ready to begin learning how to use Emacs.

With most text editors, the way to start is to learn some of the basic keystrokes —
how to move the cursor, how to page up and down, how to search for a pattern, and
so on — and then practice, practice, practice.

With Emacs you need a different strategy. As we discussed in Section 1.3, Emacs
is wonderful in that it is a full-fledged working environment. However, it is this very
same exhaustive complexity that makes Emacs difficult to learn. So, here then, are
three helpful guidelines. First, what *not* to do:

1. Do not jump in and start by learning the basic keystrokes. Keystrokes are easy
to learn. To really understand Emacs, you must first have the proper background
(Chapters 1 and 2 of this book).

2. As you will see in Section 12.4, Emacs comes with a built-in tutorial. Do not begin
by starting Emacs and firing up the tutorial. All that will happen is you will become
confused and discouraged. (At least, that's what happened to me.)

So what should you do?

3. After you have read Chapters 1 and 2, continue by reading each section of this
chapter in order. I will start by teaching you all the basic concepts (and there are a lot
of them). At the proper time, I will show you how to use the fundamental keystrokes,
and *then* you can practice, practice, practice. When you get to Section 12.4, I will
explain how to run the Emacs tutorial, and you can use it as a post-graduate course.

© Harley Hahn 2016
H. Hahn, *Harley Hahn's Emacs Field Guide*, DOI 10.1007/978-1-4842-1703-0_4

Section 4.2: The Ctrl Key

Emacs has a lot of key combinations, referred to as "key sequences". (We'll talk about key sequences Section 6.1, at which time I will give you a technical definition.) There are far more key sequences than you will ever memorize. In Section 4.5, I will explain why there are so many. First, though, you need to understand how Emacs uses the keyboard.

Like all text editors, Emacs uses all the regular keys (letters of the alphabet, numbers, punctuation, and so on). However, Emacs also uses two special keys: Ctrl and Meta.

The Ctrl key is used in the usual way. You hold down <Ctrl> as you press another key. For example, the command <Ctrl-H> starts the built-in Help facility: hold down the Ctrl key and press the letter **h**. No surprise here.

What will be new to you is that many Emacs commands consist of more than one Ctrl combination in a row, or a Ctrl combination followed by a single letter. Here are two examples:

- To quit Emacs, you use <Ctrl-X> <Ctrl-C>. That is, press <Ctrl-X> and then press <Ctrl-C>.

- To start the built-in tutorial, you use <Ctrl-H> **t**. That is, you press <Ctrl-H> and then press the letter **t**.

In order to make the description of such key sequences readable, Emacs uses its own notation. As you may know, the Unix convention for describing the Ctrl key sequences is to use a ^ (circumflex) character to represent <Ctrl>. For example, in the Unix world, **^X** means <Ctrl-X>. Another part of this convention is that when we describe a Ctrl key sequence, we write the letter of the alphabet in uppercase. For instance, we write **^X**, not **^x**. We do this because it is easier to read. (You don't actually press the Shift key when you type the **x**.)

In Emacs, the Ctrl key is represented by **C-** (the uppercase letter "C" followed by a hyphen), and the letters are written in lowercase. For example, instead of writing <Ctrl-X> or **^X**, we write **C-x**. Similarly, the combination <Ctrl-X> <Ctrl-C> is written as **C-x C-c**; and <Ctrl-H> followed by the letter **t** is written as **C-h t**. It is important that you recognize this notation because that is what you will see when you read about Emacs. To help you get used to these conventions, I will use them consistently throughout the rest of the book.

Section 4.3: The Meta (Alt) Key

In addition to the Ctrl key, Emacs uses the Alt key which, for historical reasons, is referred to as the META KEY, written as <Meta>, so whenever you see a reference to the Meta key, just press <Alt>. (With a Macintosh keyboard, the Meta key is the Option key.)

The Meta key is used in the same way you use the Ctrl and Shift keys. That is, you hold it down while you press another key. For example, to type an uppercase "A", you hold down the Shift key and press the letter **a**. To type <Ctrl-A>, you hold down <Ctrl> and press **a**. And, to use <Meta-A>, you hold down <Alt> and press **a**. (Or, with a Macintosh keyboard, you hold down <Option> and press **a**.)

The Emacs notation used to indicate a Meta key sequence is similar to what we use with the Ctrl key, except that we use **M-** instead of **C-**. For instance, to indicate the combination <Meta-A>, we write **M-a**. Here is an example:

- When you are editing a file, the command to move down one screenful is **C-v**. The command to move up one screenful is **M-v**.

This means, to move down one screenful, you press <Ctrl-V>. To move up one screenful, you press <Meta-V> (that is, <Alt-V>).

As an alternative, you can also use the Escape key (<Esc>) as a Meta key. However, when you use <Esc>, you do not hold it down. You press it, let go, and then press the second key. For example, if you want use the **M-v** command I mentioned above, you can either press <Meta-V> or type the two keys <Esc> **v**. (This alternative way of using <Meta> was created because, at one time, there were keyboards that didn't have a Meta key or an Alt key.)

You will occasionally see key sequences that use both the Meta key and the Ctrl key. For example, **M-C-s**. To type this command, you have two choices. You can either hold down <Ctrl> and <Meta> and press **s**, or you type the two keys <Esc> <Ctrl-S>.

Thus, there are four possible ways to use each letter of the alphabet. For instance, the letter "a" can be used as a:

- Lowercase letter (**a**)
- Uppercase letter (**A**)
- Ctrl combination (**C-a**)
- Meta combination (**M-a**)
- Meta-Ctrl combination (**M-C-a**)

When you have a Meta-Ctrl combination, you hold down both keys at the same time. For example, the following two combinations are equivalent, and you will see it written both ways.

```
M-C-a
C-M-a
```

I know this all may sound confusing when you read it, but in practice it is easy.

Section 4.4: Special Key Names

When you read about Emacs, you will see special names used to represent specific keys. These names are shown in Figure 4-1. It is important that you memorize them, as you will see these names when you read Emacs documentation, especially reference information about commands and Lisp functions.

Name	Key
C-	Ctrl
M-	Meta
M-C-	Meta-Ctrl
BS	Backspace
DEL	Delete
ESC	Esc
RET	Return
SPC	Space
TAB	Tab

FIGURE 4-1. **Emacs names for special keys.**

When you read about Emacs, you will sometimes see abbreviated names used for special keys. These names are derived from the technology of the 1970s, and they are important enough that it is a good idea to memorize them.

What you see in Figure 4-1 comes from very old technology of the 1970s, when Unix and Emacs were originally developed. Except for the Meta key (which we'll talk about in a moment) and the Tab key, all the keys in Figure 4-1 can be traced back to the earliest Unix terminal, the Teletype Model 33 ASR we discussed in Section 2.4.

We have already met the Ctrl key and Meta key. To summarize:

- C- stands for "hold down the Ctrl key"
- M- stands for "hold down the Meta key"
- M-C- stands for "hold down both the Meta key and the Ctrl key"
- As an alternative to the Meta key, you can press <Esc>.

For example, **M-x** means you can use either <Meta-X> or <Esc> **x**. **M-C-x** means you can use either <Meta-Ctrl-X> or <Esc> <Ctrl-X>.

You will see the Meta-Ctrl double-key sequences written in three different ways, but they all mean the same thing. For example, the three commands below are equivalent. They mean either "hold down the Meta and Ctrl keys and press **s**, or" press the Esc key, let it go, and then press <Ctrl-S>.

```
C-M-s
M-C-s
ESC C-s
```

Here is another, more complex example. While I was researching this chapter, I found a reference that contained a long list of Emacs commands. It the middle of the list was a line that said:

ESC-!   **Enter a shell command.**

In other words, while you are working within Emacs, you can enter a shell command by typing **ESC !** (followed by the shell command). The moment I saw this, my mind changed **ESC-!** to <Meta-!>. (This is the type of thinking I want you to train you mind to do automatically.)

But there is more. Look at your keyboard and notice that the **!** (exclamation mark) character is actually an "uppercase" **1** (the number 1). Thus, the sequence **ESC !** is actually **ESC** <Shift-1>, which is the same as <Meta-Shift-1>, which is actually <Alt-Shift-1> on my keyboard.

So when I read that the way to enter a shell command is by using **ESC !**, my mind immediately knew to press <Alt-Shift-1>, type the shell command, and then press <Enter>. One day, your mind will do the same and, on that day, you will know you are an Emacs person.

To continue with the discussion of Figure 4-1. The **BS, DEL, ESC, RET, SPC,** and **TAB** keys are simple to understand: they represent the following keys: Backspace, Delete, Esc (Escape), Return (Enter), Space, and Tab. (**DEL** refers to the same Delete key we discussed in Section 2.10.)

▨ **Note**

On a Macintosh keyboard, BS refers to the Delete key at the top-right corner of the main part of the keyboard. This is the primary Delete key, which corresponds to the Backspace key on a PC keyboard. DEL refers the secondary Delete key, the one to the left of the End key.

The secondary Delete key is available only with a full-sized Macintosh keyboard. If you have a compact keyboard, you won't have this key. Instead, you can use either <fn-Delete> or <Control-D>.

Section 4.5: The Meta Key, Bucky Bits, and Much More

As soon as you start to use Emacs, you will find out how important the Meta key is. In fact, the use of the Meta key is one of the defining characteristics of Emacs. And yet, I hear you say, "What Meta key? Ain't no stinkin' Meta key on my keyboard." Indeed, modern keyboards don't have a Meta key, we use <Alt> instead (or <Option> with a Macintosh). So why don't we just call it the Alt key?

The Meta key is a legacy from the early days of Emacs and Lisp at MIT (see Section 1.4), when there actually were keyboards that had this key. In fact, there were at least two such keyboards that were used with Lisp machines. (Remember, Emacs is tightly integrated with the Lisp programming language.) These keyboards were called the Knight keyboard and the Space Cadet keyboard. I'll talk more about them in a moment but, first, I want to explain a few technical details.

In Section 1.2 we talked about ASCII (the American Standard Code for Information Interchange). The list of all the ASCII characters and their meanings is called the ASCII CODE. The ASCII code uses 8-bit bytes to store characters, one character per byte. The original, plain vanilla ASCII code used only 7 of the 8 bits and, thus, defined 128 characters from 0 to 127. The original purpose of the Meta key was to turn on the top (8th) bit to allow the use of characters 128 through 255. In other words, using a Meta key effectively doubled the number of different characters from 128 to 256.

The tradition of using a special key to modify the top bits of a character began with the Stanford University SAIL KEYBOARD, developed in 1971 for special-purpose Lisp computers at the Stanford Artificial Intelligence Lab (SAIL). These keyboards had a number of extra keys, including Meta, Control and Alt.

Shortly afterwards, the West Coast SAIL keyboard began to influence the design of keyboards used by the East Coast AI (artificial intelligence) community. First, the so-called KNIGHT KEYBOARD was created by Tom Knight to be used on the legendary MIT Lisp Machines at MIT's AI Lab, where Emacs was later developed. (A LISP MACHINE was a single-user computer, optimized to run the Lisp programming language.) This keyboard and the Lisp working environment heavily influenced Richard Stallman when he designed Emacs.

Later, Tom Knight enhanced the Knight keyboard to create the more complex SPACE CADET keyboard (see below). Finally, the Space Cadet keyboard was adapted into several versions of a simpler SYMBOLICS KEYBOARD, used on commercial Lisp machines in the early 1980s.

All of these keyboards had a Meta key, which is how it found its way into Emacs. However, there was more. The Knight keyboard had four modifier keys: Top, Shift, Meta, and Ctrl. The Space Cadet keyboard had seven such keys: Top, Greek, Shift, Hyper, Super, Meta, and Ctrl.

Each key on the Space Cadet keyboard had three markings: in the regular place, higher up (top), and on the front of the key. In the regular place were the standard characters: letters, numbers, and punctuation, exactly like a regular keyboard. Above the regular character were special symbols, mostly mathematical. In fact, the "top" keys on the Space Cadet keyboard contained the complete APL character set. (APL is a mathematical programming language created by Ken Iversen in the 1960s.) On the front of the keys were Greek letters. To access the extra keys, you used <Shift>, <Top>, and <Greek>.

In this way, the Space Cadet keyboard lets you to type four completely different sets of characters. First, you type lowercase characters, numbers and punctuation in the regular way. Second, you hold down the Shift key to type uppercase letters and punctuation, also in the regular way. Third, you hold down the Top key to type the mathematical symbols and the Greek key to type the Greek letters. In other words, the Shift, Top, and Greek keys worked like regular shift keys. (Note: Because the Greek letters are on the front of the keys, you will sometimes see the Greek key referred to as the Front key.)

The other four modifier keys — Ctrl, Meta, Hyper, Super — used extra bits that were tacked on to the actual characters. For example, in the same way that you can type, say, <Ctrl-A> to send a special signal to the computer, you could also type <Meta-A>, <Hyper-A>, and <Super-A>, all of which were different. (In fact, in is actually possible to still use a Hyper key and a super Key with Emacs. All you have to do is use Emacs Lisp commands to make specific keys on your keyboard become the Hyper and Super keys. You can then connect Emacs commands that don't already have a key sequence — of which there are many — to use whichever Hyper and Super key sequences you want. By the way, if you are using a PC keyboard with Linux, by default, the Windows key is the Super Key.)

To return to the Space Cadet keyboard, in all, you could use it to type more than 8,000 different characters. This phenomenon gave rise to the Emacs (and the general hacker) philosophy that it is worthwhile to memorize the meanings of a very large number of strange, complicated key sequences, if it will reduce typing time.

Note

If you are experienced enough with Unix to have encountered the never-ending debate of Emacs vs. the **vi** text editor, here is the gist of it in one sentence:

Emacs people believe that it is worthwhile to memorize the meanings of a very large number of strange, complicated key sequences, if it will reduce typing time.

The extra bits used by the Ctrl, Meta, Hyper, and Super keys are known as BUCKY BITS. They are named after Niklaus Worth, the inventor of the Pascal programming language, whose nickname was Bucky. When Worth was at Stanford in 1964-1965, he suggested adding an extra key (called <Edit>) to use the 8th bit within bytes that stored 7-bit ASCII characters. Although this exact suggestion was never implemented, it did inspire the idea to use extra keys (and extra bits) to extend a keyboard's character set. As the story goes, Worth had prominent front teeth (buck teeth), so behind his back some people called him Bucky. Hence the name bucky bits.

One last point: the Knight keyboard was named after Tom Knight, one of the Lisp Machine's principal designers. However, the name also has more metaphysical connotations in that it recalls a semi-mythical organization of Lisp hackers called the Knights of the Lambda Calculus. (The lambda calculus is the mathematical theory upon which the Lisp programming language is based.)

Section 4.6: Meta Key Problems When Using a Terminal Window

When you run Emacs within a terminal window (see Section 2.6 and Section 5.2), you may encounter a problem using the Meta key.

With most keyboards, the Meta key is the Alt key. However, terminal windows are GUI-based programs that use the Alt key to access top-level menus. For example, it is common to access the File menu by pressing <Alt-F>. This can interfere with using the Meta key, because when you type certain key sequences, the terminal window program will grab the <Alt> key, instead of leaving it for Emacs to interpret. Here is a common example.

With Ubuntu Linux, the default terminal window is a Free Software Foundation program called Gnome Terminal. By default, Gnome Terminal uses <Alt> key combinations to let you access menus. For instance, to access the View menu, you type <Alt-V>. This means that the Emacs command **M-v** (which you will meet in Section 7.1 and Section 8.5) won't work properly. All that will happen is you will pull-down the View menu for the terminal window program.

In you have this problem, you need to find an option to disable <Alt> as a menu shortcut key. For example, with Gnome Terminal, pull down the View menu and select "Keyboard Shortcuts". You will see the following option:

Enable menu access keys (such as Alt+F to open the File menu)

Once you turn off this option, Gnome Terminal will ignore the Alt key, and your Emacs Meta key will work properly.

Of course, none of this matters when you run Emacs within a virtual terminal (see Section 2.6).

CHAPTER 5

■ ■ ■

Starting and Stopping Emacs

Section 5.1: Starting Emacs

In Chapter 3, we talked about how to install Emacs on different types of systems. If you are working with a GUI and at the time of installation you created an Emacs icon, all you need to do is click (or double-click) that icon to start Emacs. In this section, I will show you how to start Emacs from the command line. (We discussed how to enter Unix commands in Section 2.9.)

To start Emacs, you enter the Emacs command. The basic syntax is:

emacs [*option...*] [*file...*]

where *file...* indicates one or more files you want to edit.

The Emacs command has a lot of options, but you probably won't need them. I'll talk about a few of the options, but if you want to see all of them, use the **man** emacs command to look at the Emacs man page. (The online manual is explained in Section 2.13.)

The recommended way to start Emacs is to simply enter the command by itself:

emacs

Once Emacs starts, you can either create a brand new file or tell Emacs to read an existing file.

When you start Emacs, it automatically displays a screenful of useful information called the SPLASH PAGE. Although this is helpful, after a while, you won't need it. To start Emacs without a splash page, use the **-Q** (quick start) option:

emacs -Q

(Be sure to use an uppercase **-Q**. The **-q** option is completely different, and is something you probably don't want.)

H. Hahn, *Harley Hahn's Emacs Field Guide*, DOI 10.1007/978-1-4842-1703-0_5

■ **Note**

When Emacs starts, it looks for an initialization file named `.emacs` in your home directory. If an initialization file exists, Emacs will read it and execute all the commands it contains as part of the startup process. By placing commands in your `.emacs` file, you can customize your working environment (see Section 11.8).

When you learn more about Emacs, you will want to create an initialization for yourself. However, once you do, you need to stop using the `-Q` option. The reason is that, although -Q option tells Emacs not to display a splash screen (which is why we are using it), it also tells Emacs to ignore your initialization file. Thus, if you start Emacs with `-Q`, you won't have your personal customizations.

The solution is to create a `.emacs` file that contains the following command to suppress the splash screen. Once you have this command in your `.emacs` files, you can omit the `-Q` option. (The line that starts with a semicolon is a comment.)

```
; Do not display the splash screen
(setq inhibit-startup-screen t)
```

If none of this makes sense to you right now, don't worry about it.

If you specify the name of a file when you start the program, Emacs will automatically load the file you specified. For example, say that you want to edit an existing file named **document** in the current directory (see Section 2.17). You can enter:

```
emacs document
emacs -Q document
```

Once Emacs has started, you will be ready to edit the file. If you want, you can enter more than one file name. For example:

```
emacs document names addresses phone-numbers
emacs -Q document names addresses phone-numbers
```

Emacs will read each file into its own work area, and you can switch back and forth as necessary.

If you are experimenting as you read, the quick way to stop Emacs is to type **C-x C-c**. We'll talk more about stopping Emacs in Section 5.5.

▓ **Note**

Although it is possible to specify a file name (or multiple file names) when you start Emacs, this is not the recommended procedure. Why? Because it runs counter to the Emacs philosophy.

Emacs was designed to provide a total working environment. Unlike other editors, Emacs makes it easy to handle more than one file at the same time (as well as use email, work with directories, write and debug programs, enter shell commands, and so on).

The intention is that you should start Emacs by entering the command without file names, and then initiate as many different tasks as you want, switching from one to another as the mood takes you. Once you get good at Emacs, you can do just about anything you want from within it. Indeed, some people virtually live within Emacs (leaving only to get something to eat).

So, although you *can* specify a file name when you start Emacs, in the long run, you are better off thinking of Emacs as home away from home and not simply a text editor.

Section 5.2: Starting Emacs in a Terminal Window

When you start Emacs from a terminal window, you are working within the GUI. (For a discussion of terminal windows compared to virtual terminals, see Section 2.6.) Emacs knows when you start it within a GUI and, by default, it will use a GUI-based format. For example, if you are in a terminal window and you enter the following command, you will get the GUI version of Emacs:

```
emacs
```

If you prefer using Emacs like this, and you don't want to tie up your terminal window, you can tell the shell to run the program in its own window, that is, as a separate process. To do so, all you need to do is append an **&** (ampersand) character to the end of the command. Here are some examples:

```
emacs &
emacs document &
emacs document names addresses phone-numbers &
```

When you enter the command in this way, the GUI version of Emacs runs in its own window, and your terminal window is still available for other work.

Alternatively, if you prefer to use Emacs with a purely text-based format, such as you would use with a virtual terminal (which is my preference), you can start Emacs using the **-nw** (no window system) option:

```
emacs -nw
emacs -nw document
emacs -nw document names addresses phone-numbers
```

■ **Note**

If you prefer the Emacs text-based format, here is a very cool trick I think you will like. What you are about to read is highly technical, so if you don't understand it, you can ignore it.

When you start Emacs using the following command, the program runs in an extra-large window:

```
printf '\e[8;50;100 t' ; emacs -nw
```

The details of how this works will take us too far afield, so I won't explain it all. Suffice to say that the **printf** command above changes the size of the terminal window, and the *;* (semicolon) separates two commands that are executed one after the other.

Of course, you wouldn't type this command every time you want to use Emacs. Instead, you can create an alias and use that to start the program. The following command creates a suitable alias named **e**:

```
alias e="printf '\e[8;50;100 t' ; emacs -nw"
```

To make this convenient, all you have to do is put the **alias** command in your **.bashrc** file. (For a discussion of dotfiles, see Section 2.18.)

Once that is done, you can start a text version of Emacs in a large terminal window whenever you want simply by entering:

```
e
```

Section 5.3: Starting Emacs as a Read-Only Editor

There may be times when you want to use Emacs to look at an important file that should not be changed. To do this, start Emacs using the following syntax:

emacs *file* -f read-only-mode

For example, say that you need to look at a file named **secrets**. You want to use Emacs to look at the file, but you want to be sure you don't accidentally make any changes to it. Enter the command:

```
emacs secrets -f read-only-mode
```

When Emacs starts, the file will be marked as being read-only. This means you can look at it, but not make any changes.

■ **Note**   When you start Emacs by using the **-f** option, it tells Emacs to execute the Lisp function that is specified after the option. In this case, you are telling Emacs to execute a function named **toggle-read-only**. This function tells Emacs to consider the file you are editing as being read-only.

Section 5.4: Recovering Data After a System Failure

As a general rule, if your work is interrupted abnormally, you stand to lose all the data you entered since the last time you saved. For this reason, it is a good idea to pause and save your work regularly.

Still, accidents do happen, and Emacs works behind the scenes to protect you from losing data in case of a system failure. Whenever you are editing a file, Emacs automatically saves a copy of that file at regular intervals (by default, every 300 keystrokes). This backup file is called the AUTO-SAVE FILE.

Emacs creates the auto-save file in the same directory as the file you are editing. (We discussed directories in Section 2.15.) The name of the file will be the same as the file you are editing, except that there will be a # (number sign) character at the beginning and end of the name. For example, if you are editing a file named **document**, Emacs will create an auto-save file named **#document#**. So if you are looking at a directory and you see a file with such a name, you will understand what it is and how it got there.

Whenever you save a file, Emacs automatically removes the auto-save file. If you make more changes to the file, Emacs creates a new auto-save file. Thus, under normal circumstances, you should never see an auto-save file. However, if your Emacs session is terminated abnormally — before you have a chance to save your work — the auto-save file is preserved.

Each time you tell Emacs to begin work with an existing file, Emacs first checks to see if there exists a corresponding auto-save file. If so, it means that the last time you edited the file, you were unable to save your work properly. In such cases, Emacs will display a message like the following:

`Auto save file is newer; consider M-x recover-file`

This means Emacs thinks that you need to recover your file. To do so, simply follow the instructions. Enter the command:

`M-x recover-file`

Emacs will display the name of the original file. If this is correct, press <Enter>. Emacs will now ask your permission to restore the auto-save file. At the same time, Emacs will create a new window and display the directory information for the original file. (We discussed directories in Section 2.15.)

If you decide to restore the file, type **yes**. Emacs will replace the text you are editing with the contents of the auto-save file. If you do not want to restore the auto-save file, just type **no**.

To summarize, if your work is interrupted abnormally, Emacs will probably have saved what you were doing in an auto-save file. If so, you will see a message suggesting that you recover the file the next time you start to edit that file. To recover the file, enter:

M-x recover-file

When Emacs displays the name of the file, press <Enter>. Then, when Emacs asks for permission to restore the file, enter **yes**.

Section 5.5: Stopping Emacs

To stop Emacs, use the command **C-x C-c**. If there is no need to save any files, you may see a message like this:

(No files need saving)

Regardless, Emacs will quit, and you will be returned to the shell prompt.

If you have been working with one or more files that have not yet been saved, Emacs will give you a chance to save your work before it quits. For each file that has not been saved, Emacs will display the name of the file along with several choices.

Here is an example. You have been working with a file named **document** that has not as yet been saved. You press **C-x C-c** and you see the following:

Save file /home/harley/document? (y, n, !, ., q, C-r or C-h)

Emacs is asking if you want to save the file. Notice that Emacs displays the full pathname of the file:

/home/harley/document

This shows the file name and the directory in which it resides (see Section 2.17).

At this point, you have a number of choices. Most likely, you will want to save the file and quit. To do so, press **y** (for yes). If you don't want to save the file, press **n** (for no), and Emacs will quit without saving. Be careful: if you press **n**, any changes you have made to the file since the last time you saved it will be lost.

■ **Note**   If you are editing an existing file and you happen to make a lot of mistakes, you may decide to abandon everything you have done. Simply press **C-x C-c**, and then press **n** to quit without saving.

When you are editing more than one file, Emacs will display the name of each file that needs to be saved, one at a time, and ask you what to do. As before, you can press **y** to save and **n** to not save. However, you also have a few other choices.

To save all of the files at once and then quit, press ! (exclamation mark). To quit immediately, without saving anything more, press q. To save the current file only, but quit without saving anything else, press . (period).

If you try to quit when there are still files that are not saved, Emacs will ask you to confirm your intentions. You will see a message like:

Modified buffers exist; exit anyway? (yes or no)

In this case, you must enter either the full words **yes** or **no**.

Notice that the message refers to "buffers". I will explain what they are in a moment. For now, you can consider each buffer to be a separate working area.

Note   When Emacs wants to be especially sure you are making the right decision, it will ask you to answer **yes** or **no** (as opposed to **y** or **n**). In such cases, you must type the full word. This prevents you from making a serious mistake by accidentally pressing a single wrong key.

When you are working with only a single file, you can see the file on your screen when Emacs asks if you want to save it. However, when you are editing more than one file, Emacs will ask you about each file in turn, and you may have forgotten what was in one of the files. If so, when Emacs asks what to do with that particular file, press C-r. Emacs will show you the file, so you can make an informed decision. As you are looking at the file, you will be in VIEW MODE, which means you can read the file, but not make any changes. To quit viewing the file, press q (for quit).

Finally, if you forget what any of the choices mean, press C-h to display a quick help summary. To get rid of the help information, press q.

To summarize, you stop Emacs by pressing C-x C-c. If there are files to be saved, you have the choices summarized in Figure 5-1.

y	Save the specified file
n	Do not save the specified file
!	Save all the remaining files
q	Quit immediately without saving
.	Save the specified file and then quit
C-r	View the specified file
C-h	Display help information

FIGURE 5-1. Choosing whether or not to save files.

When you tell Emacs to quit, and you have files that have not been saved, Emacs will ask you what to do with each file in turn. Here are the responses you can use to make a choice for each such file.

CHAPTER 6

■ ■ ■

Commands, Buffers, Windows

Section 6.1: Commands and Key Bindings

In Section 4.2, I introduced the term "key sequence". However, at the time, I didn't give you a strict definition. Nor have I, as yet, given you a strict definition of an Emacs "command". However, as the poet observes:

"The time has come," the Walrus said,
"To talk of many things:
Of bindings— using Lisp commands—
Of Emacs' useful rings—
Of sequences that make you frown—
And whether keys have wings."

So, are you ready? Take a deep breath.

You know by now that the basic way you use Emacs is that you press one or more keys and something happens. Here is why.

Every Emacs COMMAND is a Lisp function (program module) that has been designed to be used interactively. All commands have a name, usually consisting of lowercase letters and hyphens. For example, the command that moves the cursor up one line is called **previous-line**. The command that moves the cursor down one line is called **next-line**.

An INPUT EVENT is anything you can do to send input to the computer: pressing a key, clicking a mouse button, moving a mouse, and so on. A KEY SEQUENCE is a series of input events that, taken as a unit, have meaning. Key sequences are used to invoke commands.

The connection between a key sequence and the command it invokes is called a KEY BINDING. Once such a connection exists, we say that the key sequence is BOUND to that specific command. For example, the key sequence **C-p** is bound to the **previous-line** command; **C-n** is bound to the **next-line** command; **C-f** is bound to the **forward-char** command; **M-f** is bound to the **forward-word** command; and so on.

© Harley Hahn 2016
H. Hahn, *Harley Hahn's Emacs Field Guide*, DOI 10.1007/978-1-4842-1703-0_6

Whenever you type a key sequence, you are actually telling Emacs to execute the command that is bound to that sequence. So, to use a specific command, you type the key sequence that is bound to that command. In our example, when you want to move the cursor up one line, you press C-p. This tells Emacs to execute the **previous-line** command. When you press C-n, you tell Emacs to execute the **next-line** command.

Here is another example. To move the cursor forward one character (that is, one position to the right), you press C-f. This invokes a command called **forward-char**. To move the cursor forward one word, you press M-f. This invokes a command called **forward-word**.

There are hundreds of Emacs commands and — in one sense — learning to use Emacs means learning how to use all the key sequences that are bound to the most useful commands. Specifically, to learn how to edit text with Emacs, you will need to memorize the key sequences for moving the cursor, displaying text, making changes, deleting characters, manipulating buffers, using windows, loading and saving files, and so on.

Most of the time, you don't need to know the names of the actual commands you are using: all you need to remember is which keys to press. However, there is a reason I am telling you all this. Emacs has so many commands that there aren't enough key sequences to go around, which means that many Emacs commands do not have their own key sequence. To use such commands, you have to type the full name of the command. To do so, you press M-x, type the name of the command, and then press <Enter>. Emacs will then execute that command.

Here is an example. The **ispell-buffer** command helps you check the spelling of all the words in your buffer. (We will discuss buffers in Section 6.2. Basically, a buffer is a work area.) The **ispell-buffer** command is not bound to any particular key sequence. Thus, you cannot run it by typing a key sequence. Instead, you must press M-x, then type **ispell-buffer** and press <Enter>.

Here are several experiments you can try for yourself. First, you might be wondering, can I use M-x to execute any command by specifying its full name rather than pressing its key? Of course.

For example, I mentioned that C-p moves the cursor to the previous line by executing the **previous-line** command. Try this. Start Emacs and type a few lines of text. Now press C-p. Notice that the cursor moves up one line. Now press M-x, type **previous-line,** and then press <Enter>. Again, the cursor moves up one line. Of course, you would never move the cursor by typing M-x **previous-line**, because pressing C-p is so easy. However, this example does show how it all works.

Here is another, more interesting example. Emacs comes with a number of games and diversions you can use by executing the appropriate programs. One such game is **doctor**: a program that acts like a therapist. (This is actually a modern version of a program called Eliza that was written many years ago at MIT.)

I will discuss the Emacs games in Section 12.7. For now, though, you may want to try talking to the built-in Emacs therapist. Press **M-x**, type **doctor**, and then press <Enter>. (Note: If Emacs displays a message saying **[No match]**, it means this program is not installed on your system.)

Once **doctor** starts, the two of you take turns talking. You can type as much as you want. When you are finished talking, press <Enter> twice, and the program will respond. When you are ready to quit, press **C-x k**, and then press <Enter>. (The **C-x k** command kills the buffer in which the program is running.)

One last point. You might wonder, why does Emacs use such long command names? After all, long names are hard to memorize and slow to type, and Emacs was designed for users who get frustrated with tools that won't let them think quickly. The answer is, when you are called upon to type a command name, Emacs will help you, so you rarely have to type the entire name. This facility is called "completion", and I will show you how it works in Section 6.7.

Note

Understanding the idea of key binding is important for several reasons. First, key binding is a basic part of Emacs, and until you understand it, you won't really understand Emacs.

Second, if there is a command you find useful but the key sequence is awkward for you to use, you can change it to a key sequence you like better.

Finally, as I mentioned above, there are many commands that do not have their own key sequences. To use these commands, you need to invoke them manually, using **M-x**. Once you understand key binding, you can learn how to bind a specific key sequence to any command you want, which makes it much easier to use that command.

To be sure, being able to customize your work environment in this way is an advanced skill, but it all starts with a firm understanding of key binding.

Section 6.2: Buffers

One of the nice features of Emacs is that it lets you do more than one thing at a time. For example, you can edit as many files as you want, jumping from one to another as the mood takes you.

In order to offer this flexibility, Emacs keeps a separate storage area, called a BUFFER, for each particular task. For example, if you are editing three different files, Emacs will maintain three separate buffers, one for each file.

Understanding buffers and how to use them is a crucial skill you must develop in order to become comfortable with Emacs. So let's take a few moments to explore what these things are and just how they work.

There are two ways in which buffers are created. First, you can make a new buffer whenever you want. Second, Emacs will automatically create a buffer when the need arises.

The thing to remember is that everything you see and everything you type is kept in one buffer or another. For example, Emacs contains a comprehensive, built-in help system called the Info facility that you can use whenever you want. When you press the key sequence to ask for help (it happens to be `C-h i`), Emacs creates a new buffer to hold the help information.

Here is another example. In Section 6.1, I mentioned that Emacs comes with a program called `doctor` that acts like a therapist. (You tell it your problems, and it responds with meaningless platitudes.) When you enter the command to start it (`M-x doctor`), Emacs creates a new buffer in which to run the program.

One last example. To keep track of your resources, you can use a command that tells Emacs to display a list of all your buffers (the command is `C-x C-b`). When you use this command, Emacs creates yet another buffer to hold the actual list as it is being displayed.

To keep track of all your buffers, Emacs assigns each one of them a unique name. When Emacs is called upon to create a buffer on its own, it will choose an appropriate name. For example, when you start the Info facility, Emacs creates a buffer named `*info*`, and when you run the `doctor` program, Emacs creates a buffer named `*doctor*`. When you start editing a file, Emacs creates a buffer with the same name as the file. Thus, if you tell Emacs you want to edit a file named `document`, it will create a buffer named `document` to hold that file.

At all times, Emacs makes sure that you have at least one buffer. When you start Emacs by specifying a file to edit, Emacs will create a buffer by that name. If the file exists, Emacs will read its contents into the buffer. If not, Emacs will create a brand new file by that name, and the buffer will be empty. For example, to start working with a file named `document`, you enter the command:

`emacs document`

When you start Emacs without a file name:

`emacs`

you will find yourself with an empty buffer named `*scratch*`. Since Emacs does not know what file you want to use, it creates the `*scratch*` buffer, so you will have someplace to work.

One of the most important uses for a buffer is to act as a temporary work area when you need to make some quick notes. For example, say that your mother calls you on the phone as you are working on an essay. She tells you to write down the name of a wonderful book you should read (*Harley Hahn's Guide to Unix and Linux*), but you don't want to take the time to look for a piece of paper and a pen. Instead, you quickly create a new buffer and type the information. Once your mother hangs up, you switch back to the buffer that contains the essay you are typing. The new buffer remains hidden from view, where you can deal with it at your leisure.

In Section 6.2, I will discuss the commands you can use to manipulate your buffers. For now, just remember the following five important ideas:

- Everything you do with Emacs is contained in a buffer.
- Each buffer has a unique name.
- You can create a new buffer whenever you want.
- You can kill (delete) a buffer whenever you want.
- Some buffers are created by you; some are created automatically by Emacs.

Note   Buffers are your friends.

Section 6.3: Windows

As we discussed in Section 6.2, everything you do with Emacs takes place within a buffer. You can have as many buffers as you want and, much of the time, you will have several things going on at once.

But how do you see what is in your buffers? The answer is that Emacs creates one or more WINDOWS on your screen and, within each window, you can view the contents of a single buffer. Some people prefer to use one large window and look at only one buffer at a time. Other people like to use multiple windows to look at more than one buffer at a time. For example, say that you are working with three different files. You might decide to have three windows, each of which displays a different file in its own buffer.

As you become experienced with Emacs, you will develop your own personal style. Most of the time, you will probably use just one or two windows, creating and deleting extra ones as the need arises.

So you can see what it looks like, Figure 6-1 shows a typical Emacs screen with a single window; Figure 6-2 shows a screen with two windows.

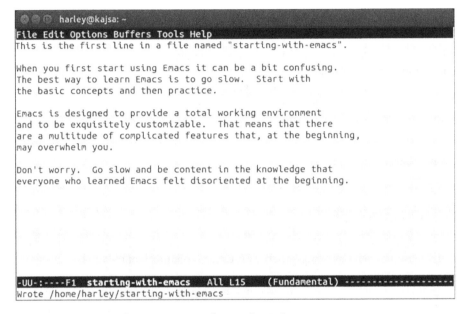

FIGURE 6-1. A typical Emacs screen with a single window.

This is the simplest Emacs configuration: one window displaying the contents of a buffer.

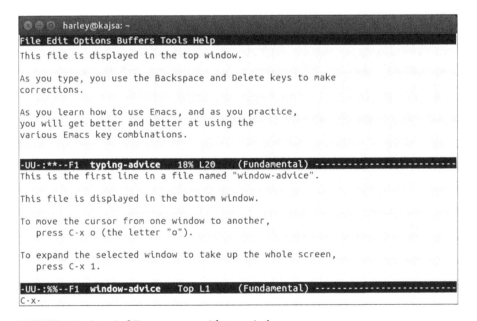

FIGURE 6-2. A typical Emacs screen with two windows.

Emacs lets you use multiple windows, each of which displays the contents of one buffer. In this example, there are two windows displaying two different buffers.

The best way to think of a window is as a fixed-size opening into a buffer. When you look into a window, you are looking at the part of the buffer that is currently being displayed. If you want to look at another part of the buffer, you can move the window up or down (or even sideways).

One nice thing about Emacs is that it lets you display a particular buffer in more than one window at the same time. This comes in handy when the content of the buffer is too large to fit into a single window. In such cases, you can use two windows to look at different parts of the same buffer at the same time.

For example, say that you are editing a long document. You can display the beginning of the document in one window and the end of the document in another window. This makes it easy to copy or move text from one part of the buffer to another, without having to jump around and lose your place.

Here is something interesting. Let's say that you have two windows, each of which is displaying the same part of a particular buffer. What do you think will happen if you make a change to the text in one of the windows? Well, since each window is showing you the same buffer, changing the text in one window should affect the text in the other window and, indeed, that is what happens. As you type or edit the text in one window, you can see both windows change at the same time.

To see how this all works, try it for yourself. Start Emacs by using the -Q option to suppress the splash screen (see Section 5.1), so it does not get in the way of the *scratch* buffer. Either of the following commands (see Section 5.2) will do:

```
emacs -Q
emacs -Q -nw
```

Emacs will start by creating one large window containing a buffer named *scratch*. There will be a few lines at the top with some useful information. To erase these lines, use C-x h C-w. (C-x h selects the entire buffer; C-w erases the selection.)

Now create a duplicate of the window by pressing C-x 2 (the command is explained in Section 7.6. You should now have two windows, each of which shows the empty *scratch* file.

Start typing anything. Notice that everything you type shows up in both windows. Press the Backspace key a few times to erase the most recently typed characters. Notice that, as you erase a character, the change is updated in both windows. Take a moment to experiment by making some more changes, and see what happens.

When you are finished, press C-x C-c to stop Emacs.

As you work with Emacs, the cursor is always in one particular window, which we call the SELECTED WINDOW or CURRENT WINDOW. As you type, the characters are inserted into the selected window at the position of the cursor. If you want to insert characters into a different window, you must first move the focus to that window. (I will explain how to do this in Section 6.3) Once you do, the cursor will move to that window and it will become the selected window.

Section 6.4: The Mode Line / Read-Only Viewing

Near the bottom of each window is a special line called the MODE LINE. The mode line contains information about the buffer that is currently being displayed in that window. The mode line is displayed in reverse colors to make it easy to read.

Take another look at the screenshot in Figure 6-1. This screen has a single window and, hence, one mode line near the bottom of that window. You can see this mode line, by itself, in Figure 6-3. In Figure 6-2, there are two windows, so there are two mode lines, which you can see in Figure 6-4.

```
-UU-:----F1  starting-with-emacs    All L15    (Fundamental) -------------------
```

FIGURE 6-3. The mode line from Figure 6-1.

In Figure 6-1, there is only one window. Thus, there is only one mode line.

```
-UU-:**--F1  typing-advice     18% L20     (Fundamental) -----------------------
-UU-:%%--F1  window-advice     Top L1      (Fundamental) -----------------------
```

FIGURE 6-4. The two mode lines from Figure 6-2.

In Figure 6-2, there are two windows, so there are two mode lines, one for each window.

Notice that near the left-hand side of each mode line there is a colon. The two characters after the colon show you the status of the buffer. The meaning of these characters is shown in Figure 6-5. In our first example, the single mode line, the two characters are −− (two hyphens). This indicates either that the buffer has not been modified at all or has not been modified since the last time you saved the file. When you see two hyphens in this position on a mode line, it means that, if you were to quit now, there would be nothing to save.

Characters	Meaning
−−	Buffer has not been modified
**	Buffer has been modified (not yet saved)
%%	Read-only mode: buffer has not been modified
%*	Read-only mode: buffer has been modified

FIGURE 6-5. Status characters within the mode line.

On the mode line, to the right of the colon, Emacs displays two characters to show you the status of the buffer.

In the next example, the first mode line in Figure 6-4, the two characters are **
(two asterisks). This means that the buffer has been modified in some way. Whenever
you see **, it reminds you that you must save the contents of the buffer before you
quit.

In the final example, the second mode line in Figure 6-4, the two characters are
%% (two percent signs). This means that the buffer is in read-only mode and has not
been modified.

At any time, you can turn read-only mode on and off by typing C-x C-q to
execute the Emacs command **read-only-mode**. For example, if you are editing
a file in read-only mode, and you decide you want to be able to make changes, type
C-x C-q. To change back to read-only mode, type C-x C-q again.

Note

As we discussed in Section 5.3, when you start Emacs with the name of a file, you can
tell Emacs you want to work in read-only mode by using the **-f** option to execute the Lisp
function **toggle-read-only**. For example, to edit a file named **secrets** in read-only
mode, you can use the command:

```
emacs -f toggle-read-only secrets
```

If you start with a file in read-only mode in this way and you decide you want to be able to
make changes, just type C-x C-q.

To continue: the next item of information on the status line is the name of the
buffer. In our examples, you can see the names are **starting-with-emacs**,
typing-advice, and **window-advice**. These are the names I chose when
I created the buffers. As we discussed in Section 6.2, Emacs sometimes creates buffers
on its own. In particular, when you start Emacs without specifying a file name, Emacs
will create an empty buffer named ***scratch***. Also, when you start the Info
facility, Emacs creates a buffer named ***info*** to hold the help information.

To the right of the buffer name is information that gives you a rough idea of the
current position within the buffer. If the entire buffer is small enough to be contained
within the window, you will see **All**. This is the case in our first example.

If the buffer is too large to fit into the window all at once, you will see three
possible position descriptions. If the window is currently showing the beginning of
the buffer, you will see **Top**. (This is the case in our third example.) If the window is
showing the end of the buffer, you will see **Bot** (bottom). Otherwise, you will see a
number. This number indicates what percentage of the buffer is above the top in the
window. In our second example, 18 percent of the buffer is above what we see in the
window.

To the right of this, you will see the letter **L** followed by a number, indicating
the line number of the cursor position within that buffer. In our first example
(Figure 6-3), the cursor is on line 15.

Finally, to the right of the line number, you will see one or more words in parentheses. These words show you the mode in which Emacs is operating for that particular buffer. I will talk about modes in Section 11.1. For now, I will just say that Emacs can act in different ways to suit the type of work you are doing. For example, if you are editing English text, Emacs will work a little differently than if you are writing a Lisp program. The mode shows what personality Emacs is using at the moment. (This, by the way, is where we get the name "mode line".) In all three of our examples, Emacs is in Fundamental mode (which I will explain in Section 11.2).

Section 6.5: The Echo Area / Typing Emacs Commands

When you type something and you instantly see it on your screen, we say that the program you are using ECHOES what you are typing. For example, when you type a Unix command at the shell prompt, the shell echoes the command. This means that the shell displays each character as you type it.

Emacs is different: it only echoes some commands. When it does, the characters are displayed on the bottom line of your screen, which is called the ECHO AREA. Here is how it works.

Emacs does not echo any commands that consist of only a single character combination. For example, the command C-n moves the cursor to the next line. When you press this key sequence, you do not see the letters C-n in the echo area: all you see is that the cursor moves.

Emacs echoes only multi-character commands. However, it waits one second after you press a character before it echoes it. If, within that time, you press a second character, Emacs does not echo the first one.

For example, the command C-x k kills (deletes) the current buffer. When you type the first character (C-x), Emacs waits for you to type another one. If you do not type another character within one second, Emacs echoes what you have already typed. That is, the letters C-x will appear on the bottom line of the screen. However, if you complete the command quickly, nothing will echo. Emacs will simply carry out the command.

The reason that Emacs echoes in this way is to give quick typists a fast response without a distraction, while providing slower, more hesitant typists with as much feedback as possible. In practice, this means that when you type those commands with which you are the most familiar, things move fast, but when you type the commands that are still new to you, Emacs prompts you as necessary. The overall feeling is that the system speeds up or slows down to match your comfort level. (Think about that for a moment.)

The echo area is also used by Emacs to display messages. These may be error messages, warnings, or simply informative comments. Whenever it displays an error message, Emacs will make a sound to make sure to get your attention.

If you look at Figures 6-1 and 6-2, you will see examples of how Emacs uses the echo area. At the bottom of the screen in Figure 6-1 is the following message:

`Wrote /home/harley/starting-with-emacs`

This message tells us that Emacs has successfully saved the contents of the buffer to a file. At the bottom of the screen in Figure 6-2, you can see:

`C-x-`

This means that you have pressed the `C-x` key and that Emacs is waiting for you to type something else to complete the command.

As you might expect, you can type ahead as much as you want. That is, you can press the keys as fast as you can, and Emacs will remember what you type. However, when you make a mistake that generates an error message, Emacs will throw away all the pending keystrokes. This prevents a mistake from causing unexpected problems.

Finally, if you are typing a command and you change your mind, press `C-g` to cancel the command. We will discuss this in Section 6.6.

Section 6.6: The Minibuffer

Many commands require you to enter further input once you press the initial key sequences. For example, the command `C-x C-f` tells Emacs to read a file into a buffer. Once you press `C-x C-f`, Emacs will ask you for the name of the file. If the file exists, Emacs will copy it into a new buffer. If the file doesn't exist, Emacs will create it for you.

When Emacs displays a message asking for information, it writes it to the bottom line of your screen. You are expected to type the information and then press <Enter>. Whatever you type is echoed on the bottom line of the screen and, up until the time you press <Enter>, you can make corrections.

Thus, the bottom line of your screen has two purposes: First, as I explained in Section 6.5, Emacs uses this line to echo your regular keystrokes and to display messages. Second, Emacs uses this same line to ask you for information and to echo such information as you type it.

For this reason, the bottom line of your screen has two different names. When Emacs is echoing your commands or displaying messages, this line is called the echo area. When Emacs is asking you for information and reading your reply, this line is called the MINIBUFFER.

As you type information into the minibuffer, you can use the Backspace key to correct mistakes. Each time you press <Backspace>, it erases one character.

As an Emacs user, you will often find yourself typing information into the minibuffer. To help you, Emacs does two things that make your life easier. First, whenever possible, Emacs will display a default value in parentheses when it prompts you for information. This default value is Emacs' guess as to what you might want to type. If indeed this is what you want, all you need to do is press <Enter>. Otherwise, you can type a different value.

Here is an example. You are working with three different buffers: **names**, **addresses** and **phone-numbers**. At the current time, you are editing the **names** file, and you decide to switch to **addresses**. The command to change to another buffer is **C-x b**. As soon as you type this, Emacs displays the following in the minibuffer (the bottom line of your screen):

`Switch to buffer (default addresses):`

Emacs is asking you for the name of the buffer to which you want to switch. The message in parentheses is telling you that the default value is **addresses**.

Thus, if you want to switch to the **addresses** buffer, all you need to do is press <Enter>. If you want to switch to another buffer (such as **phone-numbers**), you can type its name and then press <Enter>.

The second way in which Emacs makes it easy to enter information into the minibuffer is a facility called COMPLETION. Completion is a process by which you can tell Emacs to guess what you are going to type, so you don't have to actually type all the characters yourself. Completion is an important topic, and we will discuss it in more detail in Section 6.7.

■ **Note**   Emacs uses the bottom line of your display for both the minibuffer and echo area. The difference is that the minibuffer is used for input, while the echo area is only for output.

Occasionally, Emacs will need to display something (such as an error message) while you are typing in the minibuffer. When this happens, Emacs will display the message and the minibuffer will disappear temporarily. After a few seconds, Emacs will erase the message and the minibuffer will reappear. In other words, the bottom line of your screen will have been transmogrified from the minibuffer into the echo area and then, after a few seconds, back to the minibuffer.

Occasionally, you will be typing in the minibuffer when you realize that you are making a big mistake. Emacs makes it easy to cancel the whole command: all you need to do is press **C-g** (before you press <Enter>).

This is a key worth remembering: **C-g** within Emacs acts a lot like the **^C** (intercept) key within Unix (see Section 2.11). One day this may save your life.

■ **Note**   If you get yourself into a situation within Emacs where things are getting weird and you don't know what to do, try pressing **C-g** to cancel the current command. If it doesn't work, press **C-g** a second time.

Section 6.7: Completion

One of the nice ways Emacs makes your minute-to-minute work easier is that, at various times, you can tell Emacs to guess what you are going to type and complete it for you. This facility is called COMPLETION and here is how it works.

Whenever you are typing in the minibuffer — that is, providing information in response to a prompt — you can use one of the completion commands (explained below). This is a signal to Emacs to try to complete what you are typing. Emacs will display what it thinks you want to type. If Emacs has guessed correctly, all you have to do is press <Enter>. Otherwise, you can make whatever correction is necessary and then press <Enter>.

For example, let's say that you would like to switch to a different buffer. At the current time, you have three buffers called **names**, **addresses** and **phone-numbers**. Right now, you happen to be editing the **names** buffer, but you want to switch to the **phone-numbers** buffer.

The command to switch to a different buffer is **C-x b**. When you type this command, Emacs will display a prompt in the minibuffer. In this case, you might see:

Switch to buffer (default addresses):

This means that Emacs is asking you for the name of the buffer to which you want to switch. The default is **addresses**, so if this were the buffer you want, you would press <Enter>.

In this case, however, you want to switch to a different buffer, **phone-numbers**. You could type the entire name and then press <Enter>. The shortcut, though, would be to type only a **p** and then type a completion command. Emacs will then guess what you want, and type the rest of the name for you. In this case, you would see:

Switch to buffer (default addresses): phone-number

Now all you have to do is press <Enter>.

The completion facility — like much of Emacs — has a lot of complex details. However, all you really need to know are the four completion commands. They are all single keys: **TAB** (the Tab key), **SPC** (the Space key), **RET** (the Enter key), and **?** (question mark). Figure 6-6 summarizes how these keys work.

Command	Action
TAB	Complete text in minibuffer as much as possible
C-i	Same as **TAB**
SPC	Complete text in minibuffer up to end of word
RET	Same as **TAB**, then enter the command
?	Create new window, display list of possible completions

FIGURE 6-6. Completion Commands.

*When you type in the minibuffer, Emacs helps you, whenever possible, by guessing what you want and letting you use completion commands to make choices. **TAB** and ? work for commands, files and buffer. **SPC** works for commands and buffers. **RET** works only for commands.*

The **TAB** command works for buffers, commands and files. Most of the time, **TAB** is all you will need. **TAB** tells Emacs to complete as much as possible and then wait for you to press <Enter>. Here is how it would work in our example. Emacs has just displayed the message:

Switch to buffer (default addresses):

You want to switch to the **phone-numbers** buffer, so you type the single letter **p** and press <Tab>. Emacs looks through its list of buffers to see if any of them begin with **p**. In this case, it happens there is only one, the **phone-numbers** buffer. So Emacs types the rest of the name for you. You can now press <Enter> and complete the command.

The **SPC** command works for buffers and commands, because file names can contain spaces (although it is a bad idea; see Section 2.18). **SPC** is similar to **TAB** except that **SPC** will only complete up to the end of the word. In this case, if you had pressed <Space> instead of <Tab>, Emacs would have completed only up to the hyphen after the word **phone**, and you would see:

Switch to buffer (default addresses): phone-

To complete the command, you would have to either type the rest of the name, or type **n** and press <Tab> or <Space>.

SPC is handy when you want to use part of a name and finish the rest for yourself. For example, say that you wanted to create a new buffer named **phone-messages**. You can press **C-x b**, then press **p** and **SPC** to get the response described above. Now you can type **messages** and then press <Enter>. Since this buffer does not already exist, Emacs will create it for you. In this way, you create a brand new buffer named **phone-messages**.

RET works like **TAB** with the added effect that, after the completion is finished, Emacs will enter the command for you automatically. Thus, pressing <Enter> is like pressing **TAB** followed by <Enter>. In other words, if you are sure that there is only one way for Emacs to complete what you are typing, you can simply press <Enter> instead of **TAB** <Enter> and save yourself a keystroke. **RET** works only for commands, because when you type a brand new buffer name or file name, you need to be able to press <Enter> to indicate the end of the name.

The last completion key is **?** (a question mark) which, like **TAB**, works for buffers, commands and files. If you press **?**, Emacs will create a new window and, within it, display a list of all the possible completions it can find. This is handy when there are a number of completions, and you are not sure which one you want. Once you see the one you want, you can type it and press <Enter>. If you don't see the one you want, you can press **C-g** to cancel the command.

Here is an example. There is a command named `auto-fill-mode` which is useful when you are typing English text. It tells Emacs to break long lines for you automatically as you type, so you don't have to keep pressing <Enter>. To execute this command, you would press **M-x**, type `auto-fill-mode`, and then press <Enter>.

Let's say that you want to execute this command, but you forget the full name. You remember that it starts with the word `auto`, but that is all. Press **M-x** and then type `auto`. The minibuffer now looks like this:

`M-x auto`

Now press the **?** key. Emacs will create a new window with a buffer named `*Completions*`. Within this window you will see all the possible completions. In this case, there are two:

```
auto-fill-mode
auto-save-mode
```

To finish the command, all you need to do is type `-f` and press <Enter>. Since there is only one possible completion, Emacs will type it for you and enter the command.

The power of the completion facility lies in the fact that you can use it just about any time you are called upon to type something into the minibuffer. You can use completion for file names, buffer names, Emacs commands, and so on. (Moreover, as I mentioned in Section 2.12, you can use some of the same completion shortcuts when you are entering Unix commands for the shell.) Once you get used to the completion keys — and remember, most of the time, all you really need is **TAB** — you will come to appreciate the power of Emacs.

Now you can see why it is okay that so many Emacs commands have long names. Most of the time, you never really have to type the full name.

■ **Note**

When you use the **?** completion command, Emacs creates a new buffer named ***Completions*** and, within it, displays a list of all the possible completions. If you want, you can make a choice by changing to the ***Completions*** window, moving to the selection you want, and pressing <Enter>. (I explain how to change from one window to another in Section 7.6.)

However, most of the time, it is easier to complete the command on your own by typing a few more keystrokes and then pressing either <Tab> or <Enter>.

Section 6.8: Disabled Commands

This is an advanced topic. I do want you to read this section, but if everything doesn't make sense to you right away, don't worry about it. When you need the information, it will be here waiting for you.

Some Emacs commands are troublesome for beginners because they can be confusing or even potentially destructive. To protect you, such commands are marked as being DISABLED. When you use a DISABLED COMMAND, Emacs will pause before it runs the command. You will see a message telling you the command is disabled, and you will be asked if you really want to run the command. You can then indicate yes or no. If you become comfortable with the command, you can ENABLE it permanently, which lets you use it whenever you want without looking at the warning. Here is an example to show you how it works.

In my experience the disabled commands you are most likely to encounter are two commands used to change the case of a specific area of text:

- C-x C-u converts text to all uppercase letters. This key sequence is mapped to the command **upcase-region**.

- C-x C-l converts text to all lowercase letters. This key sequence is mapped to the command **downcase-region**.

We will discuss these commands and how to use them in Section 8.8. For now, I'm just going to use them as examples.

When you type C-x C-u, Emacs displays the following message:

```
You have typed C-x C-u, invoking disabled command upcase-region.
It is disabled because new users often find it confusing.
```

Following this will be a technical description of the command. Read this carefully and decide if you really want to run it. Next you will see a question:

```
Do you want to use this command anyway?
```

This question is followed by a list of possible responses, shown in Figure 6-7. All you have to do is press one key to indicate your answer. If you want to run the command, press **y**. If you didn't really mean to use this command, press **n**. If you are confused, type C-g, the Emacs keyboard-quit command (see Section 7.4).

y	Run command; enable it for rest of the work session
n	Do not run command; leave it disabled
SPC	Run command once; leave it disabled
!	Run command; enable *all* commands for the rest of the work session

FIGURE 6-7. **Choosing whether or not to run a disabled command.**

*When you type a disabled command, Emacs tells you the command is disabled and asks you what you want to do. Most of the time, you will answer either **y** or **n**. Note: You don't need to press <Enter>.*

Note

One reason C-x C-u is disabled is that it is very similar to C-x u, the Emacs **undo** command. This is the command you use to reverse changes to the buffer (see Section 7.3), so it is used a lot.

If you mean to type C-x u but you hold down the Ctrl key a bit too long, you will accidentally type C-x C-u. In such cases, it is helpful to see a warning message, rather than unexpectedly having the entire region change to all uppercase letters.

If there is a disabled command you are comfortable using, you can enable it permanently by putting the following line in your .**emacs** initialization file. (Using the .emacs initialization file is an advanced topic, which we will discuss in Section 11.8.)

```
(put 'command 'disabled nil)
```

where *command* is the command you want to enable.

For example, to enable the C-x C-u (**upcase-region**) and C-x C-l (**downcase-region**) commands, you would put the following lines in your .**emacs** file:

```
(put 'upcase-region 'disabled nil)
(put 'downcase-region 'disabled nil)
```

If you want to disable a command permanently, put the following line in your .**emacs** initialization file:

```
(put 'command 'disabled t)
```

where *command* is the command you want to disable. You might do this if there are commands you don't want to use by accident. You can still use them, but the automatic warning will slow you down.

As an example, to disable C-x C-u (upcase-region) and C-x C-l (downcase-region), put the following lines in your .emacs file:

```
(put 'upcase-region 'disabled t)
(put 'downcase-region 'disabled t)
```

As a convenience, there are two special commands that will add such lines to your .emacs file for you. They are **enable-command** and **disable-command**. Just type **M-x** (explained in Section 6.1) followed by either **enable-command** or **disable-command**. Then type the command you want to enable or disable, and press <Enter>.

For example, to permanently enable C-x C-u, type:

M-x enable-command upcase-region <Enter>

To enable C-x C-l, type:

M-x enable-command downcase-region <Enter>

This tells **enable-command** to put the appropriate lines in your .emacs file.

To permanently disable these commands, type:

M-x disable-command upcase-region <Enter>
M-x disable-command downcase-region <Enter>

Again, **disable-command** will put the appropriate lines in your .emacs file.

Finally, I will remind you that, for exact instructions on how to use the C-x C-u and C-x C-l commands, see Section 8.8.

CHAPTER 7

■ ■ ■

The Text Editing Work Environment

Section 7.1: How to Practice Using Emacs

In order to practice with Emacs, you need to start the program and (optionally) have some text to edit. Let me show you an easy way to do that. You can do this whenever you want to practice.

Start Emacs by using one of the commands below. The −Q option suppresses the splash screen (see Section 5.1) and, if you are using a terminal window, the −nw option runs Emacs in a text-based format (see Section 5.2).

```
emacs -Q
emacs -Q -nw
```

When Emacs starts, you will see one window displaying a buffer named *scratch*. The buffer will contain several lines showing an informative message.

To begin your practice session, press C-h to start the Help facility. At the bottom of the screen, in the minibuffer (see Section 6.6), you will see a message:

```
C-h (Type ? for further options) -
```

Press b. This tells Emacs to display information about key bindings (a list of all the Emacs key sequences and what they do).

In order to display this list, Emacs will create a new buffer named *Help*. Emacs will then split your screen into two windows. The top window will contain the *scratch* buffer; the bottom window will contain the *Help* buffer. In the bottom window, you will see the beginning of the key bindings list.

At this point, your cursor will be in the top window. (In other words, the top window will be the selected window, also called the current window. See Section 6.3.) What you want to do is get rid of the top window and work exclusively with the bottom window. To do this, press C-x 0 (the number zero). This tells Emacs to kill (get rid of) the selected window.

© Harley Hahn 2016
H. Hahn, *Harley Hahn's Emacs Field Guide*, DOI 10.1007/978-1-4842-1703-0_7

You will now have one large window containing the ***Help*** buffer, which consists of a long list of key bindings. This is a good place to practice using Emacs, because, while you are practicing, you will be examining a list of Emacs key sequences and the commands to which they are bound. There are lots of ways to move through a buffer. For now, all you need to know is to type **C-v** to scroll down one screenful and **M-v** to scroll up one screenful.

■ **Note** If you are using a terminal window and typing **M-v** (<Alt-V>) pulls down a menu, it is because your terminal window program is interpreting <Alt> as a menu key. For instruction on how to fix this problem, see Section 4.6.

If you are a beginner, simply skim through the list of key bindings, reading them and trying out whatever catches your interest. Don't worry about learning everything right away. I'll take you through all the important commands in due course. When you are finished with this list, you can type **C-x C-c** to stop Emacs.

If anything weird happens while you are exploring, you can type **C-h b** to get back the list of key bindings. If this doesn't solve the problem, just bail out by pressing **C-x C-c** and start all over again.

Once you learn how to insert and modify text, you will want to practice the editing commands. However, the ***Help*** buffer is read-only, so you can't make changes. To practice editing, start Emacs with the **-Q** option and use the ***scratch*** buffer as a work area. To summarize:

Here is how to read the list of key bindings:

1. Start Emacs using **emacs -Q** or **emacs -Q -nw**.
2. Press **C-h b** to display the information about key bindings.
3. Press **C-x 0** to remove the ***scratch*** window.
4. Look at the commands, and practice as much as you want.
5. When you are finished, press **C-x C-c** to quit.

And here is how to practice editing commands:

1. Start Emacs using **emacs -Q** or **emacs -Q -nw**.
2. Use the ***scratch*** window to practice as much as you want.
3. When you are finished, press **C-x C-c** to quit.

Section 7.2: Typing and Correcting

To create text, all you have to do is move the cursor to where you want the characters to be inserted and start typing. That's all there is to it. (In Section 8.2, I will show you how to move the cursor wherever you want.)

If you want to practice, start Emacs using one of the following commands:

```
emacs -Q
emacs -Q -nw
```

You will see a single window with a buffer called *scratch*. Just start typing. When you are finished, you can stop by pressing C-x C-c.

As you type, there are two ways to make simple corrections. To erase the character you have just typed (to the left of the cursor), press <Backspace>. To erase the character at the current position of the cursor, press <Delete> or C-d. In other words, <Backspace> erases to the left; <Delete> and C-d erase to the right. (These keys are described in Figure 7-1.) These key sequences are worth practicing. As the Roman philosopher Marcus Tullius Cicero said when he first learned Emacs: "*Cuiusvis hominis est errare, nisi mentis inops, in errore perseverare.*"[1]

Key	Action
BS	Delete one character to the left of cursor
DEL	Delete one character at the position of cursor
C-d	Same as **DEL**
C-o	Open a new line
C-x u	Undo the last change to the buffer
C-_	Same as C-x u
C--	Same as C-x u
C-/	Same as C-x u
C-q	Insert the next character literally

FIGURE 7-1. **Keys to use while typing.**

 Note   C-_ is "<Ctrl>-underscore".

There are two ways to insert a new line. First, you can move to where you want the line, type whatever you want, and press the Enter key. Alternatively, you can move to where you want the line and press C-o. This will create a new line for you. (You can think of o as meaning "open".)

---

[1] Any man can make mistakes, but only an idiot persists in his error.

Here are the details for using C-o. If you are at the beginning of a line, C-o creates a new, empty line above the current line. If you are at the end of a line, C-o creates a new, empty line below the current line. If you are within a line, C-o breaks it into two separate lines. Experiment a little and it will all make sense.

As you read through this book, you will find many commands you can use to make changes in the buffer: to erase text, to replace text, to move text, and so on. As you use these commands, you will sometimes find yourself in the situation of having made a change that you really don't want. For example, you may have deleted a large chunk of the buffer and then realized that you made a horrible mistake.

In such cases, you can use the C-x u command to reverse the last change you made to the buffer. As you can see from Figure 7-1, there are three other key sequences you can use to do the same thing. Because this command is complicated, but important, I'll explain it in detail in Section 7.3.

To finish this section, I'll deal with an odd problem that comes up every now and then: entering a control character or other special character. For example, let's say you want to put an actual <Ctrl-C> or <Ctrl-H> into your text, the type of thing programmers need to do every now and then. The problem is that many of the Ctrl keys have special meanings in Emacs, as do Tab, Escape, Delete, and a few other keys.

To insert one of these characters into your text, first press C-q. This tells Emacs that the next character is to be taken literally. (Think of the q as meaning "quote"; that is, to take the next key you type literally.) Thus, to insert a <Ctrl-C> character, type C-q C-c. To insert a <Ctrl-Q>, type C-q C-q. To insert a tab, use C-q TAB.

When you type a Ctrl key into a buffer in this way, it will be displayed on your screen using the standard Unix notation: a ^ (circumflex) character representing <Ctrl>, followed by an uppercase letter (see Section 4.2). For example, if you type C-q C-c, you will see ^C on your screen. If you type C-q C-q you will see ^Q. Please remember that, even though you see two characters on your screen, they represent only a single character. (It is a good idea to become familiar with the Unix Ctrl-key notation. It is so widely used, you will see it even when you run Emacs under Microsoft Windows.)

Aside from these special keys, there is really no trick to entering characters when using Emacs: just type and be happy.

Section 7.3: The repeat and undo Commands; Redo

As you edit text, there are two needs that you will encounter frequently:

- Repeat the last command.
- Reverse the last change to the buffer.

To repeat the last command you entered, use the key sequence C-x z which is bound to the **repeat** command. To reverse that last change you made to the buffer, use C-x u, C-/ or C-_, all of which are bound to the **undo** command. If you are used to

Microsoft Windows, you can think of **C-x z** as being like **^Y** and **C-x u** as being like **^Z**. However, as you will see, there are some differences. Let's talk about the details, starting with an example using **repeat**.

Let's say you are editing a file and you want to delete from the current position, backwards, to the beginning of the sentence. The key sequence to perform this operation is **C-x BS** (<Ctrl-X> <Backspace>). You type **C-x BS** to delete a sentence, and then decide you want to delete another one in the same way. You can, of course, type **C-x BS** again. However, it is better to use **C-x z** for two reasons.

First, **C-x BS** work only in this particular case. However, since **C-x z** is the universal way to repeat the last command, it always works.

Second — and this is important — **C-x z** allows you to use a particularly handy shortcut. Once you press **C-x z** once, you can repeat it again, as many times as you want, simply by pressing the letter **z**. For example, let's say you want to use **C-x BS** to delete five sentences. It would look like this:

C-x BS C-x z z z

Let me analyze the key sequences for you:

1. **C-x BS** deletes the previous sentence.
2. **C-x z** repeats the command.
3. **z** repeats the command a third time.
4. **z** repeats the command a fourth time.
5. **z** repeats the command a fifth time.

Although this may seem complicated the first time you see it, using **C-x z** in this way is fast and easy. Once you get used to it, your fingers will know what to do automatically without your mind having to think about it.

Moving on to **undo**: In Section 7.2, I mentioned that if you make a mistake, you can reverse it by pressing **C-x u** to invoke the **undo** command. As with the **repeat** command, you can press **C-x u** more than once to reverse more than one mistake. However, in addition to **C-x u**, there are two other key sequences that are also bound to the **undo** command: **C-/** (<Ctrl> -slash) and **C-_** (<Ctrl> -underscore). (For a discussion of commands and key bindings, see Section 6.1.)

C-x u is a longer, slightly more complex key sequence than **C-/** and **C-_**. However, there is an advantage to using it. In my experience, **C-x u** will always work, while **C-/** and **C-_** will sometimes not work with particular terminals and keyboards. My suggestion is to take a moment right now, and try all three of these key sequences on your system. See which ones work for you, and pick the one you like best. (My personal preference is **C-/**.)

Before we continue, I should point out that you will often see **C-_** referred to as **C--** (<Ctrl> -hyphen). This is because, on most keyboards, the (underscore) character is actually <Shift-hyphen> and the Shift key is ignored when you press <Ctrl> (see Section 4.2). Thus, **C-_** is actually the same as **C--**, and you will see it written both ways.

So why are there so many ways to use the **undo** command? Technically speaking, C-/ is the primary key sequence bound to the **undo** command. However, C-x u is bound to **undo**, because it is easier for beginners to memorize. As you will find out, C-x is a common prefix, and it is easy to remember that u stands for "undo".

In addition, C-_ is also bound to **undo** because, on some terminals, typing C-/ actually sends the C-_ character (and, as I just mentioned, C-_ is the same as C--).

■ **Note**

When you are learning Emacs and you find something strange—for example, multiple key sequences bound to the same command—remember that there is always a good reason. You just need to find it.

Emacs has been around since 1975 (see Section 1.4), and nothing has happened by accident.

You can use **undo** repeatedly to reverse one change after another, moving backward in time, as many times as you want. This can be most useful, and combining it with **repeat** makes it even easier. Start by pressing C-x u to reverse the last change. Then press C-x z to repeat **undo** and reverse the next most recent change. You can now press z as many times as you want to reverse as many more changes as you want. For example, to reverse the last 10 changes to the buffer you would use:

C-x u C-x z z z z z z z z z z

Or, using C-/ instead of C-X u:

C-/ C-x z z z z z z z z z z

Notice that the number of repeated **undo**s is equal to the number of z's.[2]

Having talked about **undo**, I want to talk for a moment about "redo". Let's say that you are reversing multiple changes to the buffer, when you realize you have gone too far. Can you take back a few of the **undo**s? The answer is yes. If you are careful, you can use **undo** to reverse a previous **undo**. However, there is an important consideration.

When one **undo** follows another, Emacs assumes you want to reverse the previous change, going backwards in time. For example, if you type 10 **undo** commands in a row, Emacs will reverse the last 10 changes. However, the moment you type any other command, the chain is broken. Once this happens, if you type another **undo** command, it will reverse the last command, which was itself an **undo**. In this way, you can use a new **undo** as a "redo".

---

[2] This is what Paul McCartney was referring to when he wrote, in the last part of *Abbey Road*: "And in the end, the love you take is equal to the love you make."

I know that sounds confusing, so let's go slowly. Let's say you realize you have made a series of mistakes. You start using **undo** commands, one after another, to reverse the changes and go back in time. However, you accidentally go back too far. So, to break the **undo** chain, you purposely type a different command. You can now use another **undo** to go forward in time by reversing the previous **undo**.

When it comes to choosing a non-**undo** command, it is best to use something that doesn't make any changes to the buffer. A good choice is something like C-f, because all it does is move the cursor forward one position.

To show you how it works, here is an example. Look at it carefully, and then I'll explain:

C-/ C-x z z z z z z z z z C-f C-/ C-/ C-/ C-/

To start, I typed an **undo** command:

1. C-/

Then, I repeated this command 9 times:

2. C-x z z z z z z z z z

Next, I typed C-f to terminate the chain of **undo** commands:

3. C-f

Finally, I used **undo** 4 more times to reverse the previous 4 **undo**s:

4. C-/ C-/ C-/ C-/

If you want to make this even more obfuscated, remember that, after the C-f, you can use C-x z to repeat the new series of **undo** commands. So the following series of commands is equivalent to the one above:

C-/ C-x z z z z z z z z z C-f C-/ C-x z z z

Before we move on, please take a moment to re-read the last line and realize that it actually makes sense to you. Remember that I told you in Section 1.1 that using Emacs will make changes to the cells in your brain.

Sometimes, when we reverse an **undo**, we call it a "redo". Emacs doesn't have a redo command. However, as you can see, by using **undo** commands, you simulate a redo by typing a neutral command (in our case, C-f) followed by another **undo** command.

I must warn you that it will take a bit of practice to learn how to redo smoothly and successfully. This is because, behind the scenes, Emacs is doing things you will not understand at first, and it is easy to get confused. For example, if, after you end the chain of **undo** commands, you accidentally press the wrong key, another **undo** will reverse the accidental key, not the previous **undo**.

Rest assured, it all makes sense and it will come with practice, so be patient.

Section 7.4: The keyboard-quit Command (C-g)

One of the most important Emacs key sequences is C-g which is bound to the keyboard-quit command. You use C-g to cancel a partially typed command, a command that is already running, or a program that you started from within Emacs. We have talked about C-g earlier but, because it's so useful, I want to take a moment to focus on it.

The keyboard-quit command (C-g) can help you in the following situations:

Problem #1: You are in the middle of typing a command when you change your mind. You decide that you would just as soon forget the whole thing.

Solution: Press C-g to cancel the command.

Problem #2: You have started a command and it is not doing what you want.

Solution: Press C-g to cancel the command. If that doesn't work, press C-g again.

Problem #3: Something is happening that you want to stop.

Solution: Press C-g. It not only cancels commands, it stops programs (such as Lisp functions) that are running within Emacs.

Section 7.5: Emacs for vi Users

If you have some Unix experience, it is likely that you have used the vi text editor, most likely its modern version, Vim. The vi editor has two distinct modes (ways of working): COMMAND MODE and INSERT MODE. Before you can type text, you must be in insert mode, and before you can type a command, you must be in command mode. Thus, as you use vi, you will often find yourself changing back and forth from one mode to another.

Compared to vi, Emacs is a MODE-LESS editor. Specifically, since Emacs doesn't have an insert mode, you can type text whenever you want. (In vi terms, we might say that Emacs is always in insert mode.) Thus, in one sense, Emacs is simpler to use than vi, because you never have to change from one mode to another.

However, this simplicity does not come for free. In vi, the names of the commands are simple, and easy to type and remember. For example, to delete from the cursor to the end of the line, you type D. To save (write) your text to a file, you type : w. To search for a pattern using a regular expression (see Section 10.7), you press / (slash) and then type the expression.

In Emacs, all the commands require special keys like <Ctrl> and <Meta>, so they will not be confused with the letters, numbers and punctuation you might be typing. Thus, Emacs commands tend to look strange and can take longer to memorize. For example, to delete from the cursor to the end of the line, you type C-k. To save your text to a file, you type C-x C-s. To search for a pattern using a regular expression, you type M-C-s (<Meta-Ctrl-S>) and then type the expression.

Is all this complexity worth it? I think so. All you need to do is memorize 40 to 50 basic Emacs commands (which is a lot easier than you might think), and you will be as comfortable as a brother-in-law living in the spare room. Moreover, since you won't have to expend so much mental effort switching back and forth from one mode to another, a part of your brain is freed up to think about other things (such as remembering all the key sequences).

In addition, there is another important difference between vi and Emacs. When you start using vi, your main goal is to memorize and learn how to use the various commands. With Emacs, you also need to learn how to use the commands, but there is more. Emacs is designed — on purpose — so that a lot of the time, you must understand what it is doing and why.

Depending on your point of view, this is either a virtue or a flaw. However, with understanding comes acceptance. You are embarking on what will become one of the longest relationships of your life.

Section 7.6: Commands to Control Windows

One of the tricks to being an Emacs virtuoso (or, at least, looking like an Emacs virtuoso) is to become a whiz at manipulating windows. So if you like to impress other people, you will find this section particularly useful and interesting.

When you are editing a single buffer, Emacs puts it in one large window. Thus, much of the time, you will be working with one buffer and only one window.

At various times, however, Emacs will create another window. This will happen automatically whenever Emacs has some information it needs to display. For example, when you start the Help facility (explained in Section 12.3), Emacs will create a new window and, within that window, display a buffer named *Help*.

In addition, you can create a new window for yourself whenever you want. You can use the new window to display the same buffer as the old window or a completely different buffer. Remember, at any particular time, one window is designated as the selected window (see Section 6.3). This is the window that contains the cursor.

The commands to work with windows are shown in Figure 7-2. With a little practice, you will be zipping around like a greased snipe on his way home from Starbucks, moving from one window to another, manipulating windows like nobody's business.

Command	Description
C-x 0	Delete the selected window
C-x 1	Delete all windows except selected window
C-x 2	Split selected window vertically
C-x 3	Split selected window horizontally
C-x o	Move cursor to the next (other) window
C-x }	Make selected window wider
C-x {	Make selected window narrower
C-x ^	Make selected window larger
M-x shrink-window	Make selected window smaller

FIGURE 7-2. **Commands for controlling windows.**

Here is a good way to practice. Start Emacs using one of the following commands:

```
emacs -Q
emacs -Q -nw
```

You will have one large window with a *scratch* buffer. Now type C-h b to start the Help facility and display a list of all the key bindings. You now have two windows that you can use to practice the commands in Figure 7-2. When you are finished, you can stop Emacs by pressing C-x C-c.

The best way to become comfortable controlling windows is to spend time experimenting with the commands. At first, you will feel a little awkward, but it will soon become second nature to move from one window to another, delete a window, create a new one, and so on.

Please be sure you understand the difference between windows and buffers. As I explained in Section 6.2, a buffer is a work area and you can have as many as you want. A window is simply an area on your screen that Emacs uses to display the contents of a buffer. Thus, when you delete a window, you are *not* deleting the buffer that is displayed in that window. Any buffers that are not currently displayed are maintained invisibly in the background. Thus, you can have many buffers, only some of which are actually displayed in windows at the current time.

Before we leave this topic, there are a few points I would like to make about the commands in Figure 7-2. First, you will notice that there are two key sequences whose names might be a tad confusing. The "delete selected window" command is C-x 0 (the number zero). The "move cursor to next window" command is C-x o (the lowercase letter "o"). It may help if you think of the letter o as standing for "other window".

Strictly speaking, C-x o (the letter "o") moves to what is called the NEXT WINDOW. When you have more than one window on your screen, Emacs moves from one to another in a specific order. If you have only two windows, the next window is simply the other window. If you have more than two windows, Emacs cycles from one to another, going from left to right and from up to down.

If you want to check this out for yourself, try the following experiment. Start Emacs:

```
emacs -Q
emacs -Q -nw
```

You now have one large window containing an empty buffer named ***scratch***. Now press **C-x 2** and split the window into two windows, one on top of the other. Press **C-x o** a few times and watch how the cursor moves from one window to another.

Now press **C-x 3** and split one of the windows into two side-by-side windows. Again, press **C-x o** a few times and see how Emacs cycles through the three windows. Try using **C-x 2** and **C-x 3** to create some more windows and, each time, watch how **C-x o** moves the cursor. When you are finished, press **C-x C-c** to quit Emacs.

Now, take a look back at Figure 7-2. Notice that the command to make the selected window smaller (**shrink-window**) is not bound to a specific key sequence. Thus, you must execute this command explicitly by using **M-x**. Normally, though, you won't need the **shrink-window** command because whenever you make a window larger (by using **C-x ^**), Emacs automatically makes the other windows smaller. Thus, you can get by just fine simply by making a specific window larger as the need arises and letting Emacs adjust the other windows as it sees fit. Indeed, this is what most people do most of the time, which is why the **shrink-window** command does not really need its own key sequence.

▨ Note

You will notice that commands to delete and split windows are similar: **C-x** followed by a number (**0**, **1**, **2** or **3**). It looks as if there might a pattern.

There isn't, so don't bother trying to invent one. Just practice and, after a few days, you will find that each individual command will become familiar on its own.

Section 7.7: Commands to Control Buffers

As we discussed in Section 6.2, a buffer is a work area that is maintained for you by Emacs. You can have as many buffers as you want at the same time, each with its own name. At all times, you will have at least one buffer. If you start Emacs without specifying the name of a specific file, Emacs will create a buffer named ***scratch***.

Not all of your buffers need to be displayed in a window. Indeed, it is common to have an assortment of buffers to use as separate work areas, of which only one or two are actually displayed in windows. As the need arises, you can change which buffers are displayed.

▓ **Note**

It is important to realize that Emacs can handle as many buffers as you need, even though you may have only one or two windows. This means that, when you want to work with multiple files, you don't need to run a separate instance of Emacs for each file.

Once you master working with windows and buffers, you will be able to use a single instance of Emacs to edit as many files as you want at the same time, because it's so easy to switch back and forth from one buffer to another.

Figure 7-3 shows the commands you can use to control your buffers. These commands work together with the window-oriented commands I described in Section 7.6 (see Figure 7-2).

Command	Description
C-x b	Display a different buffer in selected window
C-x b	Create a new buffer in selected window
C-x C-b	Display a list of all your buffers
C-x k	Kill (delete) a buffer
C-x 4 b	Display a different buffer in next window
C-x 4 C-o	Same as **C-x 4 b**, but don't change selected window

FIGURE 7-3. **Commands for controlling buffers.**

The most important of these commands is **C-x b**. You use this command to tell Emacs that you want to work with another buffer. This new buffer will be displayed in the window in which you are currently working (the selected window). The buffer that is currently in the window will be replaced, but not lost.

When you press **C-x b**, Emacs will wait for you to enter the name of the buffer with which you want to work. If this buffer already exists, Emacs will just move it into the window. Otherwise, Emacs will create a brand new empty buffer in the window using the name you specified. Thus, **C-x b** is the command to use when you want to create a new buffer.

If you have more than a few buffers, it is easy to forget their names. To remind yourself, you can press **C-x C-b** to display a list. When you do, you will notice that Emacs has created a new buffer called ***Buffer List*** to hold the list itself.

I mentioned that when you change the contents of a window, the buffer that was replaced is not destroyed: it exists in the background and you can recall it whenever you want. However, from time to time, you may actually want to delete a buffer. To do so, use the **C-x k** (kill) command. When you do, Emacs will wait for you to enter the name of the buffer you want to kill. The default will be whatever buffer is in the selected window. If this is the buffer you want to delete, just press <Enter>. Otherwise, type the name of another buffer and press <Enter>. If you decide to cancel the command, press **C-g**, the Emacs cancel key.

Note You will not be allowed to delete all of your buffers. At the very least, Emacs will force you to have a single buffer named ***scratch***.

There will be many times when you are working with one buffer and you want to display another buffer in a different window. To do so, there are two commands you can use. The command C-x 4 b tells Emacs to display whichever buffer you specify in a different window. This new window then becomes the selected window. Thus, the C-x 4 b command allows you to switch to another buffer while still being able to see the contents of the old buffer. As with C-x b, if the buffer does not already exist, the C-x 4 b command will create a new buffer for you.

Sometimes you will want to look at the contents of another buffer without changing the selected buffer. For example, say that you are typing a letter to someone and you need to display his or her address which is in a different buffer. You will want to display the contents of this second buffer without moving away from the window in which you are typing.

In such cases, use the C-x 4 C-o command. This is similar to the C-x 4 b command, except that the selected window does not change. One restriction (which only makes sense) is that you must specify the name of a buffer that already exists. After all, there is no point in displaying an empty buffer in another window.

Note

Most Emacs commands act on the selected buffer. However, commands that begin with C-x 4 act on another buffer. Learning how to use the C-x 4 commands allows you to control your buffers smoothly and quickly.

There are also C-x 4 commands that deal with files. These commands are explained in the Section 7.8.

Section 7.8: Commands for Working With Files

The crucial thing to understand about files is how they relate to buffers. In Section 2.15 and Section 2.16, we discussed the Unix file system and talked about the technical definition of a file. In this section, we can assume that a file is a collection of information that is given a name and stored on a device (usually a disk).

In Section 5.1, I explained that when you start Emacs, you can specify the names of one or more files. If you do this, Emacs will automatically read the contents of each file into its own buffer. Once you have a lot of experience, you will find that it is better to start Emacs without file names. When you want to start working with a file (which may be right away), you use a command that tells Emacs to read the contents of the file into a buffer.

■ **Note**

Please remember: a buffer is a *temporary* work area. As such, it disappears when you quit Emacs. Thus, if you want to save the contents of a buffer to a file, you must do so before you quit.

For the same reason, as you are working, it behooves you to save your buffers regularly.

The commands to work with files are summarized in Figure 7-4. Most of the commands act on the selected window (the window in which the cursor resides.) However, the commands that begin with **C-x 4** act on the next window. This makes it easy to load a file into another window without moving from your current window. (We discussed the idea of the next window in Section 7.7.)

Command	Description
C-x C-f	Switch to buffer containing specified file
C-x C-v	Replace buffer contents with specified file
C-x C-s	Save a buffer to file
C-x C-w	Save a buffer to specified file
C-x i	Insert contents of a file into buffer
C-x 4 C-f	Read contents of file into next window
C-x 4 f	Same as **C-x 4 C-f**
C-x 4 r	Same as **C-x 4 C-f**, read-only

FIGURE 7-4. **Commands for working with files.**

If this is new to you, I realize that the commands in Figure 7-4 may look a bit confusing. To help you, here is some quick advice: the only file commands you really need to memorize are **C-x C-f** to read a file and **C-x C-w** to save a file. (Think of **f** as standing for "file" and **w** as standing for "write".)

The **C-x C-f** command tells Emacs to read the contents of a file into a buffer. Emacs will use the name of the file as the name of the buffer. If the file does not already exist, Emacs will create a new buffer by that name. When Emacs copies the contents of a file into a buffer, we say that you VISIT the file.

The idea of visiting a file is important because it implies an association between a buffer and a file. When you visit a file, Emacs remembers which buffer is associated with that particular file. Once you make changes to that buffer, Emacs will not let you quit without giving you a chance to save the contents of the buffer back to the file. The idea is to make it difficult to lose your work by accident.

However, when you create a new buffer that is not tied to a particular file, Emacs will be more than glad to let you quit without reminding you to save your work. (Read that last sentence again.)

Here is an example. You have two windows. In the first window, you have used the C-x C-f command to read in a file named **griffin** that contains a letter to a friend in the South Seas. When you entered this command, Emacs created a buffer named **griffin** in which to copy the file. It is this buffer that you are looking at in the window. In the second window, you have used the C-x b command to create a brand new buffer named **sabine**, into which you have typed a letter to a friend in England.

Now, both windows are similar in that they each contain a buffer that holds some text. However, in the first window, a file is being visited, while in the second window no file is being visited. Thus, if you were to quit Emacs, you would be asked if you want to save the contents of the **griffin** buffer back to the file, but you would *not* be asked if you want to save the **sabine** buffer.

Now, let's say you want to start working with a new buffer. You have two ways to create that buffer. You can use C-x b or you can use C-x C-f. (Remember, each of these commands will create a new buffer if the one you specify does not already exist.) The difference is that if you use C-x b, Emacs will create a buffer that is not tied to any particular file. If you use C-x C-f, the new buffer will be associated with a file of the same name. (That is, you will be visiting that file.) Thus, when you quit, you will be asked if you want to save the contents of the buffer to a file.

■ **Note**   When you want to create a new buffer for work you do *not* want to save, use the C-x b command. When you want to create a new buffer for work you do want to save, use the C-x C-f command.

The C-x C-v command copies the contents of a file into the current buffer, replacing the current contents of that buffer. You use C-x C-v when you want to switch to a new file and you don't mind losing what you are working on.

When you replace the contents of a buffer using C-x C-v, whatever was in the buffer will be deleted. For your own protection, Emacs will ask you for confirmation before it replaces a buffer that has not been saved.

If you want to insert the contents of a file into the current buffer without losing what is already in the buffer, use the C-x i command. The contents of the file you specify will be copied into the buffer at the current cursor position. The original contents of the buffer will be moved to make room for the new data, but will not be deleted.

There are two commands you can use to save the contents of a buffer to a file. Use the C-x C-s command when you are visiting a file and you want to save the contents of the buffer back to that same file. Use C-x C-w when you want to save a buffer to a different file. For example, if you are editing a file named **griffin**, the C-x C-s command will copy the current contents of the **griffin** buffer to the file named **griffin**. Obviously, this is a command you should use frequently to save your work.

Whenever you need to specify a file name, Emacs will help you by displaying the name of the current directory in the minibuffer. You can then type the name of the file you want. If the beginning of the file name is unique, you can save keystrokes by using the completion facility we discussed in Section 6.7.

Here is an example using a Unix file system (see Section 2.17). Let's say that your current directory is named **memos**. This directory lies within your home directory. When you press `C-x C-f`, Emacs will display the following prompt in the minibuffer:

`Find file: ~/memos/`

The ~ character (explained in Section 2.17) is an abbreviation for your home directory.

This particular prompt tells you that Emacs is guessing that you want a file in this particular directory. If that is the case, type the name of the file and press <Enter>. If you want a file in a different directory, you can use the Backspace key to erase the directory name and specify your own. At the end of this new directory name, type a **/** (slash), then the file name, and then press <Enter>.

As I explained in Section 7.7, key sequences that begin with `C-x 4` are used to manipulate the next window. The `C-x 4 C-f` command works like `C-x C-f` except that it acts on the next window. As a convenience, you can use `C-x 4 f` instead of `C-x 4 C-f`.

The `C-x 4 r` command is similar except that it sets the buffer to be read-only when it reads in the file. This allows you to examine an important file in another window without having to worry about changing the file by accident.

CHAPTER 8

■ ■ ■

The Cursor; Line Numbers; Point and Mark; The Region

Section 8.1: The Cursor and the Idea of Point

Emacs has a special name for the current position of the cursor. This location, within the buffer, is called POINT (not "the point", just "point".) The idea of point is important because it is at this location that whatever you type is inserted into the buffer. When you read Emacs documentation and the descriptions in the Help facility, you will see many references to point.

Although the cursor is under or on a particular character, point is actually between two characters: the one at the cursor position and the character immediately to its left. For example, say that, in your buffer, you are reading the word **tergiversate** and the cursor is on the **g**. Point is considered to be between the **r** and the **g**.

■ **What's in a Name?**

Point

The original Emacs was developed to be a set of editing macros for an obtuse text editing facility named TECO. Within TECO, you used the **.** (period) character as the command for accessing the current location within the text. Since the **.** character was really just a dot, the command that it represented was referred to as the "point" command. In Emacs, the current location within the current buffer is marked by the cursor, and is referred to as "point".

It is important to realize that each buffer has its own point which is carefully maintained by Emacs. Of course, there is only one cursor, and it is used to show where point is in the buffer that is currently active. However, Emacs remembers where point is in each buffer so that, as you switch from one buffer to another, Emacs knows exactly where to place the cursor.

© Harley Hahn 2016

H. Hahn, *Harley Hahn's Emacs Field Guide*, DOI 10.1007/978-1-4842-1703-0_8

Section 8.2: Moving the Cursor

Moving the cursor is straightforward. You can move it up and down, and backward and forward. The commands for moving the cursor are summarized in Figure 8-1.

Backward	Forward	
C-b	C-f	a single character
<Left>	<Right>	a single character
M-b	M-f	a word
C-p	C-n	a line
<Up>	<Down>	a line
M-a	M-e	a sentence
M-{	M-}	a paragraph
Beginning	End	
C-a	C-e	the current line
M-<	M->	the entire buffer

FIGURE 8-1. Commands for moving the cursor.

Notice that there are two types of commands. First, there are commands that move forward or backward a specific amount. For example, you can move to the left or right by a single character by using C-b and C-f respectively. There are similar commands to move by a single word, line, sentence or paragraph.

As a convenience, you can use the cursor control keys to move a single position at a time. Thus, pressing the Left key is the same as C-b, and pressing the Up key is the same as C-p.

Second, there are commands that move to the beginning or end of something. You will find these commands to be especially useful. For example, to jump to the very beginning of the buffer, use M-< (<Meta>-less-than sign). To jump to the end of the buffer, use M-> (<Meta>-greater-than sign).

If you look at the key sequences, you can see some patterns. For example, the letters b and f stand for "backward" and "forward"; the letters p and n stand for "previous" and "next"; and so on. Still, you don't really need to memorize Emacs keys in this way. Just practice for a few days, and you will remember without even trying.

Section 8.3: Text Modes; Paragraphs and Sentences

In Section 8.2, we talked about the commands to move the cursor through a paragraph or a sentence. You can see these commands in Figure 8-2:

Command	Description
M-}	Move forward one paragraph
M-{	Move backward one paragraph
M-e	Move forward one sentence
M-a	Move backward one sentence

FIGURE 8-2. **Commands for moving the cursor through a paragraph or a sentence.**

To use these commands, you need to know exactly how Emacs defines a "paragraph" and a "sentence", so let's talk about that.

The exact definition of a paragraph depends upon which "major mode" you are using. We will discuss major modes in Section 11.2. For now, I'll just say that the major mode controls how Emacs behaves as you are editing. When you are writing ordinary text in English (or another language), the major modes you are most likely to use are listed in Figure 8-3.

Mode	Command
Fundamental mode	`fundamental-mode`
Text mode	`text-mode`
Indented Text mode	`indented-text-mode`
Paragraph-Indent Text mode	`paragraph-indent-text-mode`

FIGURE 8-3. **Major modes to use when editing a human language.**

To change from one mode to another, type **M-x** (see Section 6.1) followed by the name of the mode, then press <Enter>:

```
M-x fundamental-mode
M-x text-mode
M-x indented-text-mode
M-x paragraph-indent-text-mode
```

Fundamental mode is the generic Emacs major mode. It is the default Emacs major mode, the one you use when you don't have a reason to use another mode. If you are writing English prose, you are better off with Text mode or Paragraph-Indent Text mode.

Text mode is for writing in a human language (as opposed to, say, a computer program). Use this mode when your paragraphs are separated by blank lines.

Paragraph-Indent Text mode is similar to text mode. Use this mode when the beginning of each paragraph is indented.

Indented Text mode is for when you are working on something that has a lot of indentation and you don't care much about paragraphs, for example, when you are creating an outline.

At this point, I am almost ready to give you the technical definition of a paragraph. I just need to define three more technical terms. (As the medieval Persian poet Saadi Shirazi (1210-1291) once said when *he* was learning Emacs, "Have patience. All things are difficult before they become easy.")

First, WHITESPACE refers to any combination of **SPC**, **TAB** or **RET**. (These characters are described in Section 4.4.) It is called whitespace because when you print on paper, it looks white.

Second, a BLANK LINE is a line that is either empty or that contains only whitespace.

Finally, an INDENTATION occurs when a line starts with one or more tabs or spaces.

With Fundamental mode, Text mode, and Indented Text mode, you indicate your paragraphs by putting a blank line between them. With Paragraph-Indent Text mode, you indicate your paragraphs by indenting them, by putting a blank line between them, or both. So here is the definition:

A PARAGRAPH is a sequence of characters that is separated from other characters by a blank line or (with Paragraph-Indent Text mode) that is indented.

Now that you know all that, take some time to experiment. Open a new buffer and type various types of text. Then use the **M-x** commands above to switch from one major mode to another and see what happens when you type **M-}** and **M-{**.

To finish, a SENTENCE is a sequence of characters that ends with a **.** (period), **?** (question mark), or **!** (exclamation mark) followed by two spaces. A sentence also begins or ends wherever a paragraph begins or ends. To make sure you understand this, open a buffer with some text, and see what happens when you use **M-a** and **M-e**.

Section 8.4: Repeating a Command: Prefix Arguments

To perform a command a specified number of times, you type what is called a PREFIX ARGUMENT in front of the command. For example, you might type the prefix argument that means "repeat the following command 6 times" and then press **C-p**. This will move the cursor up 6 lines. Because the prefix argument specifies a number, it is also referred to as a NUMERIC ARGUMENT. (The term ARGUMENT is a programming word that describes a value passed to a program when it is executed.)

To specify a prefix argument, hold down the Meta key and type a number. For example, to move the cursor up 6 lines, press **M-6 C-p**. An alternative is to use <Esc> instead of <Meta>. Thus, to move 15 characters to the right, you could press **ESC 15 C-f**.

You can use a prefix argument with any command, and Emacs will interpret the numeric value in the way that makes the most sense for that command. Where prefix arguments really come in handy is when you combine them with the cursor movement commands we discussed in Section 8.2.

Note Take a few moments and practice various combinations of prefix arguments with the cursor movement commands in Figure 8-1.

The number you specify can be either positive or negative. If you use a negative number with a cursor movement command, it will move in the opposite direction. For example, to move the cursor up 6 lines, use either M-6 C-p or M--6 C-n. (Perhaps this last command would be clearer if I wrote it as ESC -6 C-n.)

If you use the Meta key, you will hold it down as you type a prefix argument. For example, when you use the M-6 C-p command, you will have to hold down the <Meta> key as you type the 6. Some people find this inconvenient, so there are two alternatives. First, as I mentioned, you can press ESC instead of holding down <Meta>. Second, you can press C-u instead. (The name comes from the fact that this key is bound to the command universal-argument.) Thus, to move the cursor down 6 lines you can use either M-6 C-n or C-u 6 C-n. Although this looks like an extra keystroke, it is actually easier, especially when you are using a multi-digit prefix argument. For example, to move the cursor down 120 lines, you can use C-u 120 C-n.

As a final shortcut, the C-u command has a special meaning when you use it before a command *without* specifying a number. In such cases, the C-u key tells Emacs to repeat the next command 4 times. And you can type more than one C-u in a row to multiply this effect. This may seem a bit strange at first, but it is really, really useful, so take a moment to figure it out.

Here is a simple example. To move the cursor down 4 lines, you can use M-4 C-n or C-u 4 C-n. But, as a shortcut, you can use C-u by itself: C-u C-n. Similarly, to move the cursor 4 characters to the left, you can use C-u C-b.

The power of the C-u prefix comes when you use more than one in a row. Because each such prefix multiplies the next command by a factor of 4, using two in a row tells Emacs to repeat a command 16 times. Using three in a row repeats a command 64 times.

For example, to move the cursor down 16 lines, you can use C-u C-u C-n. To move the cursor 64 characters to the right, you can use C-u C-u C-u C-f. Although this may seem a bit awkward, it is actually quick and easy to type.

Once you get the hang of it, you can use more than one series of commands to combine movements. For, example, let's say you want to move the cursor down 63 lines. It is actually very fast — and totally cool — to move down 64 lines and then up one:

```
C-u C-u C-u C-n C-p
```

Try it and see if I'm not right.

To summarize, the various prefix argument combinations are shown in Figure 8-4.

Prefix	Effect
M-_number_	Repeat command specified number of times
ESC _number_	Repeat command specified number of times
C-u _number_	Repeat command specified number of times
C-u	Repeat command 4 times
C-u C-u	Repeat command 16 times
C-u C-u C-u	Repeat command 64 times
C-u C-u C-u C-u	Repeat command 256 times

FIGURE 8-4. Prefix argument combinations.

■ Note

The C-u C-u prefix is especially useful when you are working with characters and lines. This is because 16 characters are about one fifth of a line and 16 lines are about one third of a standard-sized screen. It is worth a few moments of your time to practice putting together the C-u C-u prefix with your favorite character and line commands, just to fix them firmly in your mind. For example, try:

```
C-u C-u C-f   (move 16 lines to the right)
C-u C-u C-b   (move 16 lines to the left)
C-u C-u C-n   (move 16 lines down)
C-u C-u C-p   (move 16 lines up)
```

You may find it handy to hardwire these particular combinations directly into your motor cortex (the lump of gray matter in your prefrontal gyrus, just anterior to the central sulcus). The details for doing so, however, are beyond the scope of this book.

Section: 8.5: Moving Through the Buffer

There will be many times when you want to page through the buffer. Perhaps the most common example is wanting to read something from beginning to end. You start at the top of the buffer and read one screenful at a time.

When you tell Emacs to display information that is just beyond the border of your window, we say that you are SCROLLING. For example, if you have read what is on the screen and you move down to the next screenful, we say that you scroll down. Similarly, you can display the previous screenful by scrolling up.

Notice that we talk about scrolling as if *you* do it, rather than as if Emacs is doing it. For example, you might tell a friend, "To find the secret phone number, open the file I sent you and scroll down until you see the entry for Kalle Anka." This is a common way of speaking that reminds us that computers are actually extensions of our minds.

Figure 8-5 shows the commands you can use to move throughout the buffer. The scrolling commands are completely straightforward, and there is not much I want to say about them, other than be sure to memorize **C-v** and **M-v** *this very minute*. These are two crucial commands that you will use every day of your life, so don't even leave this paragraph without committing them to memory. The right and left scrolling commands are less important: you need them only when you are dealing with unusually long lines.

Command	Description
C-v	Scroll down one screenful
\<PageDown\>	Same as **C-v**
M-v	Scroll up one screenful
\<PageUp\>	Same as **M-v**
M-C-v	Scroll down in the next window
M-<	Jump to the beginning of buffer
M->	Jump to the end of buffer
C-l	Redisplay the screen, current line in middle

FIGURE 8-5. **Commands to move throughout the buffer.**

Note   If you are using a terminal window, and typing **M-v** (\<Alt-V\>) pulls down a menu from the top of the window, it is because your terminal window program is interpreting \<Alt\> as a menu key. For instructions on how to fix this problem, see Section 4.6.

127

One variation on the scrolling commands is **M-C-v**. This command scrolls down in the next window. (We discussed the idea of the next window in Section 7.6.) Using **M-C-v**, you can scroll through the next window without having to leave the window in which you are working. Unfortunately, there is no easy way to scroll *up* in the next window.

For completeness, I have included the **M-<** (jump to the beginning of the buffer) and **M->** (jump to the end of the buffer) commands in Figure 8-5. I described these commands in Section 8.2, when we discussed moving the cursor. However, these commands also belong here because they are handy for zipping around.

Finally, there is the **C-l** (lowercase letter "L") command. This command redisplays the screen so that the line on which the cursor lies is in the middle of the screen. This command is handy when the cursor is near the bottom of the screen and you want to pull it up somewhat to read the lines underneath. **C-l** is a useful command that is all too often neglected. Take a moment and try it for yourself to see how useful it can be.

Section 8.6: Using Line Numbers

Most of the time, you will move around the buffer in small and large jumps or by searching for a specific pattern (as we will discuss in Section 10.1). However, there will be times when it is handy to be able to jump directly to a specific line based on its position in the buffer. For example, you may want to jump to line 43. There are two commands you can use in this regard. They are described in Figure 8-6.

Command	Description
M-g g	Jump to line with specified number
M-x line-number-mode	ON/OFF: display line number on mode line

FIGURE 8-6. Commands to use line numbers.

To help you orient yourself within the buffer, Emacs displays the current line number on the mode line. You can see an example in Figure 8-7. In this case, we are looking at a buffer named ***Help***. The cursor is currently on line 43, and the top line of the screen is 59 percent of the way through the buffer. (The top line of the buffer is considered to be line 1.)

```
-UUU:%%--F1   *Help*            59% L43    (Help) -------------------
```

FIGURE 8-7. The mode line showing the current line number.

Emacs displays the current line number on the mode line. In this case, the cursor is on line 43, and the top line of the screen is 59 percent of the way through the buffer.

If the current line number is not displayed on the mode line, you can display it by typing:

`M-x line-number-mode`

This command acts like a toggle, turning the line number on and off.

To jump to a particular line, type **M-g g**. Then type the line number and press <Enter>, and the cursor will jump to the line you specify. For example, to jump to line 43, type:

M-g g 43 <Enter>

Section 8.7: Mark, Point, and the Region

Within Emacs there are commands that operate on various character groupings. For example, you can work with single characters, words, lines, sentences and paragraphs. To provide flexibility, Emacs also lets you define an area of the buffer — called a REGION — which can be as long or short as you want. Once you define a region, you can operate on it using any one of several commands. For example, you can define a region of, say, thirteen and a half lines, and then erase it. Or you can define a region of ten words, and then change them all to uppercase.

Here is how it works. A region is defined as all the characters between two locations: MARK and point. Point you already know; it is the location of the cursor. Mark is a location you can set for yourself.

There are several ways to define mark. The simplest way is to move the cursor to wherever you want mark to be and then type **C-SPC** (<Ctrl-Space>). Mark is now at that location. You can then move the cursor to a new location (which becomes point). The region is now all the characters between mark and point.

The best way to understand mark and point is to think of them as two locations in the buffer, both of which you can set. However, since there is only one cursor, Emacs can only show you one of these locations (point); you will have to remember where mark is. Still, it's not all that hard once you get used to it. Most of the time you will set mark for a particular purpose, and then use it right away before you forget where it is. A simple example will make it all clear.

In order for you to understand the example I am about to show you, I will tell you that the command **M- =** counts the number of lines, words and characters in a region. Let's say you are writing an essay about the psychology of investing,[1] and you

---

[1] `www.harley.com/money-and-economics/how-thinking-affects-investing/`

have just typed the following five lines into an empty buffer. You want to know how many words you have written.

To invest well requires us to develop our ability to think well and make decisions, even in difficult situations. Doing so, however, is difficult because our feelings and our intuition can get in the way, often without our knowing what is really happening.

The plan is to define the region to consist of these five lines, and then use M-= to count the words.

To start, move the cursor to the beginning of the buffer (M-<) and type C-SPC. This sets mark to be at this location. Next, move the cursor to the end of the buffer (M->). Now mark is at the beginning of the first line, and point is at the end of the last line. Type M-= to count the words. In the echo area (the bottom line of the screen; see Section 6.5), you will see:

Region has 5 lines, 43 words, and 247 characters.

These are important concepts, so I want to take a moment to be precise. As you may remember from our discussion in Section 8.1, point is not exactly the same as the cursor. The cursor sits under or on a particular character. Point is really between two characters, the one at the cursor and the one to its left. For example, consider the line:

abcdefghijklmnopqrstuvwxyz

If the cursor were on the m, point would be between the l and the m. When you set mark, it works the same way. Say that while the cursor is on the m, you press C-SPC. Mark (and point) are now both between the l and the m. Now, you move the cursor to be on the g. Mark is still between the l and the m, and point is now between the f and the g. Thus, the region consists of the letters ghijkl. If you were to press M-=, the echo line would display:

Region has 1 line, 1 word, and 6 characters.

■ **Note**   When you are defining a region, be sure that the rightmost boundary is set to the character *after* the last one on which you want to operate.

Section 8.8: Using Mark and Point to Define the Region

A region is defined as all the contiguous characters between mark and point. Point is always at the position of the cursor. Thus, to define a region, all you need to do is set mark.

Broadly speaking, there are two ways in which mark can be set. First, as we discussed in Section 8.7, you can use a command that sets mark. Second, many commands that perform some function or other automatically set mark to a new value. When this happens, you will see a message in the echo area telling you that mark has been set.

For example, when you use a command that inserts text into the buffer, Emacs will finish the operation by setting mark at one end of the new text and point at the other end. Thus, the region will contain the newly inserted text.

Figure 8-8 shows the commands that explicitly set mark. Two of these commands set mark without changing point (C-SPC and M-@). Two other commands set both mark and point (M-h and C-x h). A final command interchanges the location of mark and point (C-x C-x).

Command	Description
C-@	Set mark to current location of point
C-SPC	Same as C-@
C-x C-x	Interchange mark and point
M-@	Set mark after next word (do not move point)
M-h	Put region around paragraph
C-x h	Put region around entire buffer

FIGURE 8-8. Commands to set mark and define a region.

Strictly speaking, the command to set mark is C-@. However, it happens that with many terminals, pressing C-SPC will generate the same character as C-@. Thus, although C-SPC is not a real character, we say that you can use it to set mark. When you do so, you are really using C-@, but C-SPC is a more convenient key sequence. If C-SPC does not work on your terminal — for example, if it generates a regular SPC character — you will have to use C-@. (On most keyboards, you use C-@ by pressing C-2, because the 2 is the same key as @. You do not need to hold down the Shift key.)

Once you set mark, it stays where it is until you change it explicitly or until another command changes it. When you define a region, it does not matter whether mark comes before or after point. Nor does it matter which one you set first.

As I explained in Section 6.2 and Section 7.7, you can work with as many buffers as you want at one time. In the same way that each buffer has its own cursor, each buffer also has its own point and mark. Thus, if you set mark in one buffer and then move to another buffer to do some work, when you move back to the first buffer, the original mark will still be there.

Because mark is invisible, you may forget where it is. Unlike point, which is marked by the cursor, there is no way to look at the screen and see mark. In such cases, you can use the C-x C-x command to exchange the location of mark and point. Thus, the new location of the cursor will be where point was. To move the cursor back to its original location, simply press C-x C-x again.

■ **Note**   Normally, you will set and use mark within a short time, so you will not forget its location. However, if you do, you can visualize the region by pressing C-x C-x twice. The cursor will jump back and forth from one boundary to the other.

You can always set mark by moving to wherever you want it and pressing C-SPC or C-@. However, there are three other commands that provide handy shortcuts.

The M-@ command sets mark after the current word. For example, let's say that you are editing some text that contains the sentence:

Okay boys, let's defenestrate him.

The cursor is currently on the **d** in **defenestrate**. You press M-@. This sets mark to be at the space at the end of the word (after the **e**). Point will not change. You can verify this by pressing C-x C-x. This is a good way to set the region to contain a particular word on which you want to perform an operation.

If you want to set mark to be more than one word away, you can use a prefix argument (explained in Section 8.4). In our previous example, for instance, let's say that the cursor is once again on the **d** in **defenestrate**, and you want to set mark to be after the end of the word **him** (2 words away). Use **ESC 2 M-@**. This leaves mark at the period. To set mark to be 10 words away, use **ESC 10 M-@**, and so on.

The next command, M-h, sets the region by moving both mark and point to contain an entire paragraph. (Within Emacs, a "paragraph" starts with one or more **space** or **tab** characters, or is preceded by a blank line.) If the cursor is within a paragraph, M-h sets point to the beginning of the paragraph and mark to the end of the paragraph. Thus, when you press M-h, it not only sets the region, it also moves the cursor to the beginning of the paragraph. If you press M-h when the cursor is on a blank line, point and mark will be set to the beginning and end of the following paragraph.

The final command, C-x h, marks the entire buffer as being in the region. It does this by moving point to the beginning of the buffer and mark to the end of the buffer.

Section 8.9: Operating on the Region

In Section 8.7 and Section 8.8, we discussed how to set mark and point, and thereby define the region. The reason we do this is to make it easy to perform an operation on all the characters in the region. Figure 8-9 shows the Emacs commands you can use.

Command	Description
C-w	Kill (erase) all the characters
C-x C-l	Convert the characters to lowercase
C-x C-u	Convert the characters to uppercase
M-=	Count the lines and characters
M-|	Run a shell command, use the characters as data

FIGURE 8-9. **Commands that act upon the region.**

Generally speaking, the most useful of these commands is C-w. This command kills (erases) the entire region. If you change your mind after the deletion, you can type C-x u (or C-/ or C-_) to undo the operation (see Section 7.3).

The C-x C-l and C-x C-u commands convert all the characters in the region to upper- and lowercase respectively. These commands work well with the mark-setting commands to change the case of a word or group of words.

For example, to change one word to uppercase, move the cursor to the beginning of the word, and press M-@ (set mark at end of word) followed by C-x C-u. To change 5 words to lowercase, move to the beginning of the first word, and press ESC 5 M-@ (set mark at end of fifth word) followed by C-x C-l.

Note When you use C-x C-l or C-x C-u, you may get a message that they are disabled. If so, read the discussion in Section 6.8 on how to enable such commands.

Here is one last example. Your cursor is in the middle of a line, and you want to change the entire line to uppercase. Type C-a (move to beginning of line), C-SPC (set mark), C-e (move to end of line), and finally, C-x C-u (change region to uppercase).

The M-= (Meta equals sign) command will count all the lines and characters in the region. This command is handy if you are a writer who has to keep measuring his output in order to convince his editor that he is making progress. (I am not mentioning any names here.) Combined with the region-defining commands, M-= works quickly and easily.

For example, say that you want to find out how many lines are in the buffer. The C-x h command will set the region to the entire buffer. Thus, to count all the lines in the buffer, all you need to type is C-x h and then M-=. Here is some typical output:

Region has 108 lines, 1724 characters

Try it: it's too cool for words.

Finally, the M-| (Meta-vertical bar) command will send the contents of the region to a shell command to be processed. To store the output, Emacs will create a buffer named *Shell Command Output*. If this buffer already exists, its contents will be replaced by the output of the new command.

This command is incredibly useful, so let's look at a few examples. First, let's say you want to sort all the lines in the buffer. All you have to do is use the C-x h command to set the region to the entire buffer, and then use M-| to run the **sort** command. To test this out, let's create a customized list of all the Emacs commands in alphabetical order.

To get the raw material, we can use the built-in Help facility (described in Section 12.3. The command to use Help is C-h. If you type C-h b, Emacs will create a new buffer, named *Help*, that contains descriptions of all the key bindings. Each line contains the name of the key, followed by the name of the command to which it is bound. Here are two examples:

```
C-h b     describe-bindings
ESC |     shell-command-on-region
```

(Notice that the <Meta> key is described as **ESC**.)

So all we have to do is generate a buffer full of key binding descriptions and sort them. When we do, we will use the Unix **sort** command with the -u (unique) option. This option eliminates all duplicate lines. In this case, the -u option will effectively eliminate all but one of the blank lines. So here is how to create your own alphabetical list of Emacs commands:

1. C-h b: Create a buffer named *Help* that contains the key descriptions.

2. C-x o: Change to the *Help* buffer.

3. C-x 1: Delete all windows except selected window.

4. C-x h: Set the region to be the entire buffer.

5. M-| sort -u <Enter>: Sort all the lines in the buffer.

6. C-x o: Change to the *Shell Command Output* buffer.

At this point, you may want to save the list to a file for future reference. If so, use the command:

7. C-x C-w: Save the buffer to a file.

Before we leave this topic, here is one more useful example. Unix has a **fmt** command you can use to format text. The **fmt** command makes your text look as uniform as possible, while preserving paragraphs and indentations. (In Emacs, this is known as "filling" text.) Using **fmt** is a nice way to smooth out ragged text that has been the victim of brutal modifications and editing.

To format the entire buffer, use **C-x h** (set the region), followed by **M-| fmt** (process the region with the **fmt** command).

Being able to use Unix commands from within Emacs is a particularly powerful tool. We will discuss this topic in detail in Section 12.1.

Note   Emacs has a command, **M-x fill-region** that has much the same effect. This main difference is that **M-x fill-region** changes the original region. Using **M-| fmt** creates a new buffer containing only the formatted text.

CHAPTER 9

■ ■ ■

Kill and Delete; Move and Copy; Correct Mistakes; Spelling; Fill

Section 9.1: Kill and Delete: Two Ways to Erase Text

There are a variety of Emacs commands you can use to erase text from the buffer. As a convenience, Emacs will remember the erased text so you can insert it back into the buffer if you want. For example, to move a paragraph from one place to another, you can erase it and then insert it somewhere else.

Once you start using these commands, it won't be long before you see there is no need for you to worry about preserving everything. For example, when you erase a single character or an empty line, there is really no need to save it. However, when you erase several lines, a whole paragraph, or an entire region, it does make sense to keep a copy of the text. In fact, this is how Emacs works.

Emacs is designed so that some commands save the erased text while others do not. In general, Emacs saves the text from commands that erase more than a single character. Such commands are called KILL COMMANDS. Emacs does not save the text from commands that erase only a single character or whitespace. These commands are called DELETE COMMANDS. (As we discussed in Section 8.3, "whitespace" refers to the **SPC**, **TAB** or **RET** characters, which are described in Section 4.4.)

The custom within Emacs is to use these two terms — kill and delete — as verbs. When we say we KILL some text, we imply that the text is being saved. When we say that we DELETE some text, we imply that the text is not saved. In other words, whatever you delete is gone for good. Whatever you kill can be resurrected.

In the next two sections, we will talk about the delete commands and then the kill commands. I will then explain how Emacs saves killed text, and what commands you can use to insert such text back into the buffer. You will find that these commands are especially useful, as you can use them to copy or move text from one part of the buffer to another, or even between two different buffers.

© Harley Hahn 2016
H. Hahn, *Harley Hahn's Emacs Field Guide*, DOI 10.1007/978-1-4842-1703-0_9

Section 9.2: Commands to Delete Text

As I explained in Section 9.1, delete commands erase only a single character or whitespace. These commands are shown in Figure 9-1. Remember, unlike the kill commands, delete characters are not saved for later recall. Still, you can't lose more than one character at a time.

Command	Description
BS	Delete one character to the left of cursor
DEL	Delete one character at the position of cursor
C-d	Same as **DEL**
M-	Delete spaces & tabs around point
M-SPC	Delete spaces & tabs around point; leave one space
C-x C-o	Delete blank lines around current line
M-^	Join two lines (delete **RET** + surrounding spaces)

FIGURE 9-1. **Commands to delete text.**

We have already covered the first three commands. **BS** <Backspace> erases the character to the left of the cursor. This is the key to use when you are typing and you need to back up, delete, and fix a mistake. **DEL** <Delete> or **C-d** erases the character that is at the cursor position. More precisely, **BS** erases to the left of point, and **DEL** and **C-d** erase to the right of point.

As with other Emacs commands, you can use a prefix argument (explained in Section 8.4) with these two commands to operate on more than one character at a time. For example, to erase 5 characters to the left, you can use **ESC 5 BS**; to erase 18 characters to the right, you can use **ESC 18 DEL** or **ESC 18 C-d**.

When you use such commands, you are erasing more than one character and, as such, you are killing and not deleting. For this reason, Emacs does save the erased text when you use **DEL** or **C-d** to erase more than one character at a time.

Secret Note

Here is a way to make a bit of money for yourself.

Take this book and go to a bar where Emacs people hang out. Look for some people who are learning Emacs and practicing on their laptops, and sit down next to them. Open the book so that Figure 9-2 in Section 9.3 is clearly visible and casually leave it where the people next to you can see it. This figure contains a summary of all the Emacs kill commands. Pretend you are not looking at the book.

Next, strike up a casual conversation with the people next to you and carefully work the topic around to the Emacs kill commands. Offer to bet them a small sum of money that they can't think of a way to kill text without pressing any upper- or lowercase letters.

When they sneak a look at the book, pretend you don't notice. When they look at Figure 9-2, they will see that **M-BS** (<Meta-Backspace> = <Alt-Backspace>) is a kill command and, thinking that you are an easy mark, they will accept the bet. When they press **M-BS**, pretend to be annoyed with yourself, pay off the bet, and tell them you would like a chance to win back your money. Offer them a much larger bet that you can kill text without using **M-BS** and without pressing any alphabetic keys.

Now, look the other way for a second, which will give them another chance to check out Figure 9-2. Aside from **M-BS**, they will not see any other kill commands that do not use a letter of the alphabet.

As soon as they take your bet, press **ESC 5 DEL** and clean up.

To continue, the **M-** (<Meta-Backslash>) command erases any **space** or **tab** characters that happen to be on either side of point. This command provides a quick way to clean up a section of whitespace. For example, say that you have typed the following text and the cursor is under one of the spaces between **tea** and **ch**:

`Everything we tea      ch you is true.`

If you press **M-**, Emacs will erase all the surrounding spaces. The line now looks like:

`Everything we teach you is true.`

The **M-SPC** (<Meta-Space>) command is similar, except that it leaves exactly one space. Here is an example. You have just typed the line:

`The sentence above is   only partially correct.`

You would like to erase the extra spaces. Move the cursor to one of the spaces between **is** and **only** and press **M-SPC**. The line is changed to the following:

`The sentence above is only partially correct.`

■ **Note**

If you are using a virtual terminal, you won't have a problem with **M-SPC**. However, with a terminal window (see Section 2.6), you may find that **M-SPC** doesn't work. This is because, in some GUIs, the sequence <Alt-Space> opens the terminal window's main context menu.

If this is a problem for you, simply use **ESC SPC** (<Esc> <Space>) instead of **M-SPC** (<Alt-Space>).

The `C-x C-o` command performs the analogous operation for blank lines. This command will erase all the blank lines surrounding the current line. For example, say that the buffer contains the following text:

`Everything we teach you is true.`

`The sentence above is only partially correct.`

`Don't believe everything you read.`

You would like only a single blank line between each line of text. Move to one of the blank lines following the first line, and press `C-x C-o`. The extra blank lines will be erased and you will be left with the following:

`Everything we teach you is true.`

`The sentence above is only partially correct.`

`Don't believe everything you read.`

Finally, the `M-^` command joins two lines into one long one. This command joins the current line to the one immediately above it, while leaving a single space between the two groups of text. Any extra spaces (at the end of the first line or at the beginning of the second line) are removed. For example, say that you have the following lines of text:

`This is the first sentence.`
`    This is the second sentence.`

You want to join these two lines. Move the cursor to the second line and press `M-^`. You will now have one long line:

`This is the first sentence. This is the second sentence.`

The cursor will be at the place where the lines were joined, in this case, at the space between the two sentences.

Section 9.3: Commands to Kill Text

Most of the commands that erase text are kill commands. When you use a kill command, Emacs saves the text that is erased in case you want to insert it back into the buffer. Figure 9-2 summarizes the various kill commands.

Command	Description
C-k	Kill from cursor to end of line
M-d	Kill a word
M-BS	Kill a word backward
M-k	Kill from cursor to end of sentence
C-x BS	Kill backward to beginning of sentence
C-w	Kill the region
M-z *char*	Kill through next occurrence of specified character

FIGURE 9-2. **Commands to kill text.**

The C-k command erases all the characters from the cursor to the end of the line. More precisely, C-k erases from point to the end of the line. (Remember, point is between the cursor and the character to its left. See Section 8.1.) If you are at the beginning of a line when you press C-k, it will erase all the characters on the line. If you are on a blank line, C-k will erase the line itself. Thus, you can erase a line completely by (1) moving to the beginning, (2) erasing all the characters, and then (3) erasing the line itself. The sequence to do this is C-a C-k C-k.

Note   To erase an entire line: if you are at the beginning of the line, press C-k C-k. If you are not at the beginning of the line, press C-a C-k C-k.

There are two kill commands that erase a word. The M-d command erases from point to the end of the word. The M-BS command erases from point to the beginning of the word. Remember that point lies between the cursor and the character to its left. Thus, M-BS does not erase the character above the cursor. (Remember that BS is <Backspace>, so M-BS = <Meta-Backspace> = <Alt-Backspace>.)

Here are a few examples. Say that you have just typed the following text:

This book is not the best Emacs book ever written.

You decide you want to erase the word **not**. There are two ways to do it. First, you can move the cursor to the **space** between **is** and **not** and press M-d to erase the next word. Or you can move to the **t** at the beginning of **the** and press M-BS to erase the previous word.

Until you practice these commands, the exact positioning may seem a little odd. However, when you look carefully at the location of point, it all starts to make sense. In Section 8.2, I explained that M-f moves the cursor forward by one word, and M-b moves the cursor backward by one word. When you use M-f, it leaves you on the **space** between two words. When you use M-b, it leaves you on the first character of a word. Take a few moments and experiment. You will see that M-f and M-d work well together when you are moving forward, and M-b and M-BS work well together when you are moving backward.

The next two kill commands erase text within a sentence. The M-k command erases forward, from point to the end of the sentence. The C-x BS command erases backward, from point to the beginning of the sentence. When you use these commands, it is helpful to remember the commands that move the cursor one sentence at a time. M-e moves forward by one sentence; M-a moves backward by one sentence. These relationships are summarized in Figure 9-3.

	WORDS			SENTENCES	
	Backward	Forward		Backward	Forward
Move:	M-b	M-f	Move:	M-a	M-e
Kill:	M-BS	M-d	Kill:	C-x BS	M-k

FIGURE 9-3. **Commands to move and kill by word or sentence.**

The next kill command, C-w, is one you will use frequently, as it allows you to kill the entire region. (As I described in Section 8.7, the region consists of all the characters between mark and point.)

■ **Note**   To erase the entire buffer, use C-x h C-w. C-x h creates a region consisting of the entire buffer (see Section 8.8). C-w kills the region.

C-w is particularly handy when you want to move a section of text. All you need to do is set mark and point to enclose the text, use C-w to kill the region, and then insert the text back into the buffer at a different location (or even into another buffer). I will discuss this idea — which is called "yanking" — in Section 9.4.

The final kill command is M-z. When you type this command, Emacs will prompt you to specify a single character. Emacs will kill all the text from point (your current position) to the next occurrence of that character. When you use this command, we say that you ZAP the characters, thus the name M-z.

Here is an example. You are editing an important document that was typed by someone who is not as smart as you. You come across a line that reads:

```
I can't imagine how anyone could prefer Emacs to vi.
```

Having read this, it is the work of a moment to move to the **space** following the I (at the beginning of the sentence) and type **M-z d**. This zaps all the characters from the **space** up to (and including) the **d** in **could**. The line now reads:

```
I prefer Emacs to vi.
```

Section 9.4: The Kill Ring and Yanking; Moving and Copying

As we have discussed, there are two types of commands that erase text. Delete commands erase single characters and whitespace (Section 9.2). Kill commands erase more than one character (Section 9.3). Whenever you use a kill command, Emacs saves the text in a KILL RING. (The name will make sense in a moment.) Because killed text is saved, you can copy it to wherever you want. Emacs has a number of commands that let you work with the kill ring and its contents. These commands are summarized in Figure 9-4.

Command	Description
C-y	Yank most recently killed text
C-u C-y	Same as **C-y**, cursor at beginning of new text
M-y	Replace yanked text with previously killed text
M-w	Copy region to kill ring, without erasing
M-C-w	Append next kill to newest kill ring entry
C-h v kill-ring	Display the actual values in the kill ring

FIGURE 9-4. **Commands to yank text.**

The kill ring is really a set of storage areas, each of which holds text that has been killed. Each storage area is called a KILL RING ENTRY. When you kill some text, it is stored as the most recent kill ring entry. To insert this text back into the buffer, you move the cursor to where you want to insert the text, and press **C-y**. When you copy such text into a buffer, we say that you YANK the text (hence the name **C-y**).

■ **What's in a Name?**

Kill, Yank

In the Emacs culture, "killing" refers to deleting text that is saved to the kill ring; "yanking" is copying this text back into the buffer. In other programs, these operations are generally referred to by the more refined names of cutting and pasting.

In other words, if you understand how to cut and paste, you know how to kill and yank.

When you use the **C-y** command to yank text into the buffer, Emacs sets mark at the beginning of the text and point at the end of the text. This means that the yanked text is now defined to be the region, in case you want to operate on it in some way. It also means that the cursor is just past the end of the text.

If you use the **C-u C-y** command instead, Emacs will yank the exact same text, but the locations of mark and point will be reversed. So, although the region will still enclose the newly inserted text, the cursor will be at the beginning. This is useful when you want to yank some text and then type something in front of it.

■ **Note**   Before you yank text, think about where you want the cursor. If you want it at the beginning of the text, use **C-u C-y**. If you want the cursor at the end of the text, use **C-y**.

Let's talk for a moment about what happens as you kill more than one section of text. The first time you kill text, Emacs stores it in a kill ring entry. Later, when you kill more text, Emacs stores it in a different entry. The kill ring has a lot of storage space, so there is no need to throw away old text until you fill up all the key ring entries. And even then, you need discard only the very oldest material in order to make room for the new text.

By default, the kill ring has 60 entries. Thus, Emacs can store the last 60 sequences of killed text. (You can change this number if you want, but it is rarely necessary.) So what happens when all the kill ring entries are filled and you kill some more text? Emacs discards the oldest entry and uses it to hold the new text.

Some people like to visualize the kill ring as 60 entries organized into a circle. As Emacs needs to store text, it works its way around the circle, using one entry after another. Thus, we have the idea of a ring.

At all times, one of the kill ring entries in the circle is the current entry. This means it is possible to yank, not only the most recent kill ring entry, but the entry before that, and the entry before that, and so on (up to 60 entries). To go through the ring, one entry at a time, you use the **M-y** command. Here is how it works.

Just after you have used a C-y or C-u C-y command, take a look and see if the newly inserted text was what you wanted. If what you wanted is stored in a previous kill ring entry, press M-y. Emacs will erase the text and replace it with the previous entry. If this is what you wanted, fine. If not, press M-y again. You can continue pressing M-y until you run out of kill ring entries. In conceptual terms, you can think of the M-y command as working its way around the kill ring, showing you one entry after another.

Note If you are using M-y repeatedly to search for an old kill ring entry and you can't find what you want, you can always use C-x u to undo the last insertion and forget the whole thing.

Emacs maintains only one kill ring for all your buffers. This means you can kill some text in one buffer, and yank it into another buffer. Indeed, this is exactly how you move text from one buffer to another: kill some text, move to another buffer, then yank the last kill ring entry.

This procedure works well, but it does have one drawback: you have to erase something before you can move it. What if you merely want to copy something without destroying the original?

The solution is to define the region (using mark and point) so as to contain the text you want to copy, and then use the M-w command. This tells Emacs to copy the text to the kill ring without erasing anything. You can then yank the text wherever you want.

To copy something from one buffer to another, you set mark and point to enclose the text, press M-w, change to the other buffer, move to where you want to insert the text, and then yank it with C-y. Of course, this will also work with two locations in the same buffer.

When you use more than one kill command in a row, Emacs will automatically collect all the killed text into the same kill ring entry. This allows you to move from place to place, killing text and accumulating it into a single large block. You can then yank all of it with a single C-y or C-u C-y command.

As soon as you use a non-kill command, Emacs stops the accumulation. The next time you kill something, it will be put into a different kill ring entry. However, there is a way to tell Emacs to place killed text into the previous entry. All you need to do is press M-C-w before you kill the text. This tells Emacs to *append* the next thing you kill to the current kill ring entry.

Here is an example of how you might use M-C-w. Let's say you want to copy three paragraphs from different places in the buffer into a new file named **summary**. Go to each paragraph in turn and copy/append it into the current kill ring entry. Then open a new buffer and yank the three paragraphs into that buffer. You can now save the buffer as a new file. Here is what the whole procedure looks like. Read it closely and slowly to make sure it makes sense to you. Then take a moment to try it for yourself.

Copy the first paragraph to the current kill ring entry:

1. Move the cursor to the beginning of the first paragraph.
2. **C-SPC**: Set mark (Section 8.7).
3. **M-}**: Move the cursor to end of the paragraph (Section 8.2).
4. **M-w**: Copy region to the current kill ring entry.
5. Move the cursor to the beginning of the second paragraph.

Append the second paragraph:

6. **C-SPC**: Set mark.
7. **M-}**: Move the cursor to end of the paragraph.
8. **M-C-w M-w**: Append region to the current kill ring entry.

Append the third paragraph:

9. Move the cursor to the beginning of the third paragraph.
10. **C-SPC**: Set mark.
11. **M-}**: Move the cursor to the end of the paragraph.
12. **M-C-w M-w**: Append region to the current kill ring entry.

Copy the current kill ring entry to a new buffer.

13. **C-b summary** <Enter>: Create a new buffer named **summary**.
14. **C-y**: Yank contents of current ring entry into buffer.
15. **C-x C-w summary** <Enter>: Save to file named **summary**.

The final kill-oriented command is **C-h v kill-ring**. This tells Emacs to display the actual contents of the kill ring. You will rarely have to use this command but, from time to time, it is interesting to look at the entire kill ring. This command makes use of the built-in Help facility (described in Section 12.3). In technical terms, Emacs stores the kill ring as a "variable" called **kill-ring** (we can ignore the details). The **C-h v** command simply tells Emacs to display the value of that variable.

Section 9.5: Correcting Common Typing Mistakes

Emacs has a number of commands that have been specifically designed to make it easy to correct typing mistakes. These commands are shown in Figure 9-5. As you can see, there are three types of commands: erasing, case changing and transposing. Notice that most of the commands act upon characters you have just typed (that is, characters to the left of the cursor). In Section 9.6, I will discuss how to correct spelling mistakes.

Command	Description
BS	Delete one character to the left of cursor
DEL	Delete one character at the position of cursor
C-d	Same as **DEL**
M-BS	Kill the previous word
C-x BS	Kill backward to beginning of sentence
M-- M-l	Change previous word to lowercase
M-- M-u	Change previous word to uppercase
M-- M-c	Change previous word to lowercase, initial cap
M-l	Change following word to lowercase
M-u	Change following word to uppercase
M-c	Change following word to lowercase, initial cap
C-t	Transpose two adjacent characters
M-t	Transpose two adjacent words
C-x C-t	Transpose two consecutive lines

FIGURE 9-5. **Commands for correcting common typing mistakes.**

■ **Note**   **BS** is <Backspace>; M-- is <Meta-hyphen>.

We have already discussed the delete and kill commands. **BS** erases the character you have just typed; **M-BS** erases the word you have just typed; and **C-x BS** erases to the beginning of the sentence.

■ **Note**

Your typing habits will influence which commands you prefer to use to make corrections when you notice a mistake.

If you are a slow typist who looks at the keys as you type, you will probably find it easier to move the cursor to the left and right, and make your corrections one character at a time. However, if you can type quickly without looking at the keys, it is a lot easier to press **M-BS** several times in a row and simply retype the last few words.

One of the most common typing mistakes is to mix up your lower- and uppercase letters. Emacs has three commands to help you. To change all the letters in the previous word to lowercase, use **M-- M-l**. To change the letters to uppercase, use **M-- M-u**. To change the letters to lowercase with the first letter capitalized, use **M-- M-c**. (M-- means <Meta-hyphen>.)

Although these three commands act on a single word, you can use a prefix argument (explained in Section 8.4) to change more than one word at a time. For example, say that you have just typed 10 words in lowercase, and you decide to make each word lowercase with an initial capital letter (as in a title). All you have to do is type **ESC 10 M-- M-c**.

The remaining commands transpose (switch around) characters, words or lines. **C-t** transposes two adjacent characters. In general, **C-t** switches the character at the cursor with the character immediately to its left. (In other words, it switches the two characters on either side of point.) Thus, if you have typed the word **Halrey** you can correct it by moving to the **r** and pressing **C-t**.

However, there is one special case. If the cursor is at the end of a line (just past the final character in the line), pressing **C-t** will transpose the last two characters. This means that if you are typing on a new line, and you press two keys in the wrong order, you can make an immediate correction by typing **C-t**. (Try it and it will make sense.)

To be more technical, the **C-t** command normally transposes the two characters on either side of point. However, at the end of a line, **C-t** switches the two characters before point. (Remember, point is between the character at the cursor, and the character on its left. For example, if the cursor is on the **r** in **Harley**, point is between the **a** and the **r**.)

The **M-t** command is similar except that it transposes two words: the word before point and the word after point. Here is an example. Say that you have just typed the line:

I should buy a copy of "Harley Hahn's Guide to Unix Linux and".

You decide to switch the last two words.

To do so, move the cursor so that point is between the words **Linux** and **and**. (The cursor should be on the space after "Linux" or on the following "a".) Now, press **M-t**. When Emacs transposes words, it does not change the punctuation, so in our example the quotation mark and the period will not be moved. You will see:

I should buy a copy of "Harley Hahn's Guide to Unix and Linux".

(Which, of course, is good advice.)

The final command is **C-x C-t**. This command switches two consecutive lines: the current line and the line above it. For example, say that the buffer contains the lines:

```
11111
22222
33333
44444
55555
```

You move the cursor to the fourth line (**44444**) and press C-x C-t. The buffer will change as follows:

```
11111
22222
44444
33333
55555
```

The only exception is when you are on the first line of the buffer. In this position, there is no line above the current line so, as you might expect, C-t switches the top two lines. In our example, if you were to move to the top line (**11111**) and press C-x C-t, you would see:

```
22222
11111
44444
33333
55555
```

Note If you place the cursor below a specific line and then press C-x C-t repeatedly, you will move that line down the buffer, one line at a time. Take a moment to try it.

Section 9.6: Correcting Spelling Mistakes

Emacs has a variety of commands to help you correct spelling. These commands are shown in Figure 9-6. Before you read this section, take a moment to create a new buffer and type some text, so you can test the various commands as I explain them.

Command	Description
M-$	Spell check: word at point, or region
M-x ispell-buffer	Spell check: buffer (only)
M-x ispell-region	Spell check: region (only)
M-x ispell	Spell check: buffer, or region
M-TAB	Complete word before point, based on dictionary
ESC TAB	Same as **M-TAB**
M-x flyspell-mode	Highlight spelling mistakes in regular text
M-x flyspell-prog-mode	Highlight spelling mistakes in programs

FIGURE 9-6. **Commands for correcting spelling mistakes.**

149

The simplest and most important command is M-$ (on most keyboards, you would press <Alt-Shift-4>). This command has two possible actions, depending on the situation.

If the region is not set — which will be the case most of the time — M-$ checks the spelling of the word at point. That is, at the position of the cursor. If the region is set, M-$ will check the spelling of all the words in the region.

Think about that for a moment. If you want to check the spelling of a single word, just move to it and press M-$. If you want to check the spelling of all the words in a section of text, or a paragraph, or the entire buffer, all you need to do is set region appropriately and press M-$.

For example, to spell check a paragraph, move point (the cursor) to that paragraph and use:

M-h M-$

To spell check the entire buffer, use:

C-x h M-$

(To learn how to set the region, see Section 8.8.)

When Emacs finds a word that is misspelled, it will create a new buffer named *Choices* to show you possible words from the dictionary. Each word will have a single number or other character in front of it. Simply press the number (or character) of the word you want to use. (It's easier than it sounds. Try it once, and you will see how it works.) If you don't see what you want, you can stop the spell check by pressing C-g.

For completeness, I will mention that there are three more specific spell check commands:

- M-x ispell-buffer: Spell checks the entire buffer (only).

- M-x ispell-region: Spell checks the region (only).

- M-x ispell: If the region is set, spell checks the region. Otherwise, spell checks the entire buffer.

As you are typing, Emacs can help you complete a partially typed word. Just type M-TAB. Emacs will then check the word to the left of point and show you a list of possible choices. Just pick the one you want and keep typing.

■ **Note**

To use **M-TAB**, you need to press <Alt-Tab>. However, if you are working in a GUI, it is likely that <Alt-Tab> will have a special meaning because, in many GUIs, this key combination is used for task switching.

If this is the case for you, you can use **ESC TAB** instead. (Using **ESC** as a substitute for the Meta key is discussed in Section 4.4.)

The final spell check tool I want to discuss is called Flyspell mode. Flyspell mode is what we call a "minor mode", which means that it is a setting you can turn on or off to provide a service. (We will discuss minor modes in Section 11.4.)

When Flyspell mode is on, Emacs will highlight all the misspelled words. This is a big help, not only as you are typing, but to let you check for spelling mistakes within the entire window, just by glancing at your screen. If you see a mistake, all you need to do is move to it and press **M-$**.

To turn on Flyspell mode, use:

```
M-x flyspell-mode
```

To turn it off, use the same command again: it acts like a toggle.

When you are editing computer programs, you can use Flyspell-Prog mode. This tells Emacs to highlight spelling mistakes, but only within comments and character strings.

The command to turn Flyspell-Prog mode on or off is:

```
M-x flyspell-prog-mode
```

Section 9.7: Filling and Formatting Text

As you type regular text (compared to say, typing a computer program), you have two special needs. First, when you reach the end of the line, you will want Emacs to start a new line for you automatically. Otherwise, you will have to keep track of the cursor position and press <Enter> each time you near the right margin.

Second, as you edit the text, you will shorten some lines and lengthen others, and you will want to be able to reformat the text to maintain as smooth a right margin as possible.

Emacs has commands to perform both of these tasks. These commands are summarized in Figure 9-7.

Command	Description
M-x auto-fill-mode	Turn on/off Auto Fill mode
M-q	Fill a paragraph
ESC 1 M-q	Fill+justify a paragraph
M-x fill-region	Fill each paragraph in the region
ESC 1 M-x fill-region	Fill+justify each paragraph in region
M-x fill-region-as-paragraph	Fill region as one long paragraph
ESC 1 M-x fill-region-as-paragraph	Fill+justify region as one paragraph
C-x f	Set the fill column value
C-h v fill-column	Display current fill column value

FIGURE 9-7. Commands to fill text.

To tell Emacs to break long lines automatically as you type, you turn on "Auto Fill mode". (We will discuss modes in Sections 11.1 through 11.7.) When Auto Fill mode is turned on, Emacs will break lines for you as you type. When Auto Fill mode is off, Emacs will not break lines.

How do you know if Auto Fill mode is on or off? When it is on, Emacs will display the word **Fill** on the mode line near the bottom of your window (see Section 6.4). You can see this in Figure 9-8.

```
-UUU:**--F1   Marta           50% L1959   (Fundamental Fill) -------------------
Auto-Fill mode enabled
```

FIGURE 9-8. Mode line showing that Auto Fill mode is enabled.

When you have turned on Auto Fill mode using **M-x auto-fill-mode** *you will see the word* **Fill** *on the mode line*

When Auto Fill mode is off, you can turn it on by using the command **M-x auto-fill-mode**. When Auto Fill mode is on, you can turn it off by using the same command. Thus, **M-x auto-fill-mode** acts as an on/off toggle switch. If you are not sure of the current status of Auto Fill mode, just look at the mode line for the word **Fill**.

If you use Emacs only for typing regular text, you will probably want Auto Fill mode to be on all the time by default. I explain how to do this in Section 11.9, when we talk about customizing Emacs.

■ **Note** You do not have to type the full command **M-x auto-fill-mode**. As with all such commands, you can use completion (discussed in Section 6.7) to ask Emacs to do some of the typing for you. In this case, all you need to type is:

M-x au SPC -f RET

One of the limitations of Auto Fill mode is that it will not automatically reformat a paragraph when you make changes. For example, when you delete and insert words, you change the length of the lines and the right margin can become ragged.

To reformat a paragraph, move the cursor to be within that paragraph (or on a blank line before the paragraph), and use the command **M-q**. Emacs will reformat by removing all the line breaks and inserting new ones as necessary. When this happens, we say that Emacs FILLS the paragraph.

There are two other fill commands you will find useful. When you want to fill part of a paragraph or more than one paragraph, you can define the region (by setting mark and point) to contain the text you want to fill. You can then fill the entire region by using **M-x fill-region.** (With completion, you only need to type **M-x fil SPC r RET**.)

A variation of this command is **M-x fill-region-as-paragraph**. This command fills an entire region as a single large paragraph. Again, with completion, you can save keystrokes by typing:

M-x fill SPC r SPC SPC RET

The fill commands can also right justify at the same time as they format. That is, they can insert spaces within the text in order to make the right margin line up. To fill and right justify at the same time, just use a prefix argument before a fill command (see Section 8.4). Any numeric value will do, so you might as well use **1**.

For example, to fill and right justify a paragraph, use the command **ESC 1 M-q**. You can also use a similar prefix argument with the other fill commands to right justify and fill the region.

When Emacs fills a paragraph, it ensures that no line is longer than a specific maximum width. By default, this width is 70 characters, but you can change it if necessary.

The value of the fill column width is kept in a variable (storage location) named **fill-column**. You can display the current value of this variable by using the command **C-h v fill-column**. (The **C-h v** command is part of the built-in Help facility. This particular command displays the value of a variable along with a short description.)

There are two ways to change the value of **fill-column**, both of which use the **C-x f** command. First, you can use this command with a prefix argument showing how many characters wide you want your lines to be. For example, to set **fill-column** to a value of 55, you can use **ESC 55 C-x f**. From now on, all lines you fill will be formatted to be no longer than 55 characters long.

The second way to change the value of **fill-column** is to move the cursor to a line that is exactly the width that you want, and then press **C-x f**. Emacs will use the width of that particular line as the new value for **fill-column**.

CHAPTER 10

Searching

Section 10.1: Introducing the Emacs Search Commands

Emacs gives you several ways to search for a pattern within the buffer. Figure 10-1 shows a summary of the different search commands. At first, it looks overwhelming, but don't worry. In almost all cases, it boils down to four simple ideas.

1. To search forward, press **C-s** and type what you want to find.

2. To search backward, press **C-r** and type what you want to find.

To remember the names, think of **s** for "search" and **r** for "reverse". As you are searching, the characters you type are called the SEARCH STRING.

3. If Emacs finds what you specified, you can search for another occurrence by pressing **C-s** (or **C-r**) as many times as you need.

4. When you find exactly what you want, press **RET** (the Enter key) to stop the search.

Most of the time, that's all you need to remember. However, this being Emacs, there are lots and lots of optional details (which we will get to in a moment).

Command	Description
C-s	Forward: Incremental search
C-s RET	Forward: Non-incremental search
M-s w	Forward: Incremental *word* search
M-C-s	Forward: Incremental *regexp* search
M-C-s RET	Forward: Non-incremental *regexp* search

Command	Description
C-r	Backward: Incremental search
C-r RET	Backward: Non-incremental search
M-s w C-r	Backward: Incremental *word* search
M-C-r	Backward: Incremental *regexp* search
M-C-r RET	Backward: Non-incremental *regexp* search

FIGURE 10-1. Search commands.

© Harley Hahn 2016

H. Hahn, *Harley Hahn's Emacs Field Guide*, DOI 10.1007/978-1-4842-1703-0_10

■ **Note** The **C-s** key sequence is bound to the command **isearch-forward**. **C-r** is bound to **isearch-backward**. **isearch** stands for "incremental search".

Section 10.2: Incremental Searching

The basic type of Emacs search is called an INCREMENTAL SEARCH. That means Emacs starts searching as soon as you type a single character. With each character you type, Emacs refines its search. Here is an example.

Let's say that you want to search for the pattern **harley**. You start by pressing **C-s**. Emacs is now waiting for you to type something. You type **h**. The search string is **h**, so Emacs jumps to the first place in the buffer that has the letter "h".

Next, you type **a**. The search string is now **ha**, so Emacs jumps to the first place in the buffer that has the letters "ha".

You then type **r**. The search string is now **har**, so Emacs jumps to the first place that has "har".

In other words, Emacs starts searching the moment you begin to type. Each time you type another character, the search string becomes more and more specific. The advantage is that, most of the time, you do not have to type the full pattern to find what you want. For instance, it is possible that you would find the pattern **harley** after typing only the first few letters.

The best way to see how this all works is to try it for yourself.

1. Start Emacs.

When you are practicing, you can start Emacs by using the **-Q** option to suppress the splash screen (see Section 5.1). Either of the following commands (see Section 5.2) will do:

```
emacs -Q
emacs -Q -nw
```

Emacs will start by creating one large window containing a buffer named ***scratch***. There will be a few lines at the top with some useful information. If you want to erase these lines, use **C-x h C-w** (see Section 9.3), although you don't have to.

2. Display something interesting to search.

Start the Help facility by pressing **C-h b**. This will display a large list of all the key bindings. Press **C-x 0** to delete the window with the ***scratch*** buffer. You will be left in the ***Help*** buffer.

3. Practice using C-s and C-r.

You can now use C-s (search forward) and C-r (search backward) as much as you want. If you are not sure what to search for, try searching for the word "command".

I suggest that you set this up right now, so as you read the following sections, you can try out the various commands.

Section 10.3: Keys to Use While Searching

While you are in the middle of a search, there are a number of keys that have special meanings. These are shown in Figure 10-2.

Key	Description
BS	Erase last character you typed
RET	Terminate the search
C-s	Search forward for same pattern
C-r	Search backward for same pattern
C-g	While search is in progress: Stop current search
C-g	While waiting for input: Abort entire command
C-w	Copy the word after point to search string
C-y	Copy current kill ring entry to search string
M-y	Copy previous kill ring entry to search string

FIGURE 10-2. **Keys to use during a search.**

While you are typing the search pattern, you can make a correction by pressing **BS** (<Backspace>) to erase the last character you typed. When you do, Emacs will back up to the place that matches those characters that remain.

Here is an example. Say that you are searching for the pattern **harley**. After you have typed the first three letters, **har**, Emacs jumps to the word **share** (because this happens to be the first word that contains these three characters). To continue, you want to type the letter **l**, but, by accident, you press the **p** key. Thus, Emacs thinks you are searching for **harp** and it jumps to the word **harpoon**. To make the correction, you press **BS**. This erases the letter **p**, whereupon Emacs jumps back to the word **share**. You now type **ley** and Emacs jumps to **harley**. (Don't worry if this is a bit difficult to follow. It will all make perfect sense when you see it.)

At any time, you can tell Emacs to find the next occurrence of the search string by pressing C-s once again. To go backward, press C-r. For example, say that you have typed **harley** and Emacs has dutifully found the first occurrence of that word. However, that is not the one you want. Simply press C-s and Emacs will find the next one.

If you press C-s and Emacs cannot find any occurrences of the search string from your current position to the end of the buffer, you will see the message:

```
Failing I-search
```

This means the incremental search has failed. That is, you are looking at the last place in the buffer that matches the search string. However, if you press C-s one more time, Emacs will wrap around and start searching at the beginning of the buffer.

In other words, you can press C-s repeatedly to search for a pattern throughout the buffer. When you get to the end (and you see the message), you can press C-s and start again from the beginning. Similarly, when you are searching backward with C-r, you can press C-r twice when you get to the top and wrap around to the bottom.

To terminate your search, you have two options. If Emacs has found what you want, simply press **RET** (<Enter>). The search command will stop and you will be left at the current position in the buffer.

If, however, you can't find what you want and you decide the whole thing was a bad idea, press C-g. This will stop the search command, but will leave you where you started, just as if nothing had happened.

There are three other keys that are handy to use during a search. If you press C-w, Emacs appends the word immediately after point (the position of the cursor) to the search string. Emacs then advances point to the end of that word. You can press C-w more than once, to pick up one word after another.

What does this mean? It means that you can search for a word in the buffer without having to actually type the word for yourself. Here is an example. You are reading an essay that contains the following quote from the writer Isaac Asimov's final autobiography:

Perhaps writers are so self-absorbed as a necessary part of their profession.

The cursor is on the space before the word **writers**. (That is, point is between the space and the **w**.) You decide to search for further occurrences of the word **writers**.

You press C-s. Emacs is now waiting for you to type a search string. Instead of typing the actual word, you press C-w and Emacs copies the word **writers** for you into the minibuffer, just as if you had typed the letters yourself. Emacs then moves the cursor to the next word (to the space before **are**). You can either press C-w again to pick up the next word, or press C-s to begin the search.

You can copy as many words as you want by pressing C-w. And you can do so not only when you start the search, but at any point along the way. Thus, whenever Emacs is paused waiting for you to type something to add to the search pattern, you can press C-w to copy the current word. If you make a mistake, you can correct it by pressing BS (<Backspace>). When you do, Emacs will erase an entire word, not just a single character. (In other words, when you are searching and you press BS, Emacs knows whether it should erase a whole word or simply one character. Pretty cool, eh?)

Aside from C-w, there are two other commands that will append text to the search string while you are searching. C-y ("yank") appends the current kill ring entry. If after using C-y, you type M-y, Emacs replaces the yanked text with the previous kill ring entry. Here is an example:

In the course of your work, you erase the word **Ignormus** (it's actually a name), and then you erase the word **heffalump**. Thus, the current key ring entry is **heffalump**, and the previous key ring entry is **Ignormus**.

You then switch to another buffer, where you are reading another quote from Isaac Asimov's autobiography:

```
I have always thought of myself as a
remarkable fellow, even from childhood,
and I have never wavered in that opinion.
```

(This, of course, is true of all good writers.)

The cursor is at the space before **always** in the first line, so point is between the space and the **a**. You press C-s to start a search, and then press C-w to copy the next word to the search string. The search string is:

```
always
```

You press <Space> to put in a single space. You then press C-y to append the current key ring entry to the end of the search sting. Since the current key ring entry is **heffalump**, the search string is now:

```
always heffalump
```

You now press M-y. This replaces **heffalump** with the previous key ring entry **Ignormus**. The search string is now:

```
always ignormus
```

▨ **Note**

If you are not familiar with a heffalump or the Ignormus, take a moment to look them up online (separately).

Be sure to spell Ignormus correctly (it is not "Ignoramus").

Section 10.4: Upper- and Lowercase Searching

One issue we have not yet discussed is what Emacs does about upper- and lowercase letters while it is searching. The general rule is that Emacs ignores all distinctions between upper- and lowercase as long as you type only lowercase letters in the search pattern. However, once you type even a single uppercase letter, Emacs will search for an exact match.

Here is an example. If you tell Emacs to search for **harley**, it will find any occurrence of these letters, whether they are upper- or lowercase or mixed. For instance, Emacs would find **harley**, **Harley**, **HARLEY**, **harLEY**, and so on. However, if you tell Emacs to search for **Harley**, it will find only this exact word.

When a program does not distinguish between upper- and lowercase, we say that it is CASE INSENSITIVE. When the distinction is made, we say the program is CASE SENSITIVE.

So let's say that you are searching for the phrase **send money to Harley**. You press **C-s** and then start to type the pattern. As you do, Emacs begins the search. So far, you have typed **send money to**. Up to this point, you have typed only lowercase letters, so Emacs is performing a case insensitive search. However, as soon as you type the **H**, Emacs switches to a case sensitive search.

At this point, you might wonder what would happen if you were to press **BS** <Backspace> and erase the only uppercase letter? Emacs would recognize what you did and switch from being case sensitive back to case insensitive.

Please realize that changing from a case insensitive search to case sensitive search requires you to actually type an uppercase letter. The change won't happen if you copy an uppercase letter to the search string from the key ring.

To see what I mean, take a look at the very last example in Section 10.2. The search string was the word **always** followed by a space:

```
always
```

We pressed **M-y** to copy an entry from the key ring to the search string. The key ring entry was the word **Ignormus**. However, the new search string was:

```
always ignormus
```

Why was the word **ignormus** in lower case? Because we had not typed an uppercase letter into the search string manually, Emacs was using a case insensitive search, so it changed **Ignormus** to **ignormus**.

If you want to test this for yourself, type **Ignormus** (with an uppercase **I**), and then press **M-BS** to kill the entire word (see Section 9.3). The current kill ring entry is now **Ignormus**.

Now press **C-s** to start a new search and type **Always**, followed by a space. The search string is:

Always

Because you typed an uppercase letter (**A**), Emacs is doing a case sensitive search. Press **C-y** to append the current kill ring entry to the search string. The new search string is:

Always Ignormus

Because you are using a case sensitive search, Emacs preserved the uppercase **I** when it copied the kill ring entry to the search string.

Section 10.5: Non-Incremental Searching

If you look back at Figure 10-1, you will see several types of search commands, and a forward and backward variation for each type. So far, we have discussed the incremental search commands (**C-s** and **C-r**). These commands begin searching as soon as you type a single character. As you type more characters, the search becomes more specific. This is called an incremental search (Section 10.2).

It may be that you want Emacs to wait until you have typed the entire pattern before it starts to search. To do so, you can use the NON-INCREMENTAL SEARCH commands listed it Figure 10-3. This is convenient if you have trouble typing and you make lots of mistakes. If so, it is a bother to have Emacs jump all over the place like a one-legged tap dancer as you fix your mistakes, one character at a time.

Command	Description
C-s RET	Forward: non-incremental search
C-r RET	Backward: non-incremental search

FIGURE 10-3. **Non-incremental search commands.**

To start a non-incremental search, simply press **RET** (<Enter>) before you start typing the search pattern. Thus, to perform a forward non-incremental search, type **C-s RET** and then type the pattern. When you are finished typing, press **RET** once again to start the search. To abort the search, press **C-g**. Similarly, you can request a non-incremental backward search by typing **C-r RET**. For reference, these commands are shown in Figure 10-3.

Section 10.6: Word Searching

A WORD SEARCH tells Emacs to search only for complete words. To use a forward word search, type **M-s w**. To use a backward word search, type **M-s w C-r**. You can now type the words you want to search for. When you are ready, press **RET** to begin searching. (The word search is actually a variation of the incremental search.)

Command	Description
M-s w	Forward: Incremental word search
M-s w C-r	Backward: Incremental word search

FIGURE 10-4. **Search commands.**

The great thing about a word search is that it ignores all punctuation, spaces, tabs and end of lines. Thus, you can look for a series of words that, for example, span more than one line. Here is an example.

You are using Emacs to read the text of Isaac Asimov's final autobiography. Within the text, you find the following passage:

```
My turn will come too, eventually, but I have
had a good life and I have accomplished all I
wanted to, and more than I had a right to expect.

So I am ready.

But not too ready.
```

Some time later, you want to find this passage again, but all you can remember are the last two lines. So you press **M-s w** to start a word search. You then type **ready but not** and press **RET** again. Emacs finds the text, even though these particular words are separated by punctuation (a period) and are broken over two lines.

Section 10.7: Searching for Regular Expressions

A REGULAR EXPRESSION or REGEXP is a compact way of specifying a general pattern of characters. Emacs has special commands that allow you to search for a regular expression. These commands are shown in Figure 10-5. As you can see, the term "regular expression" is sometimes abbreviated to "regexp". This abbreviation is worth memorizing, as you will see it a lot.

Command	Description
M-C-s	Forward: Incremental search for regexp
M-C-s RET	Forward: Non-incremental search for regexp

Command	Description
M-C-r	Backward: Incremental search for regexp
M-C-r RET	Backward: Non-incremental search for regexp

FIGURE 10-5. **Search commands for regular expressions.**

Note   If you have a problem using the key sequence **M-C-s**, you can use **ESC C-s** instead.

Notice that these commands use an **M-C** combination. This means that you must hold down both the Meta and Ctrl keys while you press the other key (either **s** or **r**). For example, to search forward for a regular expression you use **M-C-s**. To do so, you press <Meta-Ctrl-S>, which is actually <Alt-Ctrl-S>. Alternatively, instead of holding down the Meta key, you can press **ESC** (see Section 4.3). So, to search forward for a regular expression, you use **M-C-s** by typing either of the following:

```
<Alt-Ctrl-S>
<Esc> <Ctrl-S>
```

The same goes for **M-C-r**. To search backward for a regular expression, you can type either of the following:

```
<Alt-Ctrl-R>
<Esc> <Ctrl-R>
```

Note

Stop for a moment and think about what you have just read. Notice that, when you read **M-C-s**, you just know, without thinking that you must press <Alt-Ctrl-S> or type <Esc> <Ctrl-R>.

If you are an experienced Unix user and you've gotten this far, it's too late to go back to **vi**. Your brain has already changed permanently. So stick it out and read the rest of the book.

If you are using Emacs within a terminal window, you may run into trouble with **M-C-s**, because the key combination <Alt-Ctrl-S> has a special meaning with certain GUIs. If you have a problem using **M-C-s**, you can avoid it by using **ESC C-s** instead. (Isn't it nice that Emacs is so flexible?) Alternatively, if you want to fix the problem permanently, see the instructions in Section 10.9.

Section 10.8: Regular Expressions

Regular expressions allow you to expand your search capabilities enormously. For example, using the ordinary search commands, you can tell Emacs to look for an occurrence of the pattern **Harley**. But with regular expressions you could, for example, tell Emacs to search for the pattern **Harley** at the beginning of a line, or a line that consists only of the word **Harley**, or any word that starts with **Har** and ends with **y**.

Regular expressions are widely used — far beyond the world of Emacs — and understanding how they work is a *very* important skill, especially if you are a programmer. In this section, I will give you a summary of the special characters that Emacs uses for regular expressions, along with a few examples. However, if this topic is new to you, I encourage you to take time, away from Emacs, to learn all about regular expressions and how to use them well. (I cover this topic in detail in my book *Harley Hahn's Guide to Unix and Linux.*[1])

Figure 10-6 summarizes the basic characters you can use to create a regular expression with Emacs. If you already understand regular expressions, these characters will make sense to you, although you may see a few new ones.

Character	Description
Char	Any regular character matches itself
.	Match any single character except **RET**
*	Match zero or more of the preceding characters
+	Match one or more of the preceding characters
?	Match exactly zero or one of the preceding characters
^	Match the beginning of a line
$	Match the end of a line
\<	Match the beginning of a word
\>	Match the end of a word
\b	Match the beginning or end of a word
\B	Match anywhere not at the beginning or end of a word
\`	Match the beginning of the buffer
\'	Match the end of the buffer
\char	Quotes a special character
[ ]	Match one of the enclosed characters
[^]	Match any character that is not enclosed

FIGURE 10-6. Characters to use with regular expressions.

---

[1] *Harley Hahn's Guide to Unix and Linux*, McGraw-Hill Higher Education, 2008. The ISBN is 0073133612.

Here is an example of a search involving a regular expression. To search for the characters **Harley** at the beginning of a line, press **M-C-s**, then type **^Harley**. If you prefer, you can make the search non-incremental by pressing **RET** (the Enter key) before you type the regular expression. To search backward, you can use either **M-C-r** or **M-C-r RET**.

Here are a few more examples. To search for a line that consists entirely of the word **Harley**, use:

^Harley$

To search for a word that begins with **Har**, use:

\<Har

To search for a pattern that starts with **h** or **H**, and is followed by at least one **a**, use:

[hH]a+

You can use a range of characters within square brackets, for example:

[0-9] all numerals
[a-z] lowercase letters
[A-Z] uppercase letters
[a-zA-Z] all letters (uppercase and lowercase)

For instance, to search for a complete word that consists of a single letter, either upper- or lowercase, possibly followed by a single digit, use:

\<[a-zA-Z][0-9]?\>

This regular expression will match words like:

a0   a   A0   A   B5   z8   Z

If you want to search for a character that has a special meaning, you must put a \ (backslash) in front of it. For example, to search for a dollar sign followed by one or more digits, use:

\$[0-9]+

Note

When you specify all lowercase letters, Emacs does a case insensitive search. However, if you use at least one uppercase letter, the search becomes case sensitive. Examples:

The regular expression **[har]** searches for **h**, **H**, **a**, **A**, **r** or **R**.
The regular expression **[Har]** searches only for **H**, **a** or **r**.

Section 10.9: Fixing Emacs Key Conflicts

When you run Emacs within a terminal window under your GUI, you may, from time to time, run into trouble with an Emacs key combination if it has a special meaning to that particular GUI.

We saw such an example in Section 10.7. Within Unity, the default GUI used with Ubuntu Linux (see Section 2.5), <Alt-Ctrl-S> has a special meaning. However, this is the combination you need to type M-C-s, the Emacs command to search for a regular expression. One alternative is to use ESC instead of the Meta key. For example, instead of using M-C-s, you can type ESC C-s. However, you may want to fix the problem permanently.

In this section, I will show you how to do so with Unity. If you encounter a similar problem with a different Emacs key sequence, the instructions you are about to read may give you an idea how to solve it.

When you run Emacs within a terminal window under Unity, you may find that, when you press <Alt-Ctrl-S>, instead of starting a regex search, it causes your terminal window to "roll up" and disappear. This is called a "shaded state". (Think of an actual window shade that, when you pull a cord, rolls up out of the way.) To fix the problem, all you have to do is tell Unity to change the meaning of this particular key combination. Here is how to do it.

1. Open the Dash (see Section 2.6) and search for "System Settings".

2. Open "System Settings".

3. Under Hardware, open Keyboard.

4. Click the Shortcuts tab.

5. In the left-hand column, look for the category that is likely to contain the key you want to change. In our example, click Windows, because <Alt-Ctrl-S> is changing your terminal window.

6. In the right-hand column, click the offending key function. In our example, it is "Toggle Shaded State", because that is what is matched to <Alt-Ctrl-S>.

7. When you click on the key function, the key name will change to:

```
New accelerator...
```

The program is asking you to specify which key combination you want to use for an accelerator key (shortcut key) for the function "Toggle shaded state".

8. You have two choices. To disable the shortcut key completely, press <Backspace>. To specify a different key combination, simply press it.

9. Close the Keyboard window.

Now, when you return to Emacs, M-C-s will work properly and start a regular expression search.

Section 10.10: Searching and Replacing

There are several commands you can use to search for a particular pattern and then replace it once it is found. For example, say you have written a long memo to your boss in which you have used the word "jerk" several times. As you read the document a second time, it occurs to you that an overly sensitive person might take offense, so you decide to change every occurrence of **jerk** to **goofball**.

To do so, you can use one of the search and replace commands. You tell Emacs what to search for and what to use as a replacement. Emacs will start from point (the current position within the buffer) and search forward for occurrences of the search pattern. Each time it finds your search string, Emacs can make the replacement.

Note   A search and replacement operation starts from point and continues to the end of the buffer. Thus, if you want to process the entire buffer, you must jump to the beginning before you start (use the **M-<** command).

With some of the search and replace commands, Emacs will ask you for your approval, each time, before it makes a change. With other commands, Emacs makes all the changes automatically.

Figure 10-7 summarizes the Emacs search and replace commands. Notice that, of the four commands, two have a key sequence (**M-%** and **M-C-%**). The other two commands must be executed explicitly using **M-x**. However, as you will see in a moment, you can use completion (see Section 6.7), so typing these long names is actually pretty easy.

Command	Description
M-%	Query: Search and replace
M-C-%	Query: Search and replace (regexp)
M-x replace-string	No query: Search and replace
M-x replace-regexp	No query: Search and replace (regexp)

FIGURE 10-7. **Search and replace commands.**

The basic search and replace command is **M-%**. On most keyboards, the **%** (percent) character is <Shift-5>, so to use **M-%** you type <Alt-Shift-5>.

After you type **M-%**, Emacs will prompt you to type the search string, that is, the pattern for which you are searching. You will see the following message in the minibuffer:

Query replace:

Don't be confused. Emacs is not asking for the replacement string. It is simply reminding you that you are using the "Query replace" command. Type your search string and press **RET**. In our example, you would type **jerk** and press <Enter>. Emacs will then prompt you for the replacement characters. You will see:

Query replace jerk with:

Type the replacement and press **RET**. In our example, you would type **goofball** and press <Enter>.

Note

Emacs is designed to save you typing effort whenever possible. Here is a good example.

The first time in a work session that you use search and replace, Emacs asks you to type your search string and your replace string. The next time you use search and replace, Emacs will suggest the same two strings. For example, if you have already used **jerk** and **goofball**, the next time you type **M-%**, Emacs will display:

Query replace (default jerk -> goofball):

If you want to repeat the same operation, press **RET**. If you want to make changes, simply type a new search string and press **RET**.

Once you specify your search and replace strings, Emacs jumps to the first occurrence of the search string and asks you what to do. In our example, you would see:

Query replacing jerk with goofball: (? for help)

At this point, you have several choices, which are described in Figure 10-8. Notice that you can press **?** to display a help summary.

Command	Description
?	Display help summary
y	(yes) Replace
n	(no) Do not replace
q	Quit immediately
SPC	Same as y
BS	Same as n
RET	Same as q
!	Replace all remaining matches, no questions
.	(period) Replace current match and then quit
,	(comma) Replace but stay at current position
^	(circumflex) Move back to previous match
C-l	Clear screen, redisplay, and ask again
C-r	Start recursive editing (use M-C-c to return)
C-w	Delete matching pattern, start recursive edit

FIGURE 10-8. **Responses during a search and replace command.**

Most of the time, you will need only four of these responses:

- SPC (<Space>) to make a replacement and continue.

- BS (<Backspace>) to skip a replacement and continue.

- ! (exclamation mark) to make all the rest of the replacements automatically with no more questions.

- RET (<Enter>) to quit immediately

The rest of the commands (except for C-r and C-w) are straightforward and, with a little practice, you should have no trouble. The C-r and C-w commands are used for "recursive editing", which we will discuss in Section 10.11.

Please take another look at Figure 10-7. You will notice there are two other search and replace commands. These are the "no-query" commands:

M-x replace-string makes all the replacements automatically without asking you any questions. This is similar to using M-% and then pressing the ! (exclamation mark) character at the first match. The M-x replace-string is handy when you know you want to make all the replacements, and there is no point in stopping at each one to confirm your intentions.

M-x replace-regexp makes all the replacements automatically, while allowing you to use a regular expression for the search pattern.

You will have noticed that the M-% and M-C-% key sequences are short and easy to type. The no-query commands are not used as much, so they don't have their own key sequences: you need to use M-x and specify the command name explicitly. However, you don't actually have to type the entire command name. You can use completion, which we discussed in Section 6.7. (If you have not read about completion, take a moment and do so now: it is an especially handy tool. Briefly, you type part of what you want, and Emacs helps you complete the rest.)

As a reference, Figure 10-9 shows the command names for the four search and replace commands, along with the minimum number of keystrokes you need to type the command with completion. Notice, that I have described two possible key combinations for M-x query-replace-regexp. I did this so you could learn a bit more about completion. Take a moment to try both combinations, and see which type you prefer.

Key Sequence	Command	Keystrokes to Use
M-%	M-x query-replace	M-x que RET
M-C-%	M-x query-replace-regexp	M-x que TAB SPC RET
M-C-%	M-x query-replace-regexp	M-x que SPC SPC SPC RET
-none-	M-x replace-string	M-x repl SPC s RET
-none-	M-x replace-regexp	M-x repl SPC reg RET

FIGURE 10-9. **Minimum keystrokes to invoke search and replace commands.**

Section 10.11: Recursive Editing

The last search-related concept I want to discuss is RECURSIVE EDITING. This allows you to put a search and replace operation on hold temporarily, while you perform some editing. When you are finished, you can return to the search and replace that is already in progress.

Here is how you might use this facility. Let's say you are in the middle of a long search and replace operation, and you happen to notice a different change you want to make. At such times, it can be inconvenient to stop what you are doing just to make a single change. However, if you wait until your search and replace operation is finished, you may forget what it was you wanted to change.

Instead, you can press C-r. This pauses the search and replace, and puts you back into a recursive editing environment. You can now make any changes you want. When you are finished, press M-C-c <Alt-Ctrl-C>. This will stop recursive editing and return you to the search and replace operation, exactly where you left off.

Whenever you press C-r, Emacs will put square brackets, [and] , around the name of the mode on your mode line (see Section 6.4 for a discussion of the mode line). The square brackets are a reminder that you are working in a recursive editing environment.

For example, say if you are editing a buffer named **document**. Your mode line looks like the top line in Figure 10-10. You then type **C-r** to start recursive editing, your mode line now looks like the bottom line in Figure 10-10. When you press **M-C-c** to quit recursive editing, the square brackets will disappear.

```
-UUU:**--F1   document       31% L38    (Text) -------------------------------

-UUU:**--F1   document       31% L38    [(Text)] -----------------------------
```

FIGURE 10-10. Mode lines showing a change to recursive editing.
The top mode line shows a buffer named **document** *that is being edited in Text mode (see Section 8.3). The bottom line has square brackets around the name of the mode indicating that you are now in a recursive editing environment.*

Another way to start recursive editing during a search and replace operation (aside from **C-r**) is by pressing **C-w**. This will delete the current matching pattern and then start recursive editing.

Using **C-w** is handy when you want to replace the matching pattern with something that is not your specified replacement. You can delete the match, enter recursive editing, insert the replacement by hand, and then go back to where you were.

For example, say that you are in the middle of changing all the occurrences of **jerk** to **goofball**. You happen upon a particular occurrence of **jerk** that you think should really be **nice guy**. Press **C-w**. This will erase the word **jerk** and place you in recursive editing. Type **nice guy**. Then press **M-C-c** to return to the search and replace operation.

Note

While you are in recursive editing, it is possible to start another search and replace operation. While it is active, if you type **C-r** or **C-w** you will enter a second level of recursive editing. When this happens, you will see double square brackets around the mode name.

If you do the whole thing again, you will be in yet another level of recursive editing, and you will see triple square brackets around the mode name. You can see this in Figure 10-11.

In fact, you can go as deep as you want. Eventually, of course, you will have to press **M-C-c** enough times to work your way back out to the top level.

```
-UUU:**--F1   document       31% L38    [[[(Text)]]] ------------------------
```

FIGURE 10-11. Mode line showing triple-level recursive editing.
While you are in recursive editing, it is possible to start another search and replace, and put that operation into recursive editing. You can do this as many times as you want. The mode line will show you one set of square brackets for each level of recursive editing. In this case, there are three levels. To work your way back out to the top, press **M-C-c** *once for each level.*

CHAPTER 11

■ ■ ■

Modes; Customizing Using Your .emacs File

Section 11.1: Introducing Modes

Emacs was designed to be flexible, especially when you become an advanced user or if you are a programmer. The designers of Emacs realized that your needs will vary depending on what you are doing. For example, if you are writing English prose, you will be typing and editing in a different manner than if you are, say, debugging a computer program. One of the ways in which Emacs helps you is by acting slightly differently depending on what you are trying to do. For example, when you are typing a computer program, you will want to indent your lines differently than when you are composing an essay.

For this reason, Emacs uses what are called "major modes" and "minor modes" to enable you to modify your working environment. Major modes are used to edit particular types of text. For example, there are separate major modes for editing plain text (such as English, HTML, TeX, LaTeX, and outlines), and for writing programs (with Lisp, SQL, Java, JavaScript, C, C++, Ruby, Python, and so on). You use only one major mode at a time, whichever is the most appropriate for the work at hand.

Minor modes provide a variety of different features that you can turn on and off to suit your needs. You can use as many minor modes as you need.

All modes, major and minor, have names that end with **-mode**, for example, **text-mode** and **emacs-lisp-mode**. Each mode is defined by an Emacs Lisp function that has the name of the mode with the file extension **.el**, for example, **text-mode.el** and **emacs-lisp-mode.el**. (The file extension **.el** stands for "Emacs Lisp".) Once you learn how to understand modes and how to write Lisp programs, you will be able to read some such files to see exactly what they are doing. You may even choose to copy and modify some of them to create your own customized modes.

Emacs modes can be complicated, but they are important, so we are going to take some time to talk about the details. In fact, it won't be until Section 11.5 that I will actually show you how to use the commands you need to use individual modes. Until then, all I want you to do is read, think and learn. The foundation you are about to build is important.

© Harley Hahn 2016
H. Hahn, *Harley Hahn's Emacs Field Guide*, DOI 10.1007/978-1-4842-1703-0_11

Section 11.2: Major Modes

Each buffer uses one major mode, which you can change as the need arises. The MAJOR MODE affects the behavior of Emacs as you work within that buffer. For example, certain key sequences may be redefined in a way that is appropriate for the type of work you are doing. The name of the major mode is displayed in parentheses on the mode line (see Section 6.4) near the bottom of the window. You can see an example in Figure 11-1. In this example, the name of the buffer is **starting-with-emacs**, and its major mode is Fundamental mode.

```
-UU-:----F1  starting-with-emacs    All L15   (Fundamental) -------------------
```

FIGURE 11-1. Typical mode line showing the name of major mode.
In this example, the buffer is named **starting-with-emacs**, *and the buffer is in Fundamental mode.*

If you find that there is a particular major mode you use a lot of the time, you can customize your working environment so that, by default, Emacs automatically starts in that major mode (see Section 11.9). For example, if you are writing a lot of notes, you might set your default major mode to **text-mode**. If you spend most of your time working with Lisp programs, you might make **emacs-lisp-mode** your default mode.

Emacs has a great many major modes. However, almost all of them are based, directly or indirectly, on one of the four basic major modes that you see in Figure 11-2. A PARENT MODE is a mode from which other modes are created. We say that such modes are DERIVED from the parent mode. In this way, the four basic Emacs major modes are the parents (or grandparents) of almost all the other major modes.

	Name	Type of Data to Edit
Fundamental Mode	**fundamental-mode**	Anything Emacs doesn't know about
Prog Mode	**prog-mode**	Programming source code
Text Mode	**text-mode**	Human-readable text
Special Mode	**special-mode**	Special text created by Emacs

FIGURE 11-2. The Four Basic Major Modes.
Almost all the major modes are derived, directly or indirectly, from one of these four basic modes.

FUNDAMENTAL MODE is the least specialized major mode. In Fundamental mode, every Emacs command behaves in its most general manner: there are no mode-specific definitions or variable settings, and all user options are in their default state. As such, Fundamental mode is the best one to use when you are learning, or if you aren't sure what mode to use.

When Emacs loads a file into a buffer, if the file name has an extension, Emacs will set the appropriate major mode for that type of data, whenever possible. For example, if you load the file **notes.txt**, Emacs will set the major mode for that buffer to **text-mode**. If you load the file **calculate.el**, Emacs will set the major mode to **emacs-lisp-mode**. If Emacs can't figure out what type of file you are loading, it will use **fundamental-mode** as a default. This is really the main use for Fundamental mode. It is not intended to be used as a parent mode, although in a few cases, it has been customized to create other modes.

PROG MODE is for working with programming language source code. (As we discussed in Section 1.3, source code refers to instructions written in a human-readable programming language.) However, Prog mode itself is rarely used. Instead, it is the parent mode from which many specific programming major modes are derived. For example, **emacs-lisp-mode**, which is used to write Emacs Lisp programs, is derived from **prog-mode**.

TEXT MODE is used for working with human languages (as opposed to programming languages). For example, you would use Text mode for editing text in English or other languages. As such, Text mode is often used for basic editing. It is also the parent mode of other major modes designed to work with marked-up text. For example, **tex-mode**, which is used to edit TeX files, is derived from **text-mode**. And **html-mode**, which is used to edit HTML (Web page) files, is derived from **sgml-mode**, which is derived from **text-mode**.

SPECIAL MODE is the parent of major modes that are used for buffers displaying text that Emacs itself generates. For example, when Emacs creates a buffer to display a Buffer List, or Help information, or a Completion List, it uses a major mode derived from **special-mode**. Normally, you would never use Special mode yourself: it is used only by Emacs programs that need to create a buffer in which to display information.

Section 11.3: Lists of Major Modes

For reference, this section contains tables showing the most useful and popular Emacs major modes, organized into families based on their parent mode. If you want, you can think of these tables as the family trees for Emacs major modes.

You do not have to understand, or even know about, all the major modes. Read through the lists and see if any major modes relate to your work or your interests. When you gain more experience, you can come back to this section and look for an appropriate major mode for whatever you are working on at the time.

I'll show you how to set the major mode you want to use in Section 11.5, and how to learn more about a specific mode in Section 11.7. For now, just take a moment to introduce yourself to the various major modes and see how they are used in Figures 11-3 to 11-7.

Fundamental Family	Type of Data to Edit
fundamental-mode	Parent mode: General data, not specialized
array-mode	2-dimensional arrays
css-mode	CSS files (Cascading Style Sheets)
edit-abbrevs-mode	Abbreviation definitions
gud-mode	Using debuggers: **gdb, sbd, dbx, xdb**...

FIGURE 11-3. **Major Modes: Fundamental Mode Family.**

The major modes in this list are derived from Fundamental mode.

Text Family	Type of Data to Edit
text-mode	Parent mode: human-readable text
bibtex-mode	BibTeX files
change-log-mode	Change logs
html-mode	HTML files
indented-text-mode	Text with indented paragraphs
latex-mode	LaTeX-formatted files
mail-mode	Outgoing email messages
nroffmode	**nroff**- and **troff**-formatted text files
nxml-mode	XML files
org-mode	Outlines for "keeping track of everything"
outline-mode	Outlines with selective display
paragraph-indent-text-mode	Text: leading spaces start paragraphs
plain-tex-mode	TeX-formatted files
rmail-mode	Reading email
sgml-mode	SGML files
slitex-mode	SliTeX-formatted files
tex-mode	TeX-, LaTeX- or SliTeX-formatted files
texinfo-mode	TeXinfo files

FIGURE 11-4. **Major Modes: Text Mode Family.**

The major modes in this list are derived, directly or indirectly, from Text mode. These modes are used to edit human-readable text (English and other languages), as well as marked-up text (HTML, TeX, and so on).

Prog Family	Type of Data to Edit
prog-mode	Parent mode: Programming source code
ada-mode	Ada programs
antlr-mode	ANTLR grammar files (parsers, etc)
asm-mode	Assembly language programs
awk-mode	**awk** scripts
bat-mode	DOS/Windows batch files
c++-mode	C++ programs
c-mode	C programs
cperl-mode	Perl scripts (alternative to **perl-mode**)
emacs-lisp-mode	**emacs** Lisp programs
f90-mode	Fortran 90/95 programs
fortran-mode	Fortran programs
java-mode	Java programs
javascript-mode	JavaScript programs
lisp-interaction-mode	Evaluating Emacs Lisp forms
lisp-mode	Non-**emacs** lisp programs
m4-mode	M4 macros
makefile-mode	Makefiles
modula-2-mode	Modula-2 programs
opascal-mode	Object Pascal programs
pascal-mode	Pascal programs
perl-mode	Perl scripts
prolog-mode	Prolog programs
ps-mode	Postscript files
scheme-mode	Scheme programs (dialect of Lisp)
sieve-mode	Sieve (email filtering) scripts
simula-mode	Simula programs
sh-mode	Shell scripts
sql-mode	SQL programs
tcl-mode	tcl scripts

FIGURE 11-5. **Major Modes: Prog Mode Family.**

The major modes in this list are derived, directly or indirectly, from Prog mode. These modes are used to edit computer programs.

Special Family	Used for...
`special-mode`	Parent mode: built-in Emacs services
`help-mode`	Emacs Help system
`messages-buffer-mode`	Display messages in ***Messages*** buffer
`tar-mode`	Looking inside a **tar** file
`todo-mode`	Managing todo lists

FIGURE 11-6. Major Modes: Special Mode Family.

The major modes in this list are derived from Special mode. As a general rule, these modes are used by Emacs when it needs to display information, for example, `help-mode`*. However, some of these modes are also used by tools, such as* `tar-mode` *and* `todo-mode`*.*

Independent Modes	Type of Data to Edit
`conf-mode`	Configuration files
`completion-list-mode`	Display a list of possible completions
`dired-mode`	Dired directory/file tool
`doc-view-mode`	Documents: MS Office, OpenDocument, PDF, PS
`forms-mode`	Field-structured data using a form
`hexl-mode`	Hexadecimal data, ASCII data
`Info-mode`	Emacs Info system
`normal-mode`	Reset major mode to the default for this file
`picture-mode`	Text-based drawings
`ses-mode`	Simple Emacs Spreadsheet files

FIGURE 11-7. Independent Major Modes.

The major modes in this list are not derived from another major mode. Instead, they are independent tools, written to stand alone.

Section 11.4: Minor Modes

Emacs has a large number of optional features you can turn on or off that affect your work with the current buffer. These features are called MINOR MODES. Although you can set only one major mode at a time, you can turn on as many minor modes as you want.

I'll show you how to turn on the minor modes you want to use in Section 11.5, and how to learn more about a specific mode in Section 11.7. For now, just take a moment to look at the various minor modes and see what they can do for you in Figure 11-8.

Minor Mode	Description
`abbrev-mode`	Working with abbreviations
`auto-fill-mode`	Automatic filling
`auto-save-mode`	Automatic saving
`binary-overwrite-mode`	Binary overwriting
`compilation-minor-mode`	Compiling programs
`cua-mode`	Use Ctrl-X/C/V for cut/copy/paste
`delete-selection-mode`	Typed text replaces selection
`display-time-mode`	Mode line shows: time, load level, mail flag
`double-mode`	Some keys differ if pressed twice
`eldoc-mode`	Display info about Lisp function/variable
`flyspell-mode`	Highlight spelling mistakes in regular text
`flyspell-prop-mode`	Highlight spelling mistakes in programs
`font-lock-mode`	Text is fontified as you type
`hide-ifdef-mode`	Hides certain C code within `#ifdef`
`indent-according-to-mode`	Indent appropriately for major mode
`iso-accents-mode`	Display ISO accents
`ledit-mode`	Editing text to be sent to Lisp
`line-number-mode`	Mode line shows: line numbers
`outline-minor-mode`	Work with outlines
`overwrite-mode`	Overwrite/insert text
`paragraph-indent-minor-mode`	Text: leading spaces start paragraphs
`pending-delete-mode`	Same as `delete-selection-mode`
`read-only-mode`	Buffer contents cannot be changed
`resize-minibuffer-mode`	Dynamically resize minibuffer
`ruler-mode`	Header line shows: ruler
`show-paren-mode`	Highlight matching parentheses, brackets
`size-indication-mode`	Mode line shows: size of buffer
`timeclock-mode-line-display`	Track time intervals you spend working
`toggle-read-only`	Buffer contents cannot be changed
`toggle-viper-mode`	Turn **viper-mode** off and on
`tool-bar-mode`	Toggle: Display help on tool bar or mode line
`tooltip-mode`	Display Emacs toolbar
`transient-mark-mode`	Highlight region when defined
`view-mode`	Page through a file (similar to **less** pager)
`viper-mode`	Turn on (not off) emulation of **vi** text editor
`whitespace-mode`	Show all whitespace: **SPC**, **TAB**, **RET** chars
`whitespace-newline-mode`	Show **RET** characters

FIGURE 11-8. Minor modes.

As you can see from Figure 11-8, there are a great many minor modes. In fact, there are a lot more. I have shown you the ones that I think are the most useful or interesting. Choosing minor modes can be confusing at first, so to get you started, here are several minor modes that you will find particularly useful:

- `auto-fill-mode`: Sets automatic filling. As you type, automatically breaks lines, so you don't have to press the Enter key at the end of each line.

- `line-number-mode`: As you move the cursor, displays the number of the current line on the mode line.

- `overwrite-mode`: As you type, characters replace the existing text. Normally, characters are inserted.

- `read-only-mode`: The contents of the current buffer cannot be changed.

- `show-paren-mode`: When point is on one of a pair of characters — parentheses, brackets, and so on — the matching character is highlighted (very cool!).

Section 11.5: Setting Major and Minor Modes

To set a major or minor mode, type the `M-x` command (see Section 6.1) followed by the name of the mode. For example, to set the major mode to Text mode, use the command `M-x text-mode`. To set the minor mode to Overwrite mode, use `M-x overwrite-mode`. Since mode names can be long, you will want to be skillful at using completion (see Section 6.7), so Emacs will do most of the typing for you. For example, to set Overwrite mode, you need only type `M-x ov RET` (`M-x ov <Enter>`). Take a moment and try it.

■ **Note**   When you are not sure which major mode to use, use Fundamental mode.

Most of the minor modes act as on/off switches (sometimes called TOGGLES). So if Overwrite mode is off, you can turn it on by using the command `M-x overwrite-mode`. When you want to turn it off, simply use `M-x overwrite-mode` again.

Every buffer must have only one major mode, but you can use as many minor modes as you want. If you want to work with more than one type of text at the same time, all you need to do is create more than one buffer, each with its own major mode and assortment of minor modes.

To see which major mode you are using in a buffer, simply look at the mode line, the line near the bottom of the window (see Section 6.4). Emacs displays the name of the major mode, as well as some (but not all) of the minor modes. If a mode name is long, you will see an abbreviation.

Look at the example in Figure 11-9. The buffer contains **.emacs**, the Emacs initialization file (see Section 11.8). The major mode is Emacs-Lisp mode (**emacs-lisp-mode**), because the buffer contains Lisp code. There is at least one minor mode, **overwrite-mode**, which is abbreviated as **Ovwrt**. This minor mode has just been turned on, which is why you see the transient message **Overwrite mode enabled** in the echo area below the mode line. (We discuss the echo area in Section 6.5.)

```
-UU-:----F1  .emacs          All L8    (Emacs-Lisp Ovwrt) ---------------------
Overwrite mode enabled
```

FIGURE 11-9. Mode line showing the major mode as well as one minor mode.

In this example, the buffer is named **.emacs**. *The major mode is* **emacs-lisp-mode**. *In addition, there is a minor mode* **overwrite-mode**, *which is abbreviated as* **Ovwrt**.

Section 11.6: Read-Only Mode

For practice, here is an example of how to turn on a particularly useful minor mode.

On occasion, you may wish to protect a buffer so that you cannot change its contents accidentally. For example, you may want to use Emacs to read an important file that should not be modified. Or you may have typed some information that, for the time being, you want to remain completely untouched.

To protect such data, you can set Read-only mode. The command is:

M-x read-only-mode

Once read-only mode is enabled, Emacs will let you look at the contents of a buffer, but not make any changes. If you try to make a change (say, by typing something), Emacs will display a warning message:

Buffer is read-only

To turn off read-only mode, just enter the same command again. Remember, most minor modes act as toggles: off/on switches.

In Section 5.3, I showed you how to start Emacs in Read-only mode by using the command:

emacs *file* **-f read-only-mode**

If you start Emacs in this way, you can turn off Read-only mode by using the same command:

M-x read-only-mode

As a shortcut, you can also use the key sequence **C-x C-q**, which is bound to **read-only-mode** (see Section 6.4).

181

■ **Note** Setting Read-only mode within Emacs has nothing to do with Unix read-only file permissions. The Emacs Read-only mode only affects Emacs buffers.

Section 11.7: Learning About Modes

As a reference, Figure 11-10 contains a summary of commands you can use to set modes and to display descriptive information about modes. Notice that all the description commands begin with **C-h**. This is because they are part of the Emacs Help facility, which we will discuss in Section 12.3.

Command	Description
M-x *mode-name* **RET**	Set the specified major or minor mode
C-h v major-mode RET	Display information about current major mode
C-h m	Describe current major and minor modes
C-h f *mode-name* **RET**	Describe the specified mode
C-h f *-mode RET	Display names of all modes
C-h a mode	Display summary of all modes

FIGURE 11-10. **Commands to set and describe modes.**

At all times, the name of the current major mode for a buffer is stored in a variable named **major-mode**. To see information about the current value of this variable, use the Help command **C-h v**, which displays information about a specific variable:

```
C-h v major-mode RET
```

The Help facility will display information about the **major-mode** variable. Near the top will be its value, which will show you the current major mode for the buffer in which you are working.

You can also use the Help facility to describe the current major and minor modes for the buffer in which you are working. The command is:

```
C-h m
```

When you use this command you will be surprised. Of course, you will have one major mode enabled, and Emacs will show you what it is. However, you will also find that you have a number of minor modes turned on, most of which will be unknown to you. For example, while I was editing my `.emacs` file (see the example in Figure 11-9, in Section 11.5), I used the **C-h m** command. Of course, I saw that the major mode was Emacs-Lisp mode, because I was editing an Emacs Lisp file. However, I also found out that there were 14 minor modes enabled! They were:

```
Auto-Composition
Auto-Compression
Auto-Encryption
Blink-Cursor
Electric-Indent
File-Name-Shadow
Font-Lock
Global-Font-Lock
Line-Number
Menu-Bar
Mouse-Wheel
Tool-Bar
Tooltip
Transient-Mark
```

Try **C-h m** for yourself, and see what you get.

As I mentioned in Section 11.1, all modes are implemented as Emacs Lisp functions. The Help command **C-h f** displays information about a function, so you can use this command to display information about a specific mode. Just type **C-h f** followed by the name of the mode, which is also the name of the Lisp function. For example, to display information about Text mode (a major mode):

C-h f text-mode RET

To display information about Auto Fill mode (a minor mode):

C-h f auto-fill-mode RET

Take another look at the example above where I showed you all the minor modes that were enabled when I was editing my `.emacs` file. Suppose you were curious to find out about one of these modes, say, Transient-Mark mode. You can guess that the name of the mode is **transient-mark-mode**, so all you have to do is use the command:

C-h f transient-mark-mode RET

■ **Note**

Help information is easier to read if you maximize the Help window. To do so, move the cursor to the Help window (**C-x o**), and then delete all the other windows (**C-x 1**):

```
C-x o C-x 1
```

The first key sequence uses a lowercase letter "o"; the second uses the number "1".

I will remind you that **C-x 1** deletes all the other windows, but it does *not* delete any buffers, so don't worry about losing data. (All of this, including the commands I just used, is explained in Section 7.6.) Once you are finished reading the Help information, you can recall your previous buffer by using **C-x b** (see Section 7.7).

Here is an example you can use for practice:

```
C-h f transient-mark-mode RET
C-x o C-x 1
```

There are two ways to display a list of all the major and minor modes. To display a summary of all the modes, use:

```
C-h a mode
C-x o C-x 1
```

The **C-h a** command displays information about all the Emacs functions that contain a specific word. (The letter "a" stands for "apropos".) By typing **C-h a mode**, you are asking the Help facility to describe all the functions that contain the word **mode**. The key sequence **C-x o C-x 1** expands the window so it is easier to read.

When you use **C-h a mode,** Emacs will display the name of each mode followed by a one-line description. If you want more information about a specific mode, you can use **C-h f** as I described above.

The second way to look at a list of all the modes is to display only the names. To do so, use **C-h f** with a regular expression that matches all function names ending with **-mode**. (For a discussion of how Emacs uses regular expressions, see Section 10.8.) The command to use is:

```
C-h f *-mode RET
```

Emacs will display a long Completion list (see Section 6.7) containing all the names.

Once the list appears, the focus will still be in the minibuffer, because Emacs is waiting for you to type something. However, if you press **M-v**, the command to move up one screenful within a buffer (see Section 8.3), it will have the side effect of moving the focus to the buffer containing the Completion list. You can then expand the window by using **C-x 1**. This makes it easy to move through the list. The entire sequence looks like this:

```
C-h f *-mode RET
M-v
C-x 1
```

I know it looks complicated, but it makes sense and it works. Try it for yourself.

Section 11.8: Customizing With the .emacs File; Learning Lisp

Each time Emacs starts, it looks for a file named `.emacs` in your home directory. If the file exists, Emacs will read it and execute all the commands it contains as part of the initialization process. By placing commands in your `.emacs` file, you can customize just about any facet of your working environment, even to the point of eccentricity. (As we discussed in Section 2.18, files like `.emacs` — whose names begin with a period — are called dotfiles. The name `.emacs` is pronounced "dot-Emacs".)

In Section 11.9, I will introduce you to using your `.emacs` file by showing you an example of how you might customize your working environment. To prepare the way, I need to get a little technical, so don't worry if you don't understand everything right away.

As we discussed in Section 1.4, most of Emacs is written in a computer language called LISP, or more precisely, EMACS LISP. (The name stands for "List Processor".) This means that all the commands in your `.emacs` file must be written in Lisp, which can be daunting for a beginner, because Lisp programs look like nothing on Earth. It is not my intention to explain how to program in Lisp: that would be a book in itself. Rather, I will discuss some of the more important customizations you might make and show you a selection of sample commands to place in your `.emacs` file.

Note

It is worth your while to learn Lisp for two reasons. First, it will make it possible for you to read Emacs documentation and technical discussions, which often require you to be able to read basic Lisp.

Second, Lisp is fun. It is the second oldest programming language still in widespread use[1] and, once you become comfortable with the Lisp way of thinking, it is enjoyable to learn and to use. I first started to work with Lisp back in the early 1970s, and I can tell you, using Lisp is a lot of *fun*. In fact, the only programming language I can think of that is as much fun as Lisp — in an entirely different way — is APL.

The basic Lisp concept is an EXPRESSION, and the definition of a Lisp expression is deceptively simple: zero or more elements, separated by whitespace and surrounded by parentheses. Both Lisp code and Lisp data are in the form of expressions. For example, Lisp FUNCTIONS — program modules that can be executed — are built from expressions, and Lisp data also consists of expressions. Since both functions and data are built from the same type of stuff, it is possible for Lisp programs to read and modify other Lisp programs. As such, Lisp was the very first homoiconic programming language.

---

[1] See the end of Personal Note #5, "GNU's Not Unix?" (Appendix A).

When Lisp processes an expression, we say that Lisp EVALUATES it. This involves reading the expression, parsing it (making sense of it), and then performing the appropriate action. So, if you put Lisp expressions in your .emacs file, Emacs will evaluate those expressions as part of the initialization process. This is what allows you to customize your working environment. For example, you can use Lisp expressions to set modes and specify options that suit your needs.

Speaking of modes, when you are editing a Lisp program, there are two modes I suggest you set to help you. First, your major mode should be **emacs-lisp-mode**, the mode designed especially for writing Emacs Lisp programs:

M-x emacs-lisp-mode RET

Indeed, this will happen automatically, if Emacs can figure out that the file you are editing contains Lisp code.

Second, it is helpful to turn on the minor mode **eldoc-mode**. (The name stands for "Emacs Lisp documentation lookup".)

M-x eldoc-mode RET

Once this mode is enabled, whenever point is located at a Lisp function or Lisp variable, Emacs will display useful information in the echo area (the line near the bottom of the window; see Section 6.5). To see what I mean, turn on this minor mode and open a Lisp file. Move the cursor around and see what happens as you point to a function or macro, or a variable. As an example, I turned on **eldoc-mode** and opened a file. I then moved the cursor to the word **defun**. In the echo area, I saw the message:

defun: (NAME ARGLIST &optional DOCSTRING DECL &rest BODY)

This is a technical summary of the syntax for the macro **defun**, which is used to define a function.

Finally, when you create a .emacs file, you can put in descriptive COMMENTS that are ignored by Lisp. Whenever you write Lisp code — or any code for that matter — it is a good habit to use comments to make it easy for you and other people to understand the file. (If you think that your code will never be read by anyone else, think again. Tomorrow, you will be a different person.)

Lisp considers a comment to be any line that begins with a ; (semi-colon) character. You will see such comments in all our examples. When you encounter people who don't think that comments are necessary, especially in Lisp programs, feel secure in the knowledge that you and I are right, and they are wrong.

Section 11.9: Using Your .emacs File to Set Default Modes

As I explained in Section 9.7, Emacs has a minor mode called Auto Fill mode. When Auto Fill mode is turned on, Emacs will automatically break lines for you as you type. By default, this mode is turned off: if you want to turn it on, you must use the command **M-x auto-fill-mode**.

If you spend most of your time editing regular text, you will probably want to turn on Auto Fill mode (a minor mode) each time you use Text mode (a major mode). To do so, you can place the following lines in your **.emacs** file. The line that starts with the **;** (semi-colon) character is a comment.

```
; set Auto Fill mode as the default for Text mode
(setq text-mode-hook 'turn-on-auto-fill)
```

Do not leave out the parentheses or the single quote (apostrophe) character. Also, be sure to notice that there is only one single quote.

This particular Lisp expression uses what is called a VARIABLE: a quantity, with a name, that stores a particular value. Lisp and Emacs make widespread use of variables, and you can modify countless facets of Emacs' behavior simply by changing the value of some variable or another.

In this case, the variable is named **text-mode-hook**. The effect of the expression is to give this variable a value of **turn-on-auto-fill**. The single quote in front of **turn-on-auto-fill** tells Lisp that what follows is an actual value and not an expression that needs to be evaluated.

The purpose of this expression is to modify what Emacs does each time it turns on Text mode. We are making use of the fact that whenever Emacs starts Text mode, it looks at the **text-mode-hook** variable and executes its value as a command. In this case, the command will be **turn-on-auto-fill**. Thus, once you put this line of Lisp in your **.emacs** file, Auto Fill mode will be turned on automatically each time you turn on Text mode.

In Emacs, a HOOK is a variable whose value is a function that is evaluated automatically whenever a certain condition arises. For example, Emacs looks at the variable **text-mode-hook** each time Text mode is turned on.

Now let's take another look at the same expression:

```
(setq text-mode-hook 'turn-on-auto-fill)
```

Notice the word **setq**. This is the name of a FUNCTION: something that Lisp can execute. (All Lisp programs consist of one or more functions.)

For our purposes, we don't need to get too technical. All you need to understand is that when Lisp evaluates a function, something happens. In this case, what happens is that the **setq** function sets the value of a variable (**text-mode-hook**) to a particular value (**turn-on-auto-fill**). (The **q** in **setq** stands for "quote", but I can't explain why without going into esoteric details as to the basic nature of Lisp.)

Let's look at another example. Whenever you create a new buffer, Emacs will, by default, turn on Fundamental mode. However, it may be that you use Emacs only for creating regular text documents and that, for you, it would be more convenient to have all your new buffers use Text mode. To do so, use the following lines in your .emacs file:

```
; set Text mode as the default major mode
(setq-default major-mode 'text-mode)
```

Here we are using a function named `setq-default`. The purpose of `setq-default` is to set the default value of a particular variable. In this case, we are giving the variable named `major-mode` a default value of `text-mode`.

Of course, you can change this command and use another major mode as the default, simply by substituting a different mode name. (See Section 11.3 for the lists of major modes.) If you do change the command in this way, be sure not to omit the parentheses or the single quote.

A moment ago, we looked at an expression that tells Emacs to turn on Auto Fill mode each time Text mode is turned on:

```
(setq text-mode-hook 'turn-on-auto-fill)
```

You may decide that you would like Auto Fill mode to be turned on automatically for all major modes, not just for Text mode. To do so, use the following command instead of the previous one:

```
; set Auto Fill mode as the default for all major modes
(setq-default auto-fill-hook 'do-auto-fill)
```

In this example, we are telling Lisp to set the default value of the variable named `auto-fill-hook` to `do-auto-fill`.

To summarize, you can customize your Emacs environment by putting the appropriate expressions in your .emacs file. Each time Emacs starts, it will evaluate the expressions in this file and perform the appropriate actions. The expressions we discussed in this section are as follows:

- Make Text mode the default for all new buffers:
  ```
  (setq-default major-mode 'text-mode)
  ```

- Turn on Auto Fill mode automatically for Text mode only:
  ```
  (setq text-mode-hook 'turn-on-auto-fill)
  ```

- Turn on Auto Fill mode automatically for all major modes:
  ```
  (setq-default auto-fill-hook 'do-auto-fill)
  ```

CHAPTER 12

Shell Commands; Help and Info; Programs and Games

Section 12.1: Entering Shell Commands

There are several ways you can use shell commands without having to leave the Emacs environment. These tools are summarized in Figure 12-1.

Command	Description
M-!	Run a shell command
M-|	Run a shell command using region as input
M-x shell	Start a separate shell in its own buffer

FIGURE 12-1. **Running shell commands.**

To enter a single shell command, type M-! followed by the command. For example, to display a list of all the userids currently logged into your system, you could use either M-! users or M-! who. (users and who are Unix commands.)

When you run a shell command using M-!, Emacs always saves the output in a buffer named *Shell Command Output*. If this buffer does not already exist, Emacs will create it. If it does exist, the previous contents will be replaced. Thus, at any time, this buffer will hold the output from only one command.

If the shell command you enter displays a large amount of output,[1] Emacs will display the *Shell Command Output* buffer. However, if the command generates a small amount of output, Emacs will display the output in the echo area, at the bottom of the window (see Section 6.5).

---

[1] By default, greater than 25 % the height of your Emacs window.

© Harley Hahn 2016

H. Hahn, *Harley Hahn's Emacs Field Guide*, DOI 10.1007/978-1-4842-1703-0_12

Regardless, the shell output remains in the buffer until it is replaced by the next shell command. So even when the echo area is cleared, you can still switch to the ***Shell Command Output*** buffer manually, to see the output of the last shell command:

C-x b *Shell Command Output*

You can simplify this command by using completion (Section 6.7):

C-x b *S TAB

Another way to run a shell command is to use some of the data in the buffer as input for the command. For example, you may have a large number of lines you would like to sort. All you need to do is use these lines as data for the Unix **sort** program.

To perform such an operation, you use the **M-|** (<Meta>-vertical-bar) command. This will run whatever shell command you specify, using the contents of the region as input. You may remember that in Section 8.9, "Operating on the Region", we discussed an example that used the **M-|** command to create a sorted list of key descriptions. Here is another example.

You want to sort all the lines in the buffer. To do so, you set the region to the entire buffer, and then use **M-|** to run the **sort** command on the region. Use the following commands:

1. **C-x h**: Set the region to be the entire buffer.
2. **M-| sort**: Sort all the lines in the buffer.

When you use **M-|**, Emacs puts the output into a buffer named ***Shell Command Output*** just like when you use the **M-!** command. If the buffer does not exist, Emacs will create it. If the buffer does exist, its contents will be replaced.

Sometimes, though, you may want to replace the lines in your original buffer with the output of the shell command. All you need to do is use a prefix argument (explained in Section 8.4). This tells Emacs not to save the output in a special buffer. Any numeric value will do, so you might as well use **1**.

Here is an example. Say you are working with a buffer that contains people's names, one name per line. You have just typed in all the names, and now you want to sort them. However, you don't want the output of the **sort** command to be saved in a separate buffer; you want the sorted names to replace the original contents of your buffer. Use the commands:

1. **C-x h**: Set the region to be the entire buffer.
2. **ESC 1 M-| sort**: Sort all the lines in the buffer, replacing the input with the output of the **sort** command.

Note   When you use the **M- |** command with a prefix argument, the data in your buffer will be replaced by the output of the shell command. If you decide that it was all a mistake, you can undo the effects of the shell command by using the Emacs undo command: either **C-x u or C-_** or **C-/** (see Section 7.3).

Section 12.2: Shell Buffers

As we discussed in Section 11.3, you can run a shell command without leaving the buffer in which you are working by using **M- !** and **M- |** . However, sometimes you will want to use more than one shell command. In such cases, it is a lot easier to create a new buffer, just for shell commands.

To create a designated buffer just for running shell commands use **M-x shell**. This command will start a separate shell in its own buffer named ***shell***. You can then enter as many commands as you want, one after the other. Everything you type, along with all of the output, will be saved in the buffer. Whenever you want, you can switch from this buffer to another one. This means you can have a designated buffer just for running shell commands and capturing their output. This makes it easy to edit and then copy the output of a shell command to another buffer.

When you enter the **M-x shell** command, Emacs will check if a buffer named ***shell*** already exists. If not, Emacs will create it. If such a buffer already exists, Emacs will simply switch you to that buffer. When you are finished using that particular shell, you can kill the buffer and stop the shell by using **C-x k** (see Section 7.7).

As I mentioned, if you tell Emacs to create a new shell and a buffer named ***shell*** does not already exist, Emacs will create one. Thus, you can create more than one shell buffer by changing their names. Here is how it works.

The command **rename-uniquely** changes the name of a buffer to be unique. From within the ***shell*** buffer, you can use this command to change the buffer name to something else. You can then use **M-x shell** to start a brand new shell. Since there is no buffer named ***shell***, Emacs will create one and you will have two shells, each in its own buffer. Here is an example.

1. Create your first "shell in a buffer" by typing **M-x shell**. You now have a buffer named ***shell*** that contains a live shell session.

2. Type **M-x rename-uniquely**, and Emacs will change the name of the buffer to ***shell*<2>**.

3. Type **M-x shell** and Emacs will create a second shell in a new buffer named ***shell***.

If you want yet another shell buffer, you can rename the last one and use **M-x shell** again. In this way, you can create as many shell buffers as you want.

Here are two final pieces of advice. First, you do not have to type the full command **M-x rename-uniquely**. Using completion (see Section 6.7), all you need to type is **M-x ren SPC u RET**.

Second, if you are not sure what to get your mother for her birthday, a shell-in-a-buffer is something just about anyone can use.

Section 12.3: The Help Facility

Every Emacs user has access to three comprehensive help systems: the Emacs tutorial, the Emacs reference manuals, and a variety of Help tools. We'll start with the Help tools, and we'll cover the Emacs tutorial and reference manuals in Section 12.4.

To start the Help facility, you type **C-h**. Emacs will then prompt you to type a HELP OPTION. I have summarized the most important Help options in Figure 12-2. If you want to see them all, use either **C-h C-h** or **C-h ?**. if you type **C-h** and then change your mind and decide to quit, simply press **q** (quit).

Command	Description
C-h C-h	Display a summary of all the Help options
C-h ?	Same as **C-h C-h**.
C-h q	Exit from a Help command loop (quit)

Command	Description
C-h a	Show all the functions containing a specified word
C-h b	Display a full list of all the key bindings
C-h c	You specify a key, Emacs tells you what it does
C-h f	You specify a function, Emacs describes it
C-h h	Display the "Hello" file
C-h k	You specify a key, Emacs describes its function
C-h m	Describe the current major and minor modes
C-h v	You specify a variable, Emacs describes it
C-h w	You specify a function, Emacs shows you its key

Command	Description
C-h t	Emacs tutorial
C-h i	Emacs reference manuals (Info documentation browser)

FIGURE 12-2. **Help facility options.**

In a moment, I'll go over each of these commands. Before we do, here is an important technique I want you to remember.

Many of the Help options display information in a buffer named `*Help*`. This information will be a lot easier to read if you maximize the window containing the `*Help*` buffer. To do so, use `C-x o` to move the cursor to the Help window, and then use `C-x 1` to delete all the other windows. (The first key sequence uses a lowercase letter "o"; the second uses the number "1".)

```
C-x o C-x 1
```

I will remind you that when `C-x 1` deletes all the other windows, it does *not* delete any buffers, so don't worry about losing data. (All of this, including the commands I just used, is explained in Section 7.6.) Once you are finished reading the Help information, you can recall your previous buffer by using `C-x b` (see Section 7.7).

- `C-h b`: To see a full list of all the key bindings, use the `C-h b` command. This list is more interesting than you might think and is worth checking out from time to time. The more you know, the more you will find interesting key bindings to explore.

- `C-h c`: Use this option to find out the name of the function to which a key is mapped. Most of the time, this is enough to tell you what a key does, because Emacs function names are chosen to be descriptive. For example, say that you are wondering what the `C-x C-w` key sequence does. Press `C-h c C-x C-w`. You will see:

```
C-x C-w runs the command write-file
```

- `C-h k`: To display more detailed information about the function, use `C-h k`. (This is one of my favorites.) For example, to find out more about the function to which the `C-x C-w` key sequence is mapped, use the commands:

```
C-h k C-x C-w
C-x o C-x 1
```

Try it, and see what you get. Remember, the second key sequence maximizes the Help window to make it easier to read.

Note When you have a spare moment, use `C-h b` to display the master list of key bindings. Scan this list and find yourself an unfamiliar key that looks interesting. Then use the `C-h k` command to find out about that key.

- `C-h w`: Conversely, if you know the name of a function, and you want to know what key sequence it uses, type `C-h w` (the "where is?" command). For example, if you type `C-h w write-file`, you will see:

```
write-file is on C-x C-w
```

When you start working with functions and variables, there are three Help options you will find handy:

- C-h a: The "apropos" option shows you all the functions whose names contain a specific regular expression. Usually, you specify a word because you are interested in seeing all the functions whose names contain that word. For example, say that you want to see all the functions that have something to do with killing; that is, deleting text while copying it to the kill ring (see Section 9.1):

```
C-h a kill
C-x o C-x 1
```

- C-h f: If you know the name of a function, you can display a description of it by using the C-h f command, for example:

```
C-h f write-file
C-x o C-x 1
```

- C-h v: Similarly, you can use C-h v to describe a variable:

```
C-h v visible-bell
```

- C-h m: You can use C-h m to display the major and minor modes for the current buffer along with a short description of each one. (See Section 11.7 for a discussion of this command.)

- C-h h: Finally, just for fun, C-h h displays a list of how to say "Hello" in many different languages. The purpose of this file is to demonstrate a variety of the different characters sets that Emacs supports. However, this file is interesting in its own right.

Section 12.4: The Emacs Tutorial; Info and the Emacs Reference Manuals

Aside from the Help options we discussed in Section 12.3 (Figure 12-2), Emacs also comes with two full documentation systems: the Emacs tutorial and the Emacs reference manuals.

The purpose of the tutorial is to let you teach yourself basic Emacs at your own speed. However, the tutorial can be confusing for beginners, which is why I told you (in Section 4.1) that you will get a much better introduction to Emacs by reading this book. Since you have read this far, however, you already know the basics, so taking the tutorial now will actually serve as a nice review.

To start the Emacs tutorial, type C-h t. All you have to do is read from the beginning, and follow the directions as you go.

The Emacs reference manuals are more elaborate, but not for beginners. You access them by using the INFO FACILITY, or INFO, an elaborate tree-structured documentation browser. The Info facility is designed to display documentation consisting of documents that are connected to one another.

To start Info, type C-h i. Emacs will create a new buffer named *info* to display the top of the tree. This document begins with some basic instructions (worth reading carefully), followed by a table of contents for the Emacs reference manuals: a long list of topics in the form of links. (The version I looked at had 245 such topics.) To navigate, all you have to do is move the cursor to the topic you want to read, and press RET (the Enter key). Info will then display the document for that topic.

The two most important topics are Info, the manual for the Info facility itself, and Emacs, a comprehensive reference manual for Emacs concepts and commands.

As you will see, the Info facility has its own special commands. However, you can still use many of the regular Emacs commands. In particular, you can start Info, read for a while, and then use C-x b to change to another buffer. Later, you can return to Info by changing back to the *info* buffer.

The best way to learn how to use the Info facility is to start with the built-in documentation. Type the C-h i command, and then press h to start the Info tutorial. Follow the instructions and work your way through the various topics. Once you know how to use Info, you will be able to read parts of the Emacs manual whenever you want.

It is important — very important — that you learn how to use the Info facility, because it is your doorway to the Emacs reference manuals. If you don't learn how to use Info, you will have no way to find out detailed information about Emacs. The Emacs Help facility contains only summaries. The real information is in the reference manuals — and to get at them, you need Info.

I won't go into all the details of using the Info facility: they are best learned by following the Info tutorial and by practicing. However, I will cover the basic concepts and give you summaries of the important Info commands. The general commands are shown in Figure 12-3.

Command	Description
?	Display a summary of Info commands
h	Start the Info tutorial
q	Quit Info: remember current location
C-x k	Quit Info: do not remember current location

FIGURE 12-3. General Info commands.

Within the Info facility, certain keys work differently than they do with regular Emacs. For example, as you are reading a topic, you display the next screenful by pressing **SPC** (<Space>). You move back to the previous screenful, by pressing **BS** (<Backspace>). With Emacs, you would press **C-v** to move forward and **M-v** to move backward.

The Info facility organizes information into short topics called NODES. ("Node" is a technical term borrowed from a branch of mathematics called graph theory.) Each node has a name and contains information about one specific topic. As you read, you can move from one node to another.

The nodes themselves are organized into an upside-down tree. The top node is what would be the trunk in a real tree. When you start Info for the first time, you will see the top node: *The Info Directory*.

Whenever you select a node, Info will display it for you to read. As you read, there are commands to move within the node, or to jump to another node. These commands are summarized in Figures 12-4 and 12-5.

Command	Description
n	Jump to next node in the sequence
p	Jump to previous node in the sequence
u	Jump to the "up" node (the menu you came from)
l	Jump to last node you looked at
m *selection*	Pick a node from a menu
f	Follow a cross-reference
i	Look up topic in the index, then jump there
,	(comma) Jump to next match from previous **i** command

FIGURE 12-4. Info commands to select a node.

Command	Description
SPC	Go forward (down) one screenful
BS	Go backward (up) one screenful
b	Go to beginning of the node
.	Same as **b**
C-l	(<Ctrl-L>) Redisplay the current screen

FIGURE 12-5. Info commands to read a node.

When you are finished reading, you have three choices:

- Use an Emacs command (such as **C-x o** or **C-x b**) to switch to another buffer. This leaves your Info session alive in its own buffer.

- Use the **q** (quit) command to stop Info completely.

- Use the Emacs **C-x k** command to kill the Info window.

When you quit with the **q** command, Emacs remembers your location within the Info tree. If you later restart the Info facility (with another **C-h i** command), Emacs will put you back where you were when you quit. When you quit by using **C-x k** to kill the buffer, Emacs does not remember your location. The next time you start Info, you will be back at the top node of the tree (the main menu).

Note

To learn how to use the Info facility, type **C-h i** and then press **h** to start the tutorial.

To quit, press **q**. That way, the next time you start Info, you can continue from where you left off.

Section 12.5: Built-In Programs

Over the years, Emacs has provided a variety of built-in programs: tools and diversions (including games). With the growth of the Internet, some of these programs have become obsolete. Others, however, are still useful and interesting and, once in a while, someone adds a new program.

Because these programs are important (or fun), I will give you a quick guided tour so you can decide which ones appeal to you. In Section 12.6, we'll talk about the built-in Emacs tools. In Section 12.7, we'll talk about the games and diversions. Before we start, however, I want to take a moment to explain the general principles that apply to all of these programs.

- Starting a Program

To run a program, type **M-x** followed by the name of the program. For example, to run the **calendar** program, use:

M-x calendar

Emacs will create a new buffer in which to run the program.

- Stopping a Program

There are several ways to stop a program:

1. The program itself may have its own quit command, such as **q**.

2. Use the standard Emacs quit command, **C-g (keyboard-quit)**, to stop the program and preserve the buffer.

3. Use **C-x k** (see Section 7.3) to kill the buffer in which the program is running.

- Putting a program on hold

While you are using a program, you can change to a different buffer (by using, for example, the **C-x b** or **C-x o** commands). Then you can return to the program later, and work with it some more.

- Learning how to use a program

There are various ways to get information about a program. First, try the Info facility (Section 12.4). Look for the program within the Emacs reference manual and see if you can find some documentation. The larger programs have menus and submenus of their own. The smaller programs may have only a brief mention.

Second, use the Help facility to tell you what it can about the actual function. For example, to find out about **blackbox**, type **C-h f blackbox**.

Third, start the program and see if it has a built-in help command. For instance, with **dunnet**, the **help** command will display a help document. With **dired**, pressing the letter **h** will display help information.

Section 12.6: Built-In Tools, Including Dired

In this section, I will introduce you to several important tools, which are summarized in Figure 12-6.

Program	Description
calendar	Calendar and diary
customize	Tool to help you change user options
dired	Directory and file manager
eww	Web browser
ses	Create and edit spreadsheet files

FIGURE 12-6. Built-in tools.

I'm going to start with Dired because it is the most important. The **dired** ("directory editor") program provides a complete interface for working with files and directories, letting you edit a directory as easily as you can edit a text file. Specifically, you can perform all the common file and directory operations, such as copy, move, and rename. You can point to a file and tell Emacs to show it to you. You can print a file, or compress and uncompress it.

What I like best about Dired is that it makes it easy to maintain your directory tree by creating and removing directories, and by moving files from one place to another. It does so, by acting as a front end to the Unix directory and file commands, such as **ls**. (With Microsoft Windows, Dired emulates **ls**.)

Note

Dired is a powerful file manager, which makes it an important tool for everyone. However, in order to use a file manager, you need to understand files, directories, and the tree-structured file system.

These are extremely important topics, and if you need some help, please take the time to review Sections 2.15 through 2.19.

DIRED FILE MANAGER (dired)

You can start Dired in two different ways. First, you can use **M-x**, as you would for any program:

M-x dired

Alternatively, because Dired is so important, it has its own command, **C-x d**. If you want to start Dired this way, here are two possible key sequences you can use:

C-x d
C-x 4 d

C-x d starts Dired in the same way as **M-x dired**. The **C-x 4 d** key sequence starts Dired in another window (see Section 7.7).

After you type the command, press **RET** (<Enter>). Dired will ask you which directory you want to work with, and will make a suggestion. For example, you might see:

Dired (directory): ~/

In this case, Dired is suggesting that you might want to start with your home directory (~). If you do, simply press <Enter> to start the program. If not, type the name of directory you do want, and press <Enter>. (If you don't understand the abbreviation ~ for your home directory, see Section 2.17.)

Once Dired starts, there are a large number of commands you can use. I have summarized the important ones in Figure 12-7. Note that the command names are case sensitive.

Program	Description
q	Quit
h	Display Help summary
m	Mark current file/directory, move cursor down
BS	Unmark current file/directory, move cursor up
u	Unmark file/directory, move cursor down
U	Unmark all files/directories
C	Copy marked files or current file
R	Rename current file
R	Move marked files or current file to another directory
d	Flag file for deletion
x	Delete files flagged by d
g	Refresh by reading the directories again

FIGURE 12-7. Dired commands.

Here are the most important commands while using Dired, the Emacs file manager. Notice that the commands are case sensitive.

One of the most important Dired concepts is that you can MARK files and then operate on them. For example, you might mark, say, 5 files, and then move all 5 of them to another directory. Within Dired, most commands work on marked files. If no files are marked, Dired will operate on the current file (the location of the cursor).

Dired is a powerful, but complex program. There are three ways you can get the information you need to learn how to use it:

1. Use Info to look at the Dired documentation within the Emacs manual:

```
C-h i
m emacs RET
m dired RET
```

2. Within Dired, use the **h** command and read the Help summary.

3. Search online for "dired reference card". You should be able to find a Dired reference card that you can print.

■ **Note** Dired is so useful, I suggest you keep an active copy open in a buffer at all times. That way, you can switch to it instantly as the need arises.

CALENDAR AND DIARY (calendar)

The next useful program I want to talk about is **calendar**. Each time you start the program, it shows you a three-month calendar, which is handy by itself. However, **calendar** is much, much more. One of the basic **calendar** tools is a diary, which you can use to keep daily notes and reminders. Within **calendar**, you will find just about anything you can imagine that has to do with days and calendars. For example, you can display various types of calendars (such as Hebrew, Islamic, and astronomical); you can find the dates of the various phases of the moon; and you can display local times for sunrise and sunset.

To start the Emacs Calendar and Diary:

M-x calendar

Once the program has started, you can press **?** (question-mark) to display documentation about the **calendar** program. Specifically, **calendar** will jump to its Info page in the Emacs reference manual. Here you will find all the information you need to teach yourself how to use the program. To quit the program, press **q** (quit).

CUSTOMIZE (customize)

The next built-in program is **customize**. This is a very useful program that provides an interface for finding and modifying any of the huge number of Emacs settings. To start the program:

M-x customize

To quit the program, press **q** (quit).

The best way to learn how **customize** works is to use Info to read the documentation in the Emacs reference manual. To do so, start Info, then search for "easy customization interface". The key sequences to use are:

C-h i
m emacs RET
m customization RET
m easy customization RET

EMACS WEB BROWSER (eww)

The next program is a built-in Web browser named **eww**. (This program became available with Emacs version 24.) The name **eww** stands for "Emacs Web Wowser". To start the program, use:

M-x eww

Emacs will ask you to enter either a URL (Web address) or search keywords. Once you enter your response, **eww** will find the information you requested and display it in a buffer. To quit the program, press **q** (quit).

To learn about the program, use Info to look at the **eww** manual:

```
C-h i
m eww RET
```

The default search engine for **eww** is DuckDuckGo. This is a small, fast search engine that does not accumulate or share personal information. If you want to try it directly, the URL is:

```
https://www.duckduckgo.com/
```

■ **Note**

You will notice that the Web pages **eww** renders do not look nearly as elaborate or flashy as the pages you see with the popular standalone browsers. In fact, they are mostly text. That's because **eww** was not designed to compete with other browsers. Its purpose is to let you search online quickly, without leaving Emacs.

Because everything you see with **eww** is contained in an Emacs buffer (named ***eww***), it is fast and easy to copy information you find online to another Emacs buffer. That is what makes **eww** such a valuable tool.

SIMPLE EMACS SPREADSHEET (ses)

The final program I want to mention is **ses**, the Simple Emacs Spreadsheet program. Although **ses** doesn't have the power of a large, standalone spreadsheet program, it is handy because it is always available and, as the name says, it's simple.

What I like about **ses** is that, when you want to do a quick calculation that requires a spreadsheet, you don't have to leave Emacs. Moreover, because the spreadsheet you create is in an Emacs buffer, it is easy to copy data to another buffer.

Technically, **ses** is a major mode used to edit spreadsheet files. So the easiest way to start the program is to visit (open) a new file with an extension of .**ses**, for example:

```
C-x C-f calculate.ses
```

To learn how to use **ses**, start with the Help facility:

```
C-h f ses-mode
```

To use Info to read the **ses** documentation from the Emacs reference manual:

```
C-h i
m ses
```

Section 12.7: Games and Diversions

Figure 12-8 shows a summary of the most interesting games and diversions that come with Emacs. I'll go through the list, one at a time, and tell you a bit about each one. In Section 12.8, I'll show you a particularly interesting example of the **doctor** program.

Program	Description
animate	Display animated birthday message
bubbles	Game: Remove groups of bubbles until all gone
blackbox	Puzzle: Find objects inside a black box
doctor	Eliza program: acts like a psychotherapist
dunnet	Adventure-style exploration game
gomoku	Game: plays Gomoku with you
hanoi	Visual solution to Towers of Hanoi problem
landmark	Neuro-network robot that learns about landmarks
life	Game of Life: auto-reproducing patterns (not a game)
mpuz	Multiplication puzzle: guess the digits
pong	Video game: classic ping-pong game
snake	Video game: you control a growing snake
solitaire	Jump pegs across other pegs (not the card game)
spook	Generates words to get government's attention
tetris	Video game: you manipulate falling blocks

FIGURE 12-8. **Games and diversions.**

Before we begin, I will remind you how to start and stop a program, and how to display help information.

To start a program, type **M-x**, followed by the name of the program, followed by **RET** (<Enter>). For example, to start **doctor**:

M-x doctor RET

There are three ways to stop a program (see Section 12.5). Some programs stop when you press **q** (quit). If that doesn't work, try **C-g** (the **keyboard-quit** command). If all else fails, use **C-x k** to kill the buffer in which the program is running.

To display help information for a game, use **C-h f**, followed by the name of the function that runs the game (the name in Figure 12-8). For example, to learn how to play the Bubbles game, use:

C-h f bubbles RET

For long names, you can use completion (see Section 6.7).

- ANIMATE (to start: **M-x animate**)

(If this doesn't work, use **M-x animate-birthday-present**.)

This program calls upon another program that moves characters around within a buffer to create a very specific message: a birthday greeting to someone you miss who has moved away. When you start the program, **animate** will display:

Birthday present for:

It is asking you to enter the name of a friend. Type any name you want and watch the animated greeting. If you want to hack the program to make it work differently, you can find the source code in a file named **animate.el**. The easy way to edit this file is to use:

C-h f animate-birthday-greeting

Then move the cursor to the reference to **animate.el**, and press <Enter> to visit that file. (Before you start, copy the code to another file, so you don't change the original.)

- BLACKBOX (to start: **M-x blackbox**)

A puzzle game in which you use tomography to find objects hidden inside a box. "Tomography" refers to looking at X-ray images in various planes. (When a doctor talks about a CAT scan, he or she is referring to "computerized axial tomography".)

The program hides 4 balls within a box (the Blackbox) represented by an 8 by 8 grid. You "shoot" rays into the box and observe where they emerge. Your goal is to deduce the positions of the hidden balls using as few rays as possible.

This game is fun to play, but it is a bit complicated. The best way to learn how to play it is by reading the help documentation. The command to use is:

C-h f blackbox

- BUBBLES (to start: **M-x bubbles**)

A game using colored bubbles. Move the cursor to highlight contiguous bubbles of the same color. Press <Enter> to remove highlighted bubbles, and the remaining bubbles will come together. The goal is to remove as many bubbles as you can in as few moves as possible.

- DOCTOR (to start: **M-x doctor**)

The Doctor program is an old one. Originally it was called Eliza, after the Eliza Doolittle character in *Pygmalion* and *My Fair Lady*. Doctor acts like the type of psychotherapist who behaves nonjudgmentally, listening with infinite patience, and prompting you to talk about yourself. (Specifically, Doctor emulates a Rogerian psychologist using person-centered therapy.) This is the perfect program to keep someone busy at the computer, while you are in the next room working on something important.

Using Doctor is easy. You start it in the regular manner:

`M-x doctor`

All you have to do is carry on a conversation with Doctor by typing. To start, type whatever you want, then press **RET** (<Enter>) twice. This tells Doctor you are finished, and it will respond. Then you talk, then Doctor talks, and so on. Just remember to press **RET** twice whenever you want a response.

When you are ready to stop talking, type **goodbye**. Then close the buffer by using `C-x k`. Here is a short sample of a conversation you might have with Doctor. Your replies are indented and printed in italics:

`I am the psychotherapist. Please, describe your problems. Each time you are finished talking, type RET twice.`

  Hello.

`How do you do? What brings you to see me?`

  I have a problem

`Why do you say you have a problem?`

  Because my mother hates me.

`Is it because your mother hates you that you came to me?`

  Goodbye.

`My secretary will send you a bill.`

At this point, you end the conversation by closing the buffer:

`C-x k`

Because this is an example, I have kept the conversation short and simple. With a little imagination, you can make the conversation longer and more interesting. In Section 12.8, I will show you a longer, much more unusual conversation with Doctor.

- DUNNET (to start: `M-x dunnet`)

Dunnet is a wonderful text-based exploration game in the style of the original Adventure game, which is still included on many Unix systems. I can remember, in the summer of 1981, when I was in medical school, spending a lot of time playing Adventure at home, using a terminal that printed on thermal paper, connected to a remote computer using a slow modem. Playing Adventure was a lot of fun, and I advise you to spend as much time as you can playing Dunnet.

When you start the program you will see:

```
Dead end
You are at a dead end of a dirt road. The road goes to the east.
In the distance you can see that it will eventually fork off. The
trees here are very tall royal palms, and they are spaced
equidistant from each other.
There is a shovel here.
>
```

Whenever you see a > (greater-than) character, it means it is your turn to type something. When you are finished playing, type quit.

One of the challenges of Dunnet is to figure out where you are, and what you are supposed to be doing (just like real life), so I won't give you any advice. Just start typing and see what happens.

(Okay, one hint: If you are stuck, ask for help.)

- GOMOKU (to start: M-x gomoku)

Gomoku is played on a board with 15x15 squares. You play against the program. To win, you must mark off squares in such a way that you get five in a row. The program will try to block you and to mark five consecutive squares of its own.

You and the program take turns marking free squares. When it is your turn, move the cursor to a free square and mark it by pressing RET (<Enter>).

To quit, press q.

- TOWERS OF HANOI (to start: M-x hanoi)

The hanoi program displays a visual solution to a mathematical puzzle called the Towers of Hanoi. There are three poles, lined up in a row, as well as a number of different-sized discs with holes. To start, the discs are stacked from largest to smallest on the leftmost pole. The problem is to figure out how to move all the discs from the leftmost pole to another pole without ever placing a larger disc on top of a smaller disc.

If you were to design a computer program to solve this problem, you would find that it lends itself to what programmers call a "recursive" solution. The Lisp programming language (in which Emacs is written) is designed to make recursive programming easy, so it makes sense to find such a demonstration program in a Lisp-based system like Emacs.

To start the program, use ESC and a number to specify how many discs you want, followed by M-x hanoi. To stop the program, type q (quit). For example, to run the program with 5 discs, use:

ESC 5 M-x hanoi

If you don't specify a number, **hanoi** will use 3 discs. Thus, the following commands are equivalent:

```
M-x hanoi
ESC 3 M-x hanoi
```

This is a good way to test the program for the first time, as the three-disc solution is over quickly.

- GAME OF LIFE (to start: **M-x life**)

    The Game of Life is based on a simple two-dimensional grid-like universe. The Game of Life was invented by John Horton Conway and introduced publicly by Martin Gardner in the October 1970 issue of *Scientific American*.

    A number of life forms, called cells, exist. Each cell fills exactly one position in the grid, which is surrounded by eight other positions. The cells reproduce according to a few well-defined rules:

1. If a cell is surrounded by four or more cells, it dies of overcrowding.

2. If a cell is all alone or has only one neighbor, the cell dies of loneliness.

3. An empty location will be filled with a brand new cell, if that location has exactly three neighbors.

As the game progresses, you can watch the patterns change from one generation to the next.

    You start the game in the regular manner:

```
M-x life
```

The starting pattern of cells is generated randomly. Every generation, the cells change according to the rules I explained above. To quit, use **C-x k** to kill the buffer.

    By default, the length of each generation is 1 second. If you want to slow down the program, start it with a prefix number specifying the duration of a generation in seconds. For example, to run the program with 3-second generations, use:

```
ESC 3 M-x life
```

- LANDMARK (to start: **M-x landmark**)

    Landmark is a diversion in which you watch a neuro-network robot, represented by a small black rectangle, move around a flat grid labeled with the directions of the compass: north, south, east, and west. The robot's goal is to look for a tree at the center of the grid.

    The robot figures out which way to move by chemotaxis: moving in response to simulated smells it detects from each of the four directions. However, as the smell of the tree increases, the robot trains itself by adjusting its "weights". This helps it learn how to move in the direction of the tree in the future.

At first, it's mostly trial and error, but it won't take long for the robot to find the tree, and every time it does, it adjusts its weights, which makes it better and better at tree-finding.

The robot stops when it finds the tree, but you can tell it to start again by pressing <Space>. Each time, you can decide whether or not it is allowed to retain its weights (learned skills). If you tell the robot to play the game over and over, you can watch it get better and better at finding the tree. When you get tired of watching a simulated robot look for an imaginary tree using clues that you can't detect, you can quit the program by pressing q.

When you start the program, you have some control over what happens. For details, use:

C-h f landmark

In addition, within the Help information, you will see a link to **landmark.el**. Follow this link to the source code for the program, where you will find a lot of informative comments that explain about the robot. (Use **M-<** to jump to the top of the buffer and then scroll down. Be sure to look through the whole program for comments.)

• MULTIPLICATION PUZZLE (to start: **M-x mpuz**)

This program creates a multiplication calculation of medium complexity. However, each different digit is represented by a letter and not a number. Here is an example:

```
  A E C
x B H
-------
  E I I D
H B H I
I C C C D
```

Your goal is to guess which numbers are where. To do so, you press a letter, say **i** (you don't need to hold down <Shift>). The program will ask you to guess which number the letter I represents:

```
I =
```

Type a single digit, and see if you are correct. If so, the program will change all the occurrences of that letter to the correct number. For example, if you guessed that I = 6, you would see:

```
    A E C
    x  B H
    -------
    E 6 6 D
  H B H 6
  6 C C C D
```

Keep going until you have figured out all the numbers.

If you have ever played Hangman, `mpuz` is similar, except you are guessing numbers and not letters. The technical term for this type of puzzle is an ALPHAMERIC. When I was a child growing up in Canada, one of the newspapers published a daily alphameric, and I used to have fun figuring it out. Try one and see how you like it.

Solving an alphameric involves creating and using various strategies. For example, **H** and **A** can't be very low numbers, say 1 and 2, because when you multiply them together, the product has to be large enough to produce the extra digit **E**. Also, notice that when you multiply **H** times **D**, the product ends with **D**. Thus, neither of these letters can represent **1**.

To help you get started, here is the solution to the problem above:

```
    7 3 2
    x  8 5
    -------
    3 6 6 0
  5 8 5 6
  6 2 2 2 0
```

- PONG VIDEO GAME (to start: **M-x pong**)

    This is the Emacs version of Pong, the very first sports arcade video game (released in November 1972). In its time, Pong was incredibly popular.

    The goal of Pong is to beat your opponent in a simulated ping-pong game. As the ball moves left and right, you move your paddle up and down in order to reflect the ball back to your opponent. When someone misses, his opponent gets a point.

    To control the left paddle: use <Left> (paddle moves up) and <Right> (paddle moves down). To control the right paddle, use <Up> and <Down>. You can play against another person, or you can control both paddles and play against yourself.

    To pause the game, press **p**. To continue, press **p** again. To quit press **q**.

- SNAKE (to start: **M-x snake**)

    This is the Emacs version of the Snake video game. It takes place in a buffer named ***Snake***.

A yellow snake moves around a grid, leaving red blocks behind it as it moves. You control the head of the snake by using <Left>, <Right>, <Down>, and <Up>. Your goal is to earn points by maneuvering the snake's head into as many red blocks as you can. Each time the snake "eats" a red block, you get one point. However, at the same time, the snake's tail gets longer and more bothersome. At any time, you can pause the game by pressing p, and continue by pressing p again.

The game is over when the snake runs into its own tail or runs into one of the walls. At that point, the program will change to a buffer named *snake-scores* to show you how many points you have accumulated. To play another game, use C-x b to change back to the *Snakes* buffer, and press n to start a new game.

At any time, you can quit by pressing q.

• PEG SOLITAIRE (to start: M-x solitaire)

This is a very old game for one person, played on a board with holes in a particular pattern. Each hole has a peg in it, except the central hole. To play the game, you jump one peg over another in a straight line, inserting the first peg into an empty hole, and removing the peg you jumped over. The goal is to empty the board, ending up with exactly one peg in the center hole.

There are two traditional patterns for peg solitaire boards: English and European. The Emacs program uses the English pattern with 33 holes in the shape of a cross:

```
      o  o  o
      o  o  o
o  o  o  o  o  o  o
o  o  o  .  o  o  o
o  o  o  o  o  o  o
      o  o  o
      o  o  o
```

In the diagram above, all the holes are filled with pegs except the center hole, which is empty. This is the starting layout of the game.

To play, use <Left>, <Right>, <Down>, and <Up> to move the cursor to the peg you want to use to make a jump. Then press <Enter> followed by the direction in which you want to jump. The peg you jump over will disappear. Remember, your goal is to get rid of all the pegs but one, which must end up in the center hole of the grid.

At any time, if you get stuck, press <Space> and the program will tell you how many possible moves there are. To reverse a move, press one of the Emacs undo keys: C-x u, C-/ or C-_ (see Section 7.3). To quit, press q.

• SPOOK (to start: M-x spook)

Spook was designed to insert special words — with no meaningful context — into your buffer. These words are of the type that the American FBI (Federal Bureau of Investigation), CIA (Central Intelligence Agency), or NSA (National Security Agency) would be looking for within electronic messages in order to identify subversive people.

The intention is that, after composing a mail message, you execute the **spook** program to create a collection of these words to copy and paste to your outgoing message. If the FBI or CIA or NSA has a program that checks for subversive messages traveling around the Internet, your message will be snagged and archived. Later, some government flunky will have to waste time reading your mail, just to make sure you are not a bad guy.

Here is some sample output from **spook**:

```
Tuberculosis computer terrorism orthodox password
Black out NSWC Al-Qaeda AOL TOS Law enforcement
doctrine Nigeria KLM Plame Critical infrastructure
Suspicious substance
```

Of course, you don't know for sure if the FBI or CIA or NSA is really scanning your email. However, the idea is that if everyone uses Spook regularly, it would overwhelm such agencies, if they did indeed try to spy on us.

- TETRIS (to start: **M-x tetris**)

The Emacs version of the popular video game. It takes place in a buffer named ***Tetris***.

The program generates a series of geometric shapes called tetriminos. (The name is taken from the word "domino".) Each tetrimino consists of four small, square blocks stuck together. One tetrimino at a time falls slowly to the bottom of a vertical shaft. As the tetrimino falls, you can move it and rotate it. Your goal is to maneuver the tetrimino so that, when it lands at the bottom, it fits into the pattern created by the previous tetriminos (which have already fallen), without creating any empty space.

As a tetrimino falls, use <Left> and <Right> to move it sideways. Use <Up> to rotate it clockwise, and <Down> to rotate it counterclockwise. Once you get a tetrimino lined up, you can also press <Space> to force it to fall to the bottom immediately. (This speeds up the game.)

At any time, you can pause the game by pressing **p**, and continue by pressing **p** again. To quit, press **q**.

When the game ends, the program will change to a buffer named ***tetris-scores*** to show you how many points you have accumulated. To play another game, use **C-x b** to change back to the ***Tetris*** buffer, and press **n** to start a new game.

Section 12.8: Zippy the Pinhead Talks to the Emacs Psychotherapist

In this section, I'm going to show you something that used to be included with Emacs, but vanished in 2006. However, it is so interesting I thought you would like to see it — and it's a good way to end the book.

The 1970s in the United States was a time of great turmoil as the social progressive values that emerged in the late 1960s matured to take their rightful place within the popular culture: hippies, free love, drugs, anti-war protests, disco music, and Zippy the Pinhead.

Zippy the Pinhead was a creation of the American cartoonist Bill Griffith. (At the time, "pinhead" was a pejorative term for a cretin: a person with serious deformity and mental retardation, caused by a thyroid deficiency.) Zippy dressed in a baggy yellow clown suit with large red polka dots, and wore white puffy clown shoes. His point-like head was bald, except for a small sprig of hair tied with a red bow.

Zippy the Pinhead was a freakish, counterculture comic character, whose speech was characterized by repeated series of non-sequiturs. For a long time, Emacs had a program called **yow** whose purpose was to display a random quotation from Zippy the Pinhead.[2] To show you what I mean, here are three examples of what you might have seen if you had run the Emacs command **M-x yow** before 2006:

```
Equip me with MISSILES!!
*Help* I'm RELIGIOUS!!
I love a man with a HAIRPIECE!!

I don't know why but, suddenly, I want to
discuss declining I.Q. LEVELS with a blue
ribbon SENATE SUBCOMMITTEE!

My pants just went on a wild rampage through a
Long Island Bowling Alley!!
```

In Section 12.7, I described another very old Emacs program named Doctor (**doctor**). Doctor, which is still part of Emacs, acts like a nonjudgmental, infinitely patient, Rogerian psychologist using person-centered therapy. ("Tell me something about your family.")

In 2006, unfortunately, the Zippy quotations were removed for copyright reasons. However, up until that time, one of the most amusing features of Emacs was a command you could use to feed random Zippy quotations to the Doctor program. This would let you watch what happens when a nonjudgmental, infinitely patient, psychotherapist encounters a verbally iconoclastic pinhead. Because the Zippy quotations were random, the conversation was different every time. The command to use was:

```
M-x psychoanalyze-pinhead
```

---

[2] I have been able to trace it as far back as November 5, 1986.

Unfortunately, this command lives only in our memory so, to end the book, I now present you with Figure 12-9: excerpts from an authentic conversation that once took place between Zippy the Pinhead and the Emacs `doctor` program.

In order to make the conversation easy to follow, I have indented Zippy's comments and put them in italics.

```
I am the psychotherapist.
Please, describe your problems.
Each time you are finished talking, type RET twice.
```

If I am elected no one will ever have to do their laundry again!

```
Why do you say that?
```

Yow! I want my nose in lights!

```
What makes you believe you want your nose in lights?
```

I selected E5... but I didn't hear "Sam the Sham and the Pharaohs"!

```
Is it because you didn't hear sam the sham and the pharaohs that you came to me?
```

Spreading peanut butter reminds me of opera!! I wonder why?

```
Can you elaborate on that?
```

Civilization is fun! Anyway, it keeps me busy!!

```
Earlier you said you didn't hear sam the sham and the pharaohs"?
```

I'm EMOTIONAL now because I have MERCHANDISING CLOUT!!

```
When did you first know that you have merchandising clout?
```

I have seen these EGG EXTENDERS in my Supermarket... ...I have read the INSTRUCTIONS...

```
You mentioned that it keeps you busy?
```

All right, you degenerates! I want this place evacuated in 20 seconds!

FIGURE 12-9. Zippy the Pinhead talks to the Therapist.

Section 12.9: A Personal Note From Harley Hahn

To end the book, I want to ask you a question: What are the best things in life?

At the very beginning of the book, I described four characteristics about the type of people who like to use Emacs. As we end this book together, let me take a moment to recast these observations to describe *you*: the person who is reading this right now:

1. You are smart.
2. You like to use computers.
3. You enjoy teaching yourself how to use complicated, powerful tools.
4. You are able to learn on your own by reading and practicing.

Assuming this does describe you, my reader, let me repeat the question: What are the best things in life?

To be sure, we all have our own answers to this question. However, there is one important need that you and I have in common: a need that — when it is met — goes a long way to making us content. We want to work and think at the natural speed of our mind. This is why we become uncomfortable and frustrated when our thought processes are slowed down unnecessarily. When we have a problem to solve or an idea to explore, we want to be able to do it in a way that make sense to us and is enjoyable.

As such, we want computer tools that are powerful enough for the type of work and the type of thinking we enjoy. Tools that were created *by* smart people *for* smart people. Tools that will shape our minds in a *good* way as we use them. Tools we will never outgrow, that we can modify and extend and — when we feel so inclined — share with others. Finally, we want tools that are supported by a larger system that itself has these characteristics, for example, Linux and other types of Unix.

Can you see that I have just described Emacs?

No one is saying that Emacs is the only computer-based set of tools that serves people like us in that way. However, it is one of the few that has met the test of time, and it is one of the best.

True, Emacs is difficult to learn. In fact, it is very difficult to learn, which is why I spent a lot of time in the first part of this book making sure you had a strong foundation, before I even introduced you to your first Emacs commands.

Yes, it is true that Emacs is hard to learn, but it is just as true that, once you learn it, it is easy to use. And more important, Emacs is one of the few computer-based systems that will let you think and create at the natural speed of your own mind.

This is why I wrote this book: to help people like you learn how to use Emacs. As such, I thank you for spending so much time reading and thinking about what I have had to say. I am grateful for the opportunity to teach you, and to help you change your life.

HARLEY HAHN

APPENDIX A

Personal Notes

Personal Note #1: Teaching Yourself Emacs

From Section 1.1:

"Out of the 7.28 billion other people in the world, there is nobody who is ever going to teach you Emacs in person. You will have to teach it to yourself by reading and practicing."

Comment:

It wasn't always this way. In the 1970s, systems like Unix (the grandfather of Linux) and Emacs existed within a rich oral tradition among computer science students, professors, and researchers. At the time, computers were so expensive that they had to be shared, and programmers would use a terminal (a medium-sized box with a keyboard and screen) connected by a cable or a phone line to a remote computer. So when Emacs was first developed, programmers and researchers often worked in rooms with shared terminals and — believe it or not — computer programming was often a social activity. Indeed, it was common to see two programmers collaborating, sometimes even sitting at the same desk in front of the same terminal working together. In those days, it was part of the prevailing culture that if you had a problem and you had tried your best to solve it, you could ask anyone in the terminal room (or down the hall) for assistance, and they would be glad to teach you, help you, and even spend time talking about your ideas.

In the 1980s, as inexpensive, personal computers became available, programming increasingly became an individual activity. This tendency has increased to the point that, today, using a computer is very much a solitary activity, even though we are all "connected" via the Internet and mobile phones. On the other hand, because it is now easy for people all over the world to collaborate on large projects, we have a lot of high-quality, free, open source software, and many wonderful free tools.

Still, if you ask your grandparents how it was to use computers back in the 1960s and 1970s, they will tell you that it was a lot more fun than it is now because, much of the time, smart people spent their time working in person with other smart people, and they would all teach and help one another.

© Harley Hahn 2016
H. Hahn, *Harley Hahn's Emacs Field Guide*, DOI 10.1007/978-1-4842-1703-0

All of which gets back to my original point. Those days are gone and, today, no one is going to spend time, in person, teaching you how to use Emacs, so you had better be the type of person who likes to teach yourself. Of course, you do have this book, so you aren't completely alone.

Personal Note #2: Computer With a Keyboard

From Section 1.1:
"It will help a lot if you already have some experience using a computer with a keyboard."

Comment:
If you have only ever used a phone or a tablet, I do want to encourage you to learn Emacs. Just push ahead with this book, and I will help you. However, as I mentioned, you will need a computer with a keyboard, and you will have to learn how to use it. This means you will have to learn how to type and how to use all the special keys.

If you are not used to it, using a keyboard may seem a bit awkward at first. However, by the time you get half-way through this book, working with Emacs on a real computer will have permanently changed your brain cells for the better.

Personal Note #3: Usenet, Emacs, and the Growth of the Internet

From Section 1.1:
"For over 25 years, Usenet was used by a very large number of people around the world to post messages discussing every topic you can imagine, as well as to develop and share software. Many users used Emacs to create their messages, and a related program (**gnus**) to participate in Usenet discussion groups. Eventually, however, both discussions and software distribution migrated to the Web, which had no need of an external text editor."

Comment:
USENET is a vast, global system of discussion and file sharing groups. It was created in 1979 by two graduate students at Duke University, Jim Ellis and Tom Truscott, as a tool to send news and announcements between two universities in North Carolina (University of North Carolina and Duke University). Within a short time, the system had spread to other schools, and it soon developed into a very large, very popular system of discussion groups. For historical reasons, it became common to refer to Usenet as THE NEWS and to the messages in the discussion groups as ARTICLES.

Usenet, like most Internet-based services, is a client/server system. Data is stored on a large number of NEWS SERVERS; to access a server, you use a Usenet client program, called a NEWSREADER. In the 1980s, one of the more popular Usenet newsreaders was **gnus**, which was integrated with Emacs. (Both **gnus** and Emacs were created by the Free Software Foundation.)

Usenet had no central authority, so there was no one to manage the system or to make any rules (and even if there were rules, there would be no way to enforce them). For a long time, Usenet functioned well because it was put together in a clever way, and because there was a lot of cooperation among the people who managed the news servers.

Indeed, when the first primitive ancestor of the Web came along in 1991, Usenet was a robust, worldwide communication system, with many tens of thousands of discussion groups. In fact, without Usenet, it would have been impossible to develop the software and technical protocols that created the modern Internet. (Read that last sentence again.)

Eventually, however, Web-based technology became much easier to use and more powerful than Usenet. As a result, both discussion groups and software distribution migrated to the Web. Since the early 2000s, the need for the old Usenet discussions groups diminished significantly, and Usenet evolved into a large, worldwide file-sharing system.

For more information about Usenet and how to use it, visit my special Web site, *Harley Hahn's Usenet Center*:

`http://www.harley.com/usenet/`

Personal Note #4: Free/Open Source Software

From Section 1.5:
"Free software refers to programs that are distributed with a license specifying that anyone in the world is allowed to read the source code, modify the code, and share the results of their work freely. Another name commonly used for free software is open source software."

Comment:
The free software movement and the open source movement come from somewhat different motivations. As such, there are some people who will argue that, technically, "open source" is not the same as "free". My answer is: not in this book.

For practical purposes, "free software" and "open source software" refer to the same thing. Specifically, both Emacs and Linux are free/open source software (see Section 2.2).

Personal Note #5: GNU's Not Unix?

From Section 1.5:
"GNU is the name Richard Stallman chose to describe the Free Software Foundation's project to develop Unix-like tools and programs. The name GNU is an acronym for GNU's Not Unix".

Comment:

Why would Richard Stallman want to name such a large project in a negative way ("GNU's not Unix")? And why, if his goal was to create a complete, free version of Unix, would he want to tell everyone that it was not Unix? Although the name seems strange, it actually made sense in 1985.

Unix was developed in the early 1970s at Bell Labs, a New Jersey research facility that, at the time, was part of AT&T (see Section 2.2). At first, Unix was shared freely with other computer scientists and programmers. However, in 1983, AT&T decided it was time to make money from this project and changed their policy. They packaged Unix as a commercial product called UNIX System V (pronounced "System Five") and announced that the days of free Unix were over. From now on, AT&T Unix would cost money.

Moreover, they also dictated exactly how the name "Unix" should be used. Specifically, the name must be spelled in capital letters (UNIX) and could be used only as an adjective, not a noun. In other words, according to AT&T's lawyers, if you wanted to talk about Unix you must refer to it as the "UNIX Operating System", not Unix (or even UNIX). Much more important: if you wanted to use it, you now had to pay for it.

You can imagine how programmers and computer scientists felt about this ukase. On the one hand, the naming convention was ludicrous and mostly ignored. (Many people who worked with non-System V Unix started to talk about "Unix-like operating systems"; other people referred to such systems as "U*ix": two terms that you will still see today.)

On the other hand, the fees to use Unix as a commercial product were expensive, real, and highly resented; but there was no way around them: AT&T did own the operating system. Even worse, the freedom to examine and change the AT&T UNIX source code was now restricted.

The solution, of course, was to develop new versions of Unix that worked exactly like AT&T's UNIX, without trespassing on their copyrights and trademarks. To be sure, people were already hard at work, developing free versions of Unix: most notably, the BSD project at U.C. Berkeley. ("BSD" stands for Berkeley Software Distribution.) However, none of these free versions of Unix could run on personal computers, which meant they were out of reach for most of the programmers in the world.

This is why, in 1985, Richard Stallman founded the Free Software Foundation with the ambitious goal of creating a completely free version of Unix, called GNU. (You can read more about this in Section 2.2.)

But why the name GNU?

At the time, Stallman — and many, many other programmers around the world — were very uncomfortable with what AT&T (and their lawyers) had done. As a result, Stallman wanted to make it clear that what the Free Software Foundation was going to create was not going to be based, in any way, on AT&T's UNIX. Thus the name GNU: an acronym for "GNU's Not Unix".

As you can see below, within the expression "GNU's Not Unix", the word GNU can be expanded indefinitely:

```
GNU
(GNU's Not Unix)
((GNU's Not Unix) Not Unix)
(((GNU's Not Unix) Not Unix) Not Unix)
((((GNU's Not Unix) Not Unix) Not Unix) Not Unix)
```

and so on. Thus, GNU is actually a recursive acronym, a wry joke that demonstrates the sort of whimsy and irony that appeals to computer scientists.

When you expand the word GNU in this way — with each set of parentheses enclosing a list of items — you create the type of structure that is used when you program with Lisp, a language that was popular among artificial intelligence people at the time. Stallman used Lisp when he worked in the MIT AI Lab, and, in fact, Emacs itself was written in Lisp and comes with an entire Lisp programming environment called Emacs Lisp.

Lisp was created, in 1958, by John McCarthy, a computer scientist at MIT, as a mathematical notation for computer programs. As such, it is the second oldest programming language still in widespread use around the world. The name Lisp stands for "List Processor".

In case you are wondering, the oldest programming language still in use today is Fortran, which stands for "formula translation". Fortran was designed at IBM in 1954 and was implemented in 1957. (Fortran was the first programming language I ever used. This was in 1970, during my last year of high school.)

Personal Note #6: Our Tools Shape Our Minds

From Section 2.1:

"Whether you realize it or not, one of the most important choices you make in your life is which operating system you will be using."

Comment:

Imagine how a human brain develops when, from a young age, the only computer it is ever allowed to use is a touch-screen-based phone or tablet running iOS or an Android operating system. To me, this qualifies as a type of child abuse.

Personal Note #7: AT&T

From Section 2.2:

"The first primitive version of Unix was created in 1969 by Ken Thompson, a programmer at the Bell Labs research facility in New Jersey, owned by AT&T."

Comment:

When you read about the history of Unix, the C programming language, and so on, you should know that the AT&T where all this was created has absolutely nothing to do with the companies that, today, use the name AT&T.

The AT&T that, in the 1970s, owned Bell Labs is long gone. In 1984, as part of an enormous antitrust settlement, the company was broken up into eight large pieces, one of which kept the name AT&T. These pieces were sold, recombined, enlarged, diminished, and re-sold, again and again.

Although the original AT&T hasn't existed for decades, the brand is so valuable the name "AT&T" has been preserved, very carefully, for commercial purposes. In fact, I know someone who has an "AT&T" credit card, even though this particular credit card has actually been owned by Citibank since 1998.

If this sort of thing intrigues you, search online for "AT&T Brand Licensing Opportunities".

Personal Note #8: Early Unix on the West Coast

From Section 2.2:

"In 1974, the use of Unix began to spread to the West Coast [of the United States]. The result was a new Unix, called BSD (an acronym for Berkeley System Distribution), which became popular among computer scientists and programmers around the world."

Comment:

I myself first used Unix in 1976, as a graduate student at U.C. San Diego.

Personal Note #9: BSD Unix in the 1980s

From Section 2.2:

"Most of the BSD-based versions of Unix, on the other hand, were non-commercial and were distributed for free."

Comment:

The one main exception was a BSD-based version of Unix named SunOS that was created and sold by Sun Microsystems, a company co-founded in 1982 by Bill Joy, from U.C. Berkeley, and three graduates of Stanford University. Eventually, Sun merged SunOS with System V to create a new version of Unix they named Solaris. In 2010, Sun was bought by Oracle, the company that now owns Solaris, which is still a commercial product.

Personal Note #10: Hackers and Geeks

From Section 2.2:

"There was still no operating system that ran on a PC that was attractive to the type of programmer whose idea of fun was to take things apart and modify them."

Comment:

Such programmers were called "hackers". Over the years, this term has been used so often to refer to troublemakers that, although it is still used in programming circles, you will often see the term "geeks" used instead.

There was a time when such people were called "nerds", but that was before *The Big Bang Theory* TV program made the term nauseatingly mainstream.

Personal Note #11: Bash

From Section 2.2:

"The most popular shell is called Bash."

Comment:

The very first Unix shell, created in 1977 at Bell Labs, was named **sh**. In later years, this shell became known as the Bourne Shell, named after its creator Stephen Bourne. Bash was created by the programmer Brian Fox to be a replacement for the aging Bourne Shell, and was released in 1989 as part of the GNU Project.

The name Bash stands for "Bourne-again shell".

Personal Note #12: Linux Is Free

From Section 2.2:

"Linux is free, open source software."

Comment:

As I was researching this part of the book, I found some old articles from *InfoWorld* magazine which was, at the time Linux was being developed, a well-known weekly magazine for personal computing professionals. In 1990, Apple had their own version of Unix, called A/UX, which they sold as a commercial product to people who wanted to run Unix on an Apple computer. On page 40 of the May 28, 1990, issue of the *InfoWorld*, I came across the following short article:

"Apple's A/UX 2.0 will begin shipping in June. The product will cost $795 in a CD ROM version, or $995 for a tape or floppy disk version."

Let's use the second number to do a quick calculation. (I'm going to ignore the first number because, in 1990, most people didn't have CD drives.) At the time, the sales tax in California (where Apple was located) was about 6.75%. Thus, in June of 1990, the total sales price for this particular version of Unix was $1,062. To put this in perspective, $1,062 in 1990 was worth about $2,000 in 2016 dollars. Imagine living in a world where it cost $2,000 for a license for one personal computer to run a version of Unix that, by today's standards, would be horribly sub-standard.

Aren't you glad we have the Free Software Foundation and the Linux Project?

Personal Note #13: Mac OS X Is Unix

From Section 2.3:

"Almost everyone who uses Emacs does so under some type of Unix. Specifically, GNU Emacs is available in specific versions for Linux, FreeBSD, NetBSD, OpenBSD, Mac OS X, and Solaris."

Comment:

Apple's OS X operating system is Unix, because it meets the standards for being Unix and is certified as such. It is not, however, Linux, because it doesn't use the Linux kernel. Nor does it use the Free Software Foundation's GNU utilities. (For a brief discussion of kernels and utilities, see Section 2.2.)

Mac OS X uses a kernel named XNU, whose original ancestors were the Mach kernel from Carnegie-Mellon University and the BSD4.3 kernel from U.C. Berkeley. In addition, the OS X utilities are based on BSD, not the GNU utilities. What XNU does have in common with Linux and the various BSD kernels is that it has been released as free, open source software (as part of a project called Darwin).

The name XNU is an acronym for "XNU is not Unix" which is a misnomer, because OS X really is Unix.

Historical note: In the 1980s, a similar acronym, "Xinu is not Unix", was used for the name Xinu, an operating system developed as a teaching aid by Doug Comer at Purdue University. However, unlike OS X, Xinu really wasn't Unix. It was, however, a very cool operating system that, in its time, was quite popular and is still in use today.

Personal Note #14: Terminals That Print

From Section 2.3:

"Unix was developed in the 1970s, before programmers were able to have their own personal computers. To work with Unix, a person would use a terminal connected to a host. The terminal was an electronic box with a keyboard and a screen, or a keyboard and a printer."

Comment:

The oldest computer terminals produced output by printing on a continuous roll of paper. I used a number of such terminals as a student. The ones that I remember the best are the IBM 2740 and 2741 terminals based on the venerable IBM Selectric Typewriter, and the smaller Texas Instruments Silent 700 series portable terminal that printed on special thermal paper.

Before terminals with screens became cheap and ubiquitous, many people used Unix with printing terminals. In fact, the PDP-11 computer on which Unix was first developed at Bell Labs had printing terminals attached to it. (If you look at the photo in Figure 2-2, you can see these terminals.)

To this day, traditional Unix terminology uses the term "print" to refer to displaying output. For example, the Unix command to display the name of your working directory (the folder you are using at the moment) is **pwd**, which stands for "print working directory".

Personal Note #15: Why U.C. San Diego in 1976?

From Section 2.3:

"Let's pretend for a moment that we are going to take a time-travel trip back to the late 1970s. Close your eyes and pretend that it is 1976, and you and I are visiting the computer science department at U.C. San Diego."

Comment:

At the time, the two foci of Unix development were Bell Labs in New Jersey, and the computer science department at U.C. Berkeley, California.

However, in 1976, I was a grad student in San Diego and, believe me, the climate was a lot better there than in either New Jersey or Berkeley. So as long as we are going back in time, we might as well have sunshine and warmth (which is why I went to grad school in San Diego in the first place).

By the way, at U.C. San Diego in 1976, computer science was actually taught within the Department of Applied Physics and Information Science. The current Department of Computer Science and Engineering was not established until 1987.

Personal Note #16: 80- and 132-character Lines

From Section 2.4:

"The DEC VT52 terminal (introduced in July 1974) had 24 rows, each of which could display 80 characters. A few years later, the VT52 was replaced by a more powerful terminal, the DEC VT100 (August 1978), which displayed either 24 rows of 80 characters or 14 rows of 132 characters."

Comment:

With respect to character (text) output, you will find that the numbers 80 and 132 come up a lot. Here is why.

80 characters/line: In 1928, IBM introduced PUNCH CARDS that could hold 80 characters per card, which became the standard. When computers were first used commercially in the early 1960s, input data was stored on punch cards that used the same 80 characters/card form factor. These cards were created using a machine called a KEYPUNCH. The most widely used keypunches were the IBM 026 and IBM 029. Punch cards were also called COMPUTER CARDS and IBM CARDS.

Because everyone was used to 80 characters/card, the first popular video display terminals were designed to have 80-character lines, and that size became a standard for terminals, one that you will still see today with terminal emulators.

132 character/line: In 1959, IBM introduced the IBM 1403 printer, probably the best printer (for its time) in history. The most popular IBM 1403, which was extremely fast, printed 132 characters/line which became an industry standard for output.

The IBM 1403 printed on special continuous, folded and perforated paper, called COMPUTER PAPER that came in boxes. The top end of the paper would be pulled out of the box and fed into the printer. The printed paper would come out of the back of the printer as one long accordion-like PRINTOUT.

When I was a university student, the IBM 026 keypunches were just being phased out. I did use them for a bit, but I had a lot more experience with the IBM 029 keypunch, punch cards, and the 1403 printer.

Personal Note #17: Unix Workstations

From Section 2.5:

"By the end of the 1980s, many people were using Unix on inexpensive personal computers. Other people, who needed more power and larger monitors, used expensive, high-end Unix machines called workstations."

Comment:

The most popular Unix workstations were made by Sun Microsystems, Silicon Graphics, Apollo, DEC, HP, and IBM, and were not IBM PC compatible. During the 1990s, these expensive, special-purpose Unix computers began to be replaced by new generic IBM-compatible PCs that, every year, were becoming more powerful and less expensive.

As an example, in 1991, Linus Torvalds created the first Linux kernel using a generic, 386-based PC. (Trivia: Linus bought that computer on January 5, 1991.)

Personal Note #18: Time Travel

From Section 2.4:

"There are many different terminal emulators and, believe it or not, they are all based on the old DEC VT100 family of terminals we discussed in Section 2.4. This means that, even today, when you type a Unix command or run a text-based Unix program, you are using a technology that was first introduced in 1978."

Comment:

This suggests an interesting hypothetical question. Let's say you were to install the latest version of Linux on your computer. You then invent a time machine, use it to go back to 1978 and bring back an actual DEC VT100 terminal. Here is the question: If you were able to find a way to connect the VT100 to your Linux computer, would it work?

The answer is yes; it would work. Unix would have no problem communicating with a real VT100.

Of course you would have to find a way to connect a VT100 from 1978 to a modern computer, but if you are the type of person who can figure out how to make a time machine, connecting an old terminal to your computer shouldn't be much of a problem.

Personal Note #19: Midnight Commander

From Section 2.5:

"Emacs is a TUI-based program. In fact, it is one of the most powerful TUI-based programs ever written."

Comment:

If you want to see a wonderful example of another TUI-based program, I recommend that you install a file manager named "Midnight Commander". The name of the Linux version of this program is mc.

Midnight Commander is a powerful, easy-to-use program (once you get used to it) that enables you to manage files and directories using only your keyboard. If you want to see what a well-designed TUI-based program can do, Midnight Commander is a lot easier to learn than Emacs, and very useful in its own right.

The mc program is a clone of a very old TUI-based program called "Norton Commander" written by John Socha and named after Peter Norton. It was originally released in 1986 to run under DOS on PCs, but Socha's TUI-based design was so good that it is still being used, virtually unchanged, decades later on other systems, including Linux.

John Socha was a good writer and a great programmer. In 1984, he wrote an assembly language book that, in 1987, was republished as the Peter Norton assembly language book.

Believe me, assembly language books are not easy to write. I wrote my first one in 1978 (for the IBM System/360). In 1986, I wrote *The Complete Guide to IBM PC AT Assembly Language*, which was republished in 1992 as *Assembler: Inside and Out*.

At the time, we all (Peter, John, and I) had the same literary agent. Like John, when I was building my reputation, I wrote a fair bit under the Peter Norton brand name. In 1991 I wrote *Peter Norton's Guide to Unix* (my second Unix book) and, later, contributed to five other Peter Norton books. By 1995, I became accomplished enough to publish books with my own name in the title, the first one being *Harley Hahn's Internet Yellow Pages, 3rd Edition*.

I only met Peter Norton once, the day we had our photo taken together for the cover of the Unix book. I don't remember ever meeting John, but I would have liked to.

Personal Note #20: KDE and Gnome

From Section 2.5:

"With Linux, the most popular GUIs are Unity, Gnome and KDE."

Comment:

The oldest of these GUIs is KDE, first released in 1998. KDE was well-received in the Linux community, but it was based on the Qt Toolkit which, at the time, was not totally free software. This was a concern for some of the Free Software Foundation (FSF) programmers, who started a project to create their own, totally free GUI, called Gnome. The first version of Gnome was released in 1999. By 2000, the licensing terms for Qt had been changed so that even the FSF was satisfied, making KDE completely free.

The newest of the three GUIs is Unity, which is actually based on Gnome. Unity was first released in 2011. (For a discussion of free software and the FSF, see Section 1.5.)

Personal Note #21: Aren't All Terminals Virtual?

From Section 2.6:

"[With Linux] there are two different types of terminal emulators: virtual terminals and terminal windows. When you use a virtual terminal, the terminal emulator uses your entire screen to provide you with a totally text-based experience. When you use a terminal window, the terminal emulator runs in a window within a GUI (graphical user interface)."

Comment:

A terminal window gets its name, obviously, because it is a terminal emulator running inside a window. But what about the "virtual terminal"? What does that name mean?

In science, the term VIRTUAL refers to something that doesn't really exist. For example, when you look at an object in the mirror, what you see is a virtual image. Similarly, when a computer uses disk space to simulate memory that isn't really there, we call it virtual memory. Now you can see that the name "virtual terminal" indicates that the terminal isn't real: it's a simulation created by a program. (More formally, we say that the program emulates a terminal.)

This raises a question. As we discussed in Section 2.5, no one actually uses real terminals anymore: we use only terminal emulators. And even though *all* terminals are virtual, we apply the name "virtual" to only one type of terminal emulator.

If you say it doesn't make sense, you are right. In fact, it is often the case that computer terms don't make sense, which is why we tend to teach them to people without an explanation. (Think about that for a moment.)

To help you understand how this works, I'm going to let you in on an important secret. All professionals need a way to talk about things they don't understand in a way that doesn't detract from their processional expertise.

For this reason, when computer experts need to talk about something that doesn't make sense, something we can't really explain, we often justify it without letting on that we don't understand it. This enables us to sound like we know what we are talking about even when we don't.

Example: "For historical reasons, virtual terminals are often referred to as virtual consoles."

This is a very important part of the computer world, which I first learned in high school. (In the words of my teacher: "Computers are a snow job.")

Compare this, say, to the world of medicine. In medicine, when we don't understand something, we still need to sound like we know what we are talking about. However, human bodies are a lot more complex and problematic than computer programs, so we can't simply appeal to tradition, such as "historical reasons". Instead, we make up something that seems plausible, and we say it with authority. (Medical professionals do this all the time.)

Of course, I learned how to do this as a medical student and, over the years, I became quite good at it. However, I had an advantage. When I entered medical school, I already had a graduate degree in computer science.

Personal Note #22: Ubuntu Terminal Emulators

From Section 2.6:

"The easiest way to start a terminal window is to click on the Terminal icon in the [Ubuntu] Launcher. If you don't see the Terminal icon in the Launcher, click the top icon on the Launcher to open the Dash and type `terminal`. You will see the Terminal icon, which you can click to start the program."

Comment:

The Ubuntu terminal emulator, called simply "Terminal", is actually Gnome Terminal, a terminal emulator for the Gnome desktop environment. As we discussed in Section 2.5, the default Ubuntu GUI, Unity, is based on Gnome. Gnome and Gnome terminal were developed by the Free Software Foundation, the same organization that developed Emacs.

You may also see two other terminals: Xterm and UXTerm. Xterm is a terminal emulator that comes with X Window. (We discussed X Window in Section 2.4.) UXTerm is a version of XTerm that supports UNICODE, a system for encoding characters for most of the languages of the world beyond the standard Roman alphabet. You probably won't need these two programs.

Personal Note #23: How to Access the Command Line With Mac OS X and Windows

From Section 2.7:

"In this section, I am going to show you how to use the Unix command line. What you are about to read will work for any type of Unix, including Linux and Mac OS X. If you use Windows, the basic ideas will be the same, but the details and the commands will be different."

Comment:

Mac OS X:

To access the command line with Mac OS X, you need to open a terminal window. Use Finder to open the Applications folder. Then open the Utilities sub-folder and start the Terminal program.

To make it convenient to open a terminal window whenever you want, simply drag the Terminal program to the Dock.

Windows:

Windows doesn't use terminals. To access the Windows command line, you must open a Command Prompt window. With Windows 7, click the Start button. Select "All Programs", "Accessories", then click "Command Prompt". With Windows 8 or Windows 10, right-click the Start button, then click "Command Prompt".

While the Command Prompt window is open, there will be an icon in the Taskbar. To make it easy to open a Command Prompt window whenever you want, right-click this icon and select "Pin this program to taskbar" (Windows 7) or "Pin to taskbar" (Windows 8, Windows 10).

Personal Note #24: Freddy and the Men From Mars

From Section 2.15:

"You might create a directory named `circus` to hold a collection of photos from a trip to Centerboro, New York, where you saw Boomschmidt's Stupendous and Unexcelled Circus. If you have a lot of photos, you might organize them by using three subdirectories: `friends`, `animals`, and `martians`."

Comment:

Boomschmidt's Stupendous and Unexcelled Circus appears in several of the Freddy the Pig books. The specific references above are from the book *Freddy and the Men from Mars*. As an Emacs user, it will probably do you a lot of good to read all the Freddy books, so here is the basic information.

Between 1927 and 1958, the American writer Walter R. Brooks (1886-1958) wrote 26 children's books about Freddy the Pig. Freddy lives on a farm owned by Mr. and Mrs. Bean, near the town of Centerboro in upstate New York, along with many other animals. All the animals can talk, but Freddy is, by far, the most talented. In the course of the books he becomes a detective, a poet, a newspaper publisher, a banker, a pilot, a football player, a politician, a magician, a baseball coach, and much more. *Freddy and the Men from Mars* was published in 1954.

I have a large Freddy collection and have read each book many times. In fact, much of what I know about human nature, I learned from Freddy and his friends. For more information, see the Freddy the Pig page on my Web site:

`http://www.harley.com/freddy-the-pig/`

Personal Note #25: Special Files and Proc Files

From Section 2.15:

"Pseudo files provide services to programs using the same methods that are normally used to read and write data from ordinary files. The three most important types of pseudo files are special files, named pipes, and proc files. Special files (also called device files) represent physical or emulated devices. Named pipes connect the output of one program to the input of another. Proc files provide technical information about the system itself."

Comment:

You can use special files to read or write using a physical device, for example, a display or printer (for output); a keyboard or mouse (for input); or a disk partition (input and output). You can also read and write using special files that emulate a physical device, such as a terminal.

Finally, there are special files that create virtual devices that provide esoteric services. For example, a program can obtain random numbers by reading from the special file **/dev/random**. Another example: there is a special file called **/dev/null** that discards anything you write to it. In fact, this is how Unix programmers get rid of a stream of data they don't want: they redirect it to **/dev/null**.

Proc files provide technical information directly from the kernel, the central part of the operating system (see Section 2.2). For instance, you can obtain information about your computer's memory (RAM) by reading from the file **/proc/meminfo**. To show you how it works, the following command uses the **less** program (see Section 2.14) to read from the file **/proc/meminfo** and to display the data one screenful at a time. Try it, and see what you get.

```
less /proc/meminfo
```

Here is a similar command that uses the **cat** program (used to display very short files) to read from the file **/proc/sys/kernel/hostname**. Reading this file accesses the kernel to obtain the name of the computer you are using:

```
cat /proc/sys/kernel/hostname
```

A program can read from this file to find out the name of the computer on which the program is running. Finally, here is a command that displays information about the processors (CPUs) in your computer:

```
less /proc/cpuinfo
```

Personal Note #26: How Many Files Are on Your Unix System?

From Section 2.16:

"A typical Unix system contains well over 300,000 files."

Comment:

To count the number of files and directories on a Unix system, use the following command:

```
sudo ls -R / | wc -l
```

We can take this command apart as follows:

- **sudo** runs the command as superuser, so you will have permission to count all the files on the system, not just your own. (You will need the superuser/administrator password to run this command.)

- **ls -R /** lists the name of every file and directory in the system, one name per line.

- | (the pipe symbol) sends the output of `ls` to the `wc` program.

- `wc -l` counts the number of lines.

I ran this command on a newly installed Linux system (Ubuntu Desktop Linux 14.04.3 LTS) without any extra software installed. It took 24 seconds to find that there were 340,615 files. When you have a few moments, try this command on your own computer.

If you have a lot of time and you want to see the names of all these files, you can pipe (send) the output of the `ls` command to the **less** pager (Section 2.14), which will display the output one screenful at a time:

`sudo ls -R / | less`

If you view one screenful every half-second, it will take you 47 hours and 19 minutes to look at all the names. If you get bored, you can stop **less** by pressing `q` to quit.

Alternatively, if you want to save the output to a file and print it out, you could have the pages bound into books with a nice cover. At 60 lines/page, you would have 5,637 pages. If you were to bind 200 pages/book, you would end up with 29 volumes, which would make a wonderful Mother's Day gift.

The point is, Unix systems come with a *lot* of files. (And remember, we are only taking about the *names* of the files, not the actual contents.)

Personal Note #27: Comparing Unix Packages to Commercial Apps

From Section 3.1:

"A package manager automates the various processes required to install, upgrade, configure, and uninstall software. All you have to do is tell the package manager what you want, and it does all the work."

Comment:

If the description of how a package management system functions sounds familiar, it is because package managers are also used to download consumer apps from app stores. This is the case with mobile devices, such as phones and tablets, and with personal computers running Mac OS X and some versions of Windows.

The Unix package managers differ from app package managers in several ways. The biggest difference is that the consumer app market is very tightly controlled by the companies that sell the operating system. They run the apps stores as they see fit, in their own interests, and most of the software (which is not open source) is designed for the money-driven consumer market. This is why commercial apps are secret, inflexible programs that either cost money, force you to look at advertisements, try to sell you something, capture and use your personal data, or all of the above.

The package management systems used with Linux and BSD systems are open source and non-commercial. As such, they are designed for the benefit of users. Generally speaking, the software you download is free, does not show you ads, does not try to sell you something, and is designed to respect your privacy. (All of which, by the way, is true for Emacs.)

APPENDIX B

Command Summaries

Throughout the book, there are 60 figures that have summaries of various Emacs or Unix/Linux commands. For reference, I have collected them all in this appendix.

To make it easy for you to find what you want, here is a list of the summaries in the same order that you will find them in the book. All you have to do is scan the list, find what you want, and look below for the actual command summary. In case you need more information, I have included the section number in which each figure appears, so you can read about the summary in its original context.

- Accessing a virtual terminal from the GUI. (Figure 2-4)
- Changing from one virtual terminal to another. (Figure 2-5)
- Keys to make corrections when typing a command. (Figure 2-7)
- Key combinations to use when typing a command. (Figure 2-8)
- Commands to use with less. (Figure 2-9)
- Important directories in filesystem hierarchy standard. (Figure 2-10)
- The most important file commands. (Figure 2-11)
- The most important directory commands. (Figure 2-12)
- Bash configuration files. (Figure 2-13)
- Linux package management systems. (Figure 3-1)
- BSD package management systems. (Figure 3-2)
- Emacs names for special keys. (Figure 4-1)
- Choosing to save files after stopping Emacs with **C-x C-c**. (Figure 5-1)
- Status characters within the mode line. (Figure 6-5)
- Completion commands. (Figure 6-6)
- Choosing whether or not to run a disabled command. (Figure 6-7)
- Keys to use while typing. (Figure 7-1)
- Commands for controlling windows. (Figure 7-2)
- Commands for controlling buffers. (Figure 7-3)
- Commands for working with files. (Figure 7-4)
- Commands for moving the cursor. (Figure 8-1)
- Commands for moving cursor through a paragraph/sentence. (Figure 8-2)
- Major modes to use when editing a human language. (Figure 8-3)
- Prefix argument combinations. (Figure 8-4)

© Harley Hahn 2016
H. Hahn, *Harley Hahn's Emacs Field Guide*, DOI 10.1007/978-1-4842-1703-0

- Commands to move throughout the buffer. (Figure 8-5)
- Commands to use line numbers. (Figure 8-6)
- Commands to set mark and define a region. (Figure 8-8)
- Commands that act upon the region. (Figure 8-9)
- Commands to delete text. (Figure 9-1)
- Commands to kill text. (Figure 9-2)
- Commands to move and kill by word or sentence. (Figure 9-3)
- Commands to yank text. (Figure 9-4)
- Commands for correcting common typing mistakes. (Figure 9-5)
- Commands for correcting spelling mistakes. (Figure 9-6)
- Commands to fill text. (Figure 9-7)
- Search commands. (Figure 10-1)
- Keys to use during a search. (Figure 10-2)
- Non-incremental search commands. (Figure 10-3)
- Search commands. (Figure 10-4)
- Search commands for regular expressions. (Figure 10-5)
- Characters to use with regular expressions. (Figure 10-6)
- Search and replace commands. (Figure 10-7)
- Responses during a search and replace command. (Figure 10-8)
- Minimum keystrokes to invoke search/replace commands. (Figure 10-9)
- The four basic major modes. (Figure 11-2)
- Major modes: Fundamental mode family. (Figure 11-3)
- Major modes: Text mode family. (Figure 11-4)
- Major modes: Prog mode family. (Figure 11-5)
- Major modes: Special mode family. (Figure 11-6)
- Independent major modes. (Figure 11-7)
- Minor modes. (Figure 11-8)
- Commands to set and describe modes. (Figure 11-10)
- Running shell commands. (Figure 12-1)
- Help facility options. (Figure 12-2)
- General info commands. (Figure 12-3)
- Info commands to select a node. (Figure 12-4)
- Info commands to read a node. (Figure 12-5)
- Built-in tools. (Figure 12-6)
- Dired commands. (Figure 12-7)
- Games and diversions. (Figure 12-8)

Figure 2-4 (from Section 2.6). Accessing a Virtual Terminal From the GUI.

Terminal	Key Combination
1	<Ctrl-Alt-F1>
2	<Ctrl-Alt-F2>
3	<Ctrl-Alt-F3>
4	<Ctrl-Alt-F4>
5	<Ctrl-Alt-F5>
6	<Ctrl-Alt-F6>

To switch from the GUI to a specific virtual terminal, use <Ctrl-Alt-F1> through <Ctrl-Alt-F6>. To return to the GUI, use <Alt-F7> or <Ctrl-Alt-F7>.

Figure 2-5 (from Section 2.6). Changing From One Virtual Terminal to Another.

Terminal	Key Combination
Next	<Alt-Right>
Previous	<Alt-Left>
1	<Alt-F1> or <Ctrl-Alt-F1>
2	<Alt-F2> or <Ctrl-Alt-F2>
3	<Alt-F3> or <Ctrl-Alt-F3>
4	<Alt-F4> or <Ctrl-Alt-F4>
5	<Alt-F5> or <Ctrl-Alt-F5>
6	<Alt-F6> or <Ctrl-Alt-F6>
Return to GUI	<Alt-F7> or <Ctrl-Alt-F7>

To switch from one virtual terminal to another, you have several choices. <Alt-Right> changes to the terminal with the next highest number. <Alt-Left> changes to the terminal with the previous number. <Alt-F1> through <Alt-F6> changes to a specific terminal. Finally, <Alt-F7> will return you to the GUI (the Desktop Environment). Please note that, for convenience, the function key combinations can use either <Alt> or <Ctrl-Alt>.

Figure 2-7 (from Section 2.10). Keys to Make Corrections When Typing a Command.

Key	Function
<Left>	Move cursor left one position
<Right>	Move cursor right one position
<Backspace>	Delete character to the left of the cursor
<Delete>	Delete character at the cursor
<Ctrl-W>	Delete the previous word
<Ctrl-U>	Delete the entire line (on some systems <Ctrl-X>)

As you enter a command, here are the most important keys you can use to make corrections. These keys work with all Unix systems, including Mac OS X. The first four keys also work when you type commands with Microsoft Windows. However, <Ctrl-W> and <Ctrl-U> do not work with Windows, as they are Unix keys.

Figure 2-8 (from Section 2.12). Key Combinations to Use When Typing a Command.

Unix Keys	Function
\<Up>	Display previous line in history list
\<Down>	Display next line in history list
\<Left>	Move cursor left one position
\<Right>	Move cursor right one position
\<Backspace>	Delete character to the left of the cursor
\<Delete>	Delete character at the cursor
\<Ctrl-W>	Delete the previous word
\<Ctrl-U>	Delete the entire line (on some systems \<Ctrl-X>)

Emacs Keys	Function
\<Ctrl-P>	Display previous line in history list
\<Ctrl-N>	Display next line in history list
\<Ctrl-A>	Move cursor to beginning of the line
\<Ctrl-E>	Move cursor to end of the line
\<Ctrl-B>	Move cursor left (backward) one position
\<Ctrl-F>	Move cursor right (forward) one position
\<Alt-F>	Move cursor right (forward) one word
\<Alt-B>	Move cursor left (backward) one word
\<Ctrl-K>	Delete from cursor to end of the line
\<Ctrl-A> \<Ctrl-K>	Delete the entire line

The top list shows the keys we discussed in Section 2.10 that you can use to make corrections when you are typing a command. The bottom list shows some of the key combinations copied from Emacs as part of the GNU Readline facility. You can use the keys in both these lists to move within the current line and the history list, and to help you make changes.

Figure 2-9 (from Section 2.14). Commands to use with `less`.

Letters	Function
h	Display help information
q	Quit the program
g	Go to first line of text
G	Go to last line of text
<Space>	Move forward (down) one screenful
b	Move backward (up) one screenful
/pattern	Search forward for specified pattern
?*pattern*	Search backward for specified pattern
n	Repeat search in the same direction (next)
N	Repeat search in the opposite direction
! *command*	Run the specified shell command

Special Keys	Function
<Home>	Go to first line of text
<End>	Go to last line of text
<PageDown>	Move forward (down) one screenful
<PageUp>	Move backward (up) one screenful

*The default Unix pager program is named **less**. The purpose of **less** is to display text, one screenful at a time. While you are reading, there are many commands you can use. Here are the most important ones.*

Figure 2-10 (from Section 2.16). The Most Important Directories Within the Filesystem Hierarchy Standard.

Directory	Description
`/`	Root directory
`/bin`	Essential user commands (binaries)
`/boot`	Boot loader files
`/dev`	Device files (special files)
`/etc`	System configuration files
`/home`	User home directories
`/lib`	Essential shared libraries and kernel modules
`/media`	Mount point: removable media
`/mnt`	Mount point: temporarily mounted filesystems
`/opt`	Application programs ("optional" software)
`/proc`	Proc files
`/root`	Home directory for the root userid (superuser)
`/run`	Temporary data used by programs that are running
`/sbin`	System programs (binaries)
`/srv`	Data for system services
`/tmp`	Temporary files, not preserved between reboots
`/usr`	Sharable, read-only data
`/var`	Variable (changeable) system data

All Unix systems organize files and directories into a tree-structured filesystem using a single root directory. The Filesystem Hierarchy Standard is the basic plan followed by Linux systems. To see the details for your particular system, look at the `hier` *man page.*

Figure 2-11 (from Section 2.17). The most important file commands.

Command	Description
`cat`	Display a very short file
`cat`	Combine (catenate) multiple files
`chmod`	Modify (change) file permissions
`cmp`	Compare two files to see if they are the same
`cp`	Copy files
`du`	Display disk usage for files
`file`	Analyze file type
`find`	Search for files in directory tree, then process results
`head`	Display the beginning of a file
`less`	Display contents of file, one screenful at a time
`ls`	Display (list) information about files
`ls -l`	Display full information (long listing) about files
`mv`	Move files
`mv`	Rename files
`od`	Display contents of a binary file (octal dump)
`pwd`	Display name of current directory
`rm`	Delete (remove) files
`tail`	Display the end of a file
`touch`	When file does not exist: create brand new empty file
`touch`	When file exists: update access and modification times
`whereis`	Find files associated with a command

When you use Emacs there will be many times when you need to manipulate your files. Sometimes you can do it from within Emacs, but a lot of the time, it will be easier and faster to use the standard Unix file commands. These are the most important ones, and I recommend you learn how to use them all. (Notice that `cat`, `mv`, *and* `touch` *each perform two different functions.)*

Figure 2-12 (from Section 2.17). The most important directory commands.

Command	Description
cd	Change your current (working) directory
chmod	Modify (change) directory permissions
du	Display disk usage for directories
ls	Display (list) information about directories
ls -l	Display full information (long listing) about directories
mkdir	Create (make) a directory
mv	Move directories
mv	Rename directories
pwd	Display name of current directory
rmdir	Delete (remove) an empty directory
tree -d	Display a diagram of a directory tree

*Unix uses a very large, tree-structured file system. Within that file system, starting from your home directory, you can build a tree structure of your own in a way that suits you. This will become more and more important, as you develop a facility with Emacs. Here are the commands you can use to build, maintain, and use your own personal directory tree. (Notice that **mv** performs two different functions.)*

Figure 2-13 (from Section 2.18). Bash Configuration Files.

File	Description
.bash_profile	Login file
.bash_login	Login file
.profile	Login file (POSIX mode)
.bashrc	Environment file
.bash_logout	Logout file

Many programs use dotfiles to hold configuration information. These are the files used by Bash, the default shell on many Unix systems (including most types of Linux as well as Mac OS X). Once you learn how to use Emacs, I suggest that you take some time to learn about these files and customize them.

Figure 3-1 (from Section 3.2). Linux Package Management Systems.

Package Manager	Linux Family	Linux Distributions
APT	Debian-based	Debian, Mint, Ubuntu
RPM	Fedora-based	Fedora, Mageia, Manjaro, RHEL, CentOS
RPM	SUSE-based	OpenSUSE
Pacman	Arch-based	Arch
Portage	Gentoo-based	Gentoo
pgktool	Slackware-based	Slackware

To make software easy to share and download, most Unix systems use a package management system. The most widely used Linux package managers are shown in this table.

Figure 3-2 (from Section 3.2). BSD Package Management Systems.

Package Manager	BSD System
pkg	FreeBSD
pkg_add	NetBSD
pkg_add	OpenBSD

This table shows the package managers you are most likely to encounter when you use a BSD-based version of Unix.

Figure 4-1 (from Section 4.4). Emacs names for special keys.

Name	Key
C-	Ctrl
M-	Meta
M-C-	Meta-Ctrl
BS	Backspace
DEL	Delete
ESC	Esc
RET	Return
SPC	Space
TAB	Tab

When you read about Emacs, you will sometimes see abbreviated names used for special keys. These names are derived from the technology of the 1970s, and they are important enough that it is a good idea to memorize them.

Figure 5-1 (from Section 5.5). Choosing whether or not to save files.

y	Save the specified file
n	Do not save the specified file
!	Save all the remaining files
q	Quit immediately without saving
.	Save the specified file and then quit
C-r	View the specified file
C-h	Display help information

When you tell Emacs to quit, and you have files that have not been saved, Emacs will ask you what to do with each file in turn. Here are the responses you can use to make a choice for each such file.

Figure 6-5 (from Section 6.4). Status characters within the mode line.

Characters	Meaning
--	Buffer has not been modified
**	Buffer has been modified (not yet saved)
%%	Read-only mode: buffer has not been modified
%*	Read-only mode: buffer has been modified

On the mode line, to the right of the colon, Emacs displays two characters to show you the status of the buffer.

Figure 6-6 (from Section 6.7). Completion Commands.

Command	Action
TAB	Complete text in minibuffer as much as possible
C-i	Same as **TAB**
SPC	Complete text in minibuffer up to end of word
RET	Same as **TAB**, then enter the command
?	Create new window, display list of possible completions

*When you type in the minibuffer, Emacs helps you, whenever possible, by guessing what you want and letting you use completion commands to make choices. **TAB** and ? work for commands, files and buffer. **SPC** works for commands and buffers. **RET** works only for commands.*

Figure 6-7 (from Section 6.8). Choosing whether or not to run a disabled command.

y	Run command; enable it for rest of the work session
n	Do not run command; leave it disabled
SPC	Run command once; leave it disabled
!	Run command; enable *all* commands for the rest of the work session

*When you type a disabled command, Emacs tells you the command is disabled and asks you what you want to do. Most of the time, you will answer either **y** or **n**. Note: You don't need to press <Enter>.*

Figure 7-1 (from Section 7.2). Keys to use while typing.

Key	Action
BS	Delete one character to the left of cursor
DEL	Delete one character at the position of cursor
C-d	Same as DEL
C-o	Open a new line
C-x u	Undo the last change to the buffer
C-_	Same as C-x u
C--	Same as C-x u
C-/	Same as C-x u
C-q	Insert the next character literally

Note: C-_ is "<Ctrl>-underscore".

Figure 7-2 (from Section 7.6). Commands for controlling windows.

Command	Description
C-x 0	Delete the selected window
C-x 1	Delete all windows except selected window
C-x 2	Split selected window vertically
C-x 3	Split selected window horizontally
C-x o	Move cursor to the next (other) window
C-x }	Make selected window wider
C-x {	Make selected window narrower
C-x ^	Make selected window larger
M-x shrink-window	Make selected window smaller

Figure 7-3 (from Section 7.7). Commands for controlling buffers.

Command	Description
C-x b	Display a different buffer in selected window
C-x b	Create a new buffer in selected window
C-x C-b	Display a list of all your buffers
C-x k	Kill (delete) a buffer
C-x 4 b	Display a different buffer in next window
C-x 4 C-o	Same as C-x 4 b, but don't change selected window

Figure 7-4 (from Section 7.8). Commands for working with files.

Command	Description
C-x C-f	Switch to buffer containing specified file
C-x C-v	Replace buffer contents with specified file
C-x C-s	Save a buffer to file
C-x C-w	Save a buffer to specified file
C-x i	Insert contents of a file into buffer
C-x 4 C-f	Read contents of file into next window
C-x 4 f	Same as **C-x 4 C-f**
C-x 4 r	Same as **C-x 4 C-f**, read-only

Figure 8-1 (from Section 8.2). Commands for moving the cursor.

Backward	Forward	
C-b	**C-f**	a single character
\<Left>	\<Right>	a single character
M-b	**M-f**	a word
C-p	**C-n**	a line
\<Up>	\<Down>	a line
M-a	**M-e**	a sentence
M-{	**M-}**	a paragraph

Beginning	End	
C-a	**C-e**	the current line
M-<	**M->**	the entire buffer

Figure 8-2 (from Section 8.3). Commands for moving the cursor through a paragraph or a sentence.

Command	Description
M-}	Move forward one paragraph
M-{	Move backward one paragraph
M-e	Move forward one sentence
M-a	Move backward one sentence

Figure 8-3 (from Section 8.3). Major modes to use when editing a human language.

Mode	Command
Fundamental mode	`fundamental-mode`
Text mode	`text-mode`
Indented Text mode	`indented-text-mode`
Paragraph-Indent Text mode	`paragraph-indent-text-mode`

Figure 8-4 (from Section 8.4). Prefix argument combinations.

Prefix	Effect
M-*number*	Repeat command specified number of times
ESC *number*	Repeat command specified number of times
C-u *number*	Repeat command specified number of times
C-u	Repeat command 4 times
C-u C-u	Repeat command 16 times
C-u C-u C-u	Repeat command 64 times
C-u C-u C-u C-u	Repeat command 256 times

Figure 8-5 (from Section 8.5). Commands to move throughout the buffer.

Command	Description
C-v	Scroll down one screenful
\<PageDown\>	Same as **C-v**
M-v	Scroll up one screenful
\<PageUp\>	Same as **M-v**
M-C-v	Scroll down in the next window
M-<	Jump to the beginning of buffer
M->	Jump to the end of buffer
C-l	Redisplay the screen, current line in middle

Figure 8-6 (from Section 8.6). Commands to use line numbers.

Command	Description
M-g g	Jump to line with specified number
M-x `line-number-mode`	ON/OFF: display line number on mode line

Figure 8-8 (from Section 8.8). Commands to set mark and define a region.

Command	Description
C-@	Set mark to current location of point
C-SPC	Same as C-@
C-x C-x	Interchange mark and point
M-@	Set mark after next word (do not move point)
M-h	Put region around paragraph
C-x h	Put region around entire buffer

Figure 8-9 (from Section 8.9). Commands that act upon the region.

Command	Description
C-w	Kill (erase) all the characters
C-x C-l	Convert the characters to lowercase
C-x C-u	Convert the characters to uppercase
M-=	Count the lines and characters
M-|	Run a shell command, use the characters as data

Figure 9-1 (from Section 9.2). Commands to delete text.

Command	Description
BS	Delete one character to the left of cursor
DEL	Delete one character at the position of cursor
C-d	Same as DEL
M-\	Delete spaces & tabs around point
M-SPC	Delete spaces & tabs around point; leave one space
C-x C-o	Delete blank lines around current line
M-^	Join two lines (delete **RET** + surrounding spaces)

Figure 9-2 (from Section 9.3). Commands to kill text.

Command	Description
C-k	Kill from cursor to end of line
M-d	Kill a word
M-BS	Kill a word backward
M-k	Kill from cursor to end of sentence
C-x BS	Kill backward to beginning of sentence
C-w	Kill the region
M-z *char*	Kill through next occurrence of specified character

Figure 9-3 (from Section 9.3). Commands to move and kill by word or sentence.

| | WORDS | | | SENTENCES | |
	Backward	Forward		Backward	Forward
Move:	M-b	M-f	Move:	M-a	M-e
Kill:	M-BS	M-d	Kill:	C-x BS	M-k

Figure 9-4 (from Section 9.4). Commands to yank text.

Command	Description
C-y	Yank most recently killed text
C-u C-y	Same as C-y, cursor at beginning of new text
M-y	Replace yanked text with previously killed text
M-w	Copy region to kill ring, without erasing
M-C-w	Append next kill to newest kill ring entry
C-h v kill-ring	Display the actual values in the kill ring

Figure 9-5 (from Section 9.5). Commands for correcting common typing mistakes.

Command	Description
BS	Delete one character to the left of cursor
DEL	Delete one character at the position of cursor
C-d	Same as DEL
M-BS	Kill the previous word
C-x BS	Kill backward to beginning of sentence
M-- M-l	Change previous word to lowercase
M-- M-u	Change previous word to uppercase
M-- M-c	Change previous word to lowercase, initial cap
M-l	Change following word to lowercase
M-u	Change following word to uppercase
M-c	Change following word to lowercase, initial cap
C-t	Transpose two adjacent characters
M-t	Transpose two adjacent words
C-x C-t	Transpose two consecutive lines

Note: BS is <Backspace>; M-- is <Meta-hyphen>.

Figure 9-6 (from Section 9.6). Commands for correcting spelling mistakes.

Command	Description
M-\$	Spell check: word at point, or region
M-x ispell-buffer	Spell check: buffer (only)
M-x ispell-region	Spell check: region (only)
M-x ispell	Spell check: buffer, or region
M-TAB	Complete word before point, based on dictionary
ESC TAB	Same as **M-TAB**
M-x flyspell-mode	Highlight spelling mistakes in regular text
M-x flyspell-prog-mode	Highlight spelling mistakes in programs

Figure 9-7 (from Section 9.7). Commands to fill text.

Command	Description
M-x auto-fill-mode	Turn on/off Auto Fill mode
M-q	Fill a paragraph
ESC 1 M-q	Fill+justify a paragraph
M-x fill-region	Fill each paragraph in the region
ESC 1 M-x fill-region	Fill+justify each paragraph in region
M-x fill-region-as-paragraph	Fill region as one long paragraph
ESC 1 M-x fill-region-as-paragraph	Fill+justify region as one paragraph
C-x f	Set the fill column value
C-h v fill-column	Display current fill column value

Figure 10-1 (from Section 10.1). Search commands.

Command	Description
C-s	Forward: Incremental search
C-s RET	Forward: Non-incremental search
M-s w	Forward: Incremental *word* search
M-C-s	Forward: Incremental *regexp* search
M-C-s RET	Forward: Non-incremental *regexp* search

Command	Description
C-r	Backward: Incremental search
C-r RET	Backward: Non-incremental search
M-s w C-r	Backward: Incremental *word* search
M-C-r	Backward: Incremental *regexp* search
M-C-r RET	Backward: Non-incremental *regexp* search

Figure 10-2 (from Section 10.3). Keys to use during a search.

Key	Description
BS	Erase last character you typed
RET	Terminate the search
C-s	Search forward for same pattern
C-r	Search backward for same pattern
C-g	While search is in progress: Stop current search
C-g	While waiting for input: Abort entire command
C-w	Copy the word after point to search string
C-y	Copy current kill ring entry to search string
M-y	Copy previous kill ring entry to search string

Figure 10-3 (from Section 10.5). Non-incremental search commands.

Command	Description
C-s RET	Forward: non-incremental search
C-r RET	Backward: non-incremental search

Figure 10-4 (from Section 10.6). Search commands.

Command	Description
M-s w	Forward: Incremental word search
M-s w C-r	Backward: Incremental word search

Figure 10-5 (from Section 10.7). Search commands for regular expressions.

Command	Description
M-C-s	Forward: Incremental search for regexp
M-C-s RET	Forward: Non-incremental search for regexp

Command	Description
M-C-r	Backward: Incremental search for regexp
M-C-r RET	Backward: Non-incremental search for regexp

Note: If you have a problem using the key sequence **M-C-s**, you can use **ESC C-s** instead.

Figure 10-6 (from Section 10.8). Characters to use with regular expressions.

Character	Description
Char	Any regular character matches itself
.	Match any single character except **RET**
*	Match zero or more of the preceding characters
+	Match one or more of the preceding characters
?	Match exactly zero or one of the preceding characters
^	Match the beginning of a line
$	Match the end of a line
\<	Match the beginning of a word
\>	Match the end of a word
\b	Match the beginning or end of a word
\B	Match anywhere not at the beginning or end of a word
\`	Match the beginning of the buffer
\'	Match the end of the buffer
char	Quotes a special character
[ ]	Match one of the enclosed characters
[^]	Match any character that is not enclosed

Figure 10-7 (from Section 10.10). Search and replace commands.

Command	Description
M-%	Query: Search and replace
M-C-%	Query: Search and replace (regexp)
M-x replace-string	No query: Search and replace
M-x replace-regexp	No query: Search and replace (regexp)

Figure 10-8 (from Section 10.10). Responses during a search and replace command.

Command	Description
?	Display help summary
y	(yes) Replace
n	(no) Do not replace
q	Quit immediately
SPC	Same as y
BS	Same as n
RET	Same as q
!	Replace all remaining matches, no questions
.	(period) Replace current match and then quit
,	(comma) Replace but stay at current position
^	(circumflex) Move back to previous match
C-l	Clear screen, redisplay, and ask again
C-r	Start recursive editing (use M-C-c to return)
C-w	Delete matching pattern, start recursive edit

Figure 10-9 (from Section 10.10). Minimum keystrokes to invoke search and replace commands.

Key Sequence	Command	Keystrokes to Use
M-%	M-x query-replace	M-x que RET
M-C-%	M-x query-replace-regexp	M-x que TAB SPC RET
M-C-%	M-x query-replace-regexp	M-x que SPC SPC SPC RET
-none-	M-x replace-string	M-x repl SPC s RET
-none-	M-x replace-regexp	M-x repl SPC reg RET

Figure 11-2 (from Section 11.2). The Four Basic Major Modes.

	Name	Type of Data to Edit
Fundamental Mode	fundamental-mode	Anything Emacs doesn't know about
Prog Mode	prog-mode	Programming source code
Text Mode	text-mode	Human-readable text
Special Mode	special-mode	Special text created by Emacs

Almost all the major modes are derived, directly or indirectly, from one of these four basic modes.

Figure 11-3 (from Section 11.3). Major Modes: Fundamental Mode Family.

Fundamental Family	Type of Data to Edit
`fundamental-mode`	Parent mode: General data, not specialized
`array-mode`	2-dimensional arrays
`css-mode`	CSS files (Cascading Style Sheets)
`edit-abbrevs-mode`	Abbreviation definitions
`gud-mode`	Using debuggers: `gdb`, `sbd`, `dbx`, `xdb`...

The major modes in this list are derived from Fundamental mode.

Figure 11-4 (from Section 11.3). Major Modes: Text Mode Family.

Text Family	Type of Data to Edit
`text-mode`	Parent mode: human-readable text
`bibtex-mode`	BibTeX files
`change-log-mode`	Change logs
`html-mode`	HTML files
`indented-text-mode`	Text with indented paragraphs
`latex-mode`	LaTeX-formatted files
`mail-mode`	Outgoing email messages
`nroffmode`	`nroff`- and `troff`-formatted text files
`nxml-mode`	XML files
`org-mode`	Outlines for "keeping track of everything"
`outline-mode`	Outlines with selective display
`paragraph-indent-text-mode`	Text: leading spaces start paragraphs
`plain-tex-mode`	TeX-formatted files
`rmail-mode`	Reading email
`sgml-mode`	SGML files
`slitex-mode`	SliTeX-formatted files
`tex-mode`	TeX-, LaTeX- or SliTeX-formatted files
`texinfo-mode`	TeXinfo files

The major modes in this list are derived, directly or indirectly, from Text mode. These modes are used to edit human-readable text (English and other languages), as well as marked-up text (HTML, TeX, and so on).

Figure 11-5 (from Section 11.3). Major Modes: Prog Mode Family.

Prog Family	Type of Data to Edit
`prog-mode`	Parent mode: Programming source code
`ada-mode`	Ada programs
`antlr-mode`	ANTLR grammar files (parsers, etc)
`asm-mode`	Assembly language programs
`awk-mode`	**awk** scripts
`bat-mode`	DOS/Windows batch files
`c++-mode`	C++ programs
`c-mode`	C programs
`cperl-mode`	Perl scripts (alternative to **perl-mode**)
`emacs-lisp-mode`	**emacs** Lisp programs
`f90-mode`	Fortran 90/95 programs
`fortran-mode`	Fortran programs
`java-mode`	Java programs
`javascript-mode`	JavaScript programs
`lisp-interaction-mode`	Evaluating Emacs Lisp forms
`lisp-mode`	Non-**emacs** lisp programs
`m4-mode`	M4 macros
`makefile-mode`	Makefiles
`modula-2-mode`	Modula-2 programs
`opascal-mode`	Object Pascal programs
`pascal-mode`	Pascal programs
`perl-mode`	Perl scripts
`prolog-mode`	Prolog programs
`ps-mode`	Postscript files
`scheme-mode`	Scheme programs (dialect of Lisp)
`sieve-mode`	Sieve (email filtering) scripts
`simula-mode`	Simula programs
`sh-mode`	Shell scripts
`sql-mode`	SQL programs
`tcl-mode`	tcl scripts

The major modes in this list are derived, directly or indirectly, from Prog mode. These modes are used to edit computer programs.

Figure 11-6 (from Section 11.3). Major Modes: Special Mode Family.

Special Family	Used for...
`special-mode`	Parent mode: built-in Emacs services
`help-mode`	Emacs Help system
`messages-buffer-mode`	Display messages in ***Messages*** buffer
`tar-mode`	Looking inside a **tar** file
`todo-mode`	Managing todo lists

The major modes in this list are derived from Special mode. As a general rule, these modes are used by Emacs when it needs to display information, for example, `help-mode`. *However, some of these modes are also used by tools, such as* `tar-mode` *and* `todo-mode`.

Figure 11-7 (from Section 11.3). Independent Major Modes.

Independent Modes	Type of Data to Edit
`conf-mode`	Configuration files
`completion-list-mode`	Display a list of possible completions
`dired-mode`	Dired directory/file tool
`doc-view-mode`	Documents: MS Office, OpenDocument, PDF, PS
`forms-mode`	Field-structured data using a form
`hexl-mode`	Hexadecimal data, ASCII data
`Info-mode`	Emacs Info system
`normal-mode`	Reset major mode to the default for this file
`picture-mode`	Text-based drawings
`ses-mode`	Simple Emacs Spreadsheet files

The major modes in this list are not derived from another major mode. Instead, they are independent tools, written to stand alone.

Figure 11-8 (from Section 11.4). Minor modes.

Minor Mode	Description
`abbrev-mode`	Working with abbreviations
`auto-fill-mode`	Automatic filling
`auto-save-mode`	Automatic saving
`binary-overwrite-mode`	Binary overwriting
`compilation-minor-mode`	Compiling programs
`cua-mode`	Use Ctrl-X/C/V for cut/copy/paste
`delete-selection-mode`	Typed text replaces selection
`display-time-mode`	Mode line shows: time, load level, mail flag
`double-mode`	Some keys differ if pressed twice
`eldoc-mode`	Display info about Lisp function/variable
`flyspell-mode`	Highlight spelling mistakes in regular text
`flyspell-prop-mode`	Highlight spelling mistakes in programs
`font-lock-mode`	Text is fontified as you type
`hide-ifdef-mode`	Hides certain C code within **#ifdef**
`indent-according-to-mode`	Indent appropriately for major mode
`iso-accents-mode`	Display ISO accents
`ledit-mode`	Editing text to be sent to Lisp
`line-number-mode`	Mode line shows: line numbers
`outline-minor-mode`	Work with outlines
`overwrite-mode`	Overwrite/insert text
`paragraph-indent-minor-mode`	Text: leading spaces start paragraphs
`pending-delete-mode`	Same as **delete-selection-mode**
`read-only-mode`	Buffer contents cannot be changed
`resize-minibuffer-mode`	Dynamically resize minibuffer
`ruler-mode`	Header line shows: ruler
`show-paren-mode`	Highlight matching parentheses, brackets
`size-indication-mode`	Mode line shows: size of buffer
`timeclock-mode-line-display`	Track time intervals you spend working
`toggle-read-only`	Buffer contents cannot be changed
`toggle-viper-mode`	Turn **viper-mode** off and on
`tool-bar-mode`	Toggle: Display help on tool bar or mode line
`tooltip-mode`	Display Emacs toolbar
`transient-mark-mode`	Highlight region when defined
`view-mode`	Page through a file (similar to **less** pager)
`viper-mode`	Turn on (not off) emulation of **vi** text editor
`whitespace-mode`	Show all whitespace: **SPC**, **TAB**, **RET** chars
`whitespace-newline-mode`	Show **RET** characters

Figure 11-10 (from Section 11.7). Commands to set and describe modes.

Command	Description
M-x *mode-name* RET	Set the specified major or minor mode
C-h v major-mode RET	Display information about current major mode
C-h m	Describe current major and minor modes
C-h f *mode-name* RET	Describe the specified mode
C-h f *-mode RET	Display names of all modes
C-h a mode	Display summary of all modes

Figure 12-1 (from Section 12.1). Running shell commands.

Command	Description
M-!	Run a shell command
M-|	Run a shell command using region as input
M-x shell	Start a separate shell in its own buffer

Figure 12-2 (from Section 12.3). Help facility options.

Command	Description
C-h C-h	Display a summary of all the Help options
C-h ?	Same as C-h C-h.
C-h q	Exit from a Help command loop (quit)

Command	Description
C-h a	Show all the functions containing a specified word
C-h b	Display a full list of all the key bindings
C-h c	You specify a key, Emacs tells you what it does
C-h f	You specify a function, Emacs describes it
C-h h	Display the "Hello" file
C-h k	You specify a key, Emacs describes its function
C-h m	Describe the current major and minor modes
C-h v	You specify a variable, Emacs describes it
C-h w	You specify a function, Emacs shows you its key

Command	Description
C-h t	Emacs tutorial
C-h i	Emacs reference manuals (Info documentation browser)

Figure 12-3 (from Section 12.4). General Info commands.

Command	Description
?	Display a summary of Info commands
h	Start the Info tutorial
q	Quit Info: remember current location
C-x k	Quit Info: do not remember current location

Figure 12-4 (from Section 12.4). Info commands to select a node.

Command	Description
n	Jump to next node in the sequence
p	Jump to previous node in the sequence
u	Jump to the "up" node (the menu you came from)
l	Jump to last node you looked at
m *selection*	Pick a node from a menu
f	Follow a cross-reference
i	Look up topic in the index, then jump there
,	(comma) Jump to next match from previous **i** command

Figure 12-5 (from Section 12.4). Info commands to read a node.

Command	Description
SPC	Go forward (down) one screenful
BS	Go backward (up) one screenful
b	Go to beginning of the node
.	Same as **b**
C-l	(<Ctrl-L>) Redisplay the current screen

Figure 12-6 (from Section 12.6). Built-in tools.

Program	Description
calendar	Calendar and diary
customize	Tool to help you change user options
dired	Directory and file manager
eww	Web browser
ses	Create and edit spreadsheet files

Figure 12-7 (from Section 12.6). Dired commands.

Program	Description
q	Quit
h	Display Help summary
m	Mark current file/directory, move cursor down
BS	Unmark current file/directory, move cursor up
u	Unmark file/directory, move cursor down
U	Unmark all files/directories
C	Copy marked files or current file
R	Rename current file
R	Move marked files or current file to another directory
d	Flag file for deletion
x	Delete files flagged by d
g	Refresh by reading the directories again

Here are the most important commands while using Dired, the Emacs file manager. Notice that the commands are case sensitive.

Figure 12-8 (from Section 12.7). Games and diversions.

Program	Description
animate	Display animated birthday message
bubbles	Game: Remove groups of bubbles until all gone
blackbox	Puzzle: Find objects inside a black box
doctor	Eliza program: acts like a psychotherapist
dunnet	Adventure-style exploration game
gomoku	Game: plays Gomoku with you
hanoi	Visual solution to Towers of Hanoi problem
landmark	Neuro-network robot that learns about landmarks
life	Game of Life: auto-reproducing patterns (not a game)
mpuz	Multiplication puzzle: guess the digits
pong	Video game: classic ping-pong game
snake	Video game: you control a growing snake
solitaire	Jump pegs across other pegs (not the card game)
spook	Generates words to get government's attention
tetris	Video game: you manipulate falling blocks

Index of Emacs Key Sequences

© Harley Hahn 2016
H. Hahn, *Harley Hahn's Emacs Field Guide*, DOI 10.1007/978-1-4842-1703-0

Index of Emacs Variables and Functions

Emacs Lisp Variables

Emacs Lisp Functions

© Harley Hahn 2016
H. Hahn, *Harley Hahn's Emacs Field Guide*, DOI 10.1007/978-1-4842-1703-0

Index of Unix Keys, Files and Commands

Unix Keys

\# (superuser shell prompt), 32
\$ (Bash shell prompt), 32, 33
% (C-Shell prompt), 32
– (command options), 34
. (current directory), 49
.. (parent directory), 49–51
/ (root directory), 45, 46
| (pipe symbol), 230
~ (home directory within
     shell prompt), 32, 33

<Backspace>, 34, 35
<Ctrl>, 72
<Ctrl-C>, 35–37
<Ctrl-D>, 35–37
<Ctrl-U>, 35
<Ctrl-W>, 35
<Ctrl-X>, 35
<Enter>, 35, 37
<Left>, 34, 35
<Right>, 34, 35

Unix Files

/dev/null, 229
/dev/random, 229

/proc/meminfo, 229
/proc/sys/kernel/hostname, 229

Unix Commands

cat, 51
cat /proc/sys/kernel/
    hostname, 229
cd, 50, 52
chmod, 51, 52
cmp, 51
cp, 51
du, 51, 52
file, 51
find, 51
fmt, 135

head, 51
less, 41, 42
less /proc/cpuinfo, 229
less /proc/meminfo, 229
logout, 19, 37
ls, 34, 49
ls -R, 229
mkdir, 52
mv, 51, 52
od, 51
pwd, 49, 51, 52
rm, 51

© Harley Hahn 2016
H. Hahn, *Harley Hahn's Emacs Field Guide*, DOI 10.1007/978-1-4842-1703-0

General Index

© Harley Hahn 2016
H. Hahn, *Harley Hahn's Emacs Field Guide*, DOI 10.1007/978-1-4842-1703-0

Get the eBook for only $5!

Why limit yourself?

Now you can take the weightless companion with you wherever you go and access your content on your PC, phone, tablet, or reader.

Since you've purchased this print book, we're happy to offer you the eBook in all 3 formats for just $5.

Convenient and fully searchable, the PDF version enables you to easily find and copy code—or perform examples by quickly toggling between instructions and applications. The MOBI format is ideal for your Kindle, while the ePUB can be utilized on a variety of mobile devices.

To learn more, go to www.apress.com/companion or contact support@apress.com.

Apress®
THE EXPERT'S VOICE™

Printed in the United States
By Bookmasters